A History of Environmentalism

A History of Environmentalism

Local Struggles, Global Histories

EDITED BY
MARCO ARMIERO AND
LISE SEDREZ

BLOOMSBURY
NEW DELHI • LONDON • OXFORD • NEW YORK • SYDNEY

BLOOMSBURY INDIA
Bloomsbury Publishing India Pvt. Ltd
Second Floor, LSC Building No. 4, DDA Complex, Pocket C–6&7,
Vasant Kunj, New Delhi 110070

BLOOMSBURY, BLOOMSBURY ACADEMIC INDIA and the Diana logo are trademarks of Bloomsbury Publishing Plc

First published in India 2022
First published 2014

This edition published with permission from Bloomsbury Publishing Plc,
50 Bedford Square, London, WC1B3DP, UK

(© Eye Ubiquitous/Universal Images Group/Getty Images)

British Library Cataloguing-in-Publication Data
A catalogue record for this book is available from the British Library.

Library of Congress Cataloging-in-Publication Data
A catalog record for this book is available from the Library of Congress

ISBN: 978-93-93715-36-4

For sale in the Indian subcontinent only

Typeset by Integra Software Services Pvt. Ltd.
Printed at Manipal Technologies Limited, Manipal

Bloomsbury Publishing Plc makes every effort to ensure that the papers used in the manufactur our books are natural, recyclable products made from wood grown in well-managed forests. O manufacturing processes conform to the environmental regulations of the country of origin.

To find out more about our authors and books
visit www.bloomsbury.com and sign up for our newsletters

To our students. With gratitude.

Our special thanks to Libby Robin, Paul Josephson, José Augusto Pádua, Mary Mackey, Stefania Barca (always), Roberto Delpiano (again), Katie Ritson and the Rachel Carson Center for Environment and Society.

CONTENTS

CONTRIBUTORS

Marco Armiero (PhD in Economic History) is an environmental historian; he has worked in Italy, the United States, Portugal and Spain. Currently, he is the director of the Environmental Humanities Laboratory at the KTH Royal Institute of Technology in Stockholm. He has co-edited with Marcus Hall *Nature and History in Modern Italy* (2010), and he is the author of *A Rugged Nation. Mountains and the Making of Modern Italy* (2011).

Mao Da is currently a postdoctoral fellow with the School of Chemistry, Beijing Normal University. He has studied environmental history since 2007, and has published a book on the early history of waste disposal in the ocean in the United States. He has extended his academic interest to other fields such as the problem of persistent organic pollutants and environmental movement. He also co-founded two environmental organizations, namely the Rock Energy and Environment Institute and Nature University, in 2012. Before that, he had been an environmental activist for seven years, and was deeply involved in environmental campaigns for integrated waste management, chemical safety and environmental health in China and globally.

Jerry Frank is an assistant professor at the University of Missouri. He specializes in US environmental history, with special attention paid to the development of consumer culture in the twentieth century. Professor Frank published *Making Rocky Mountain National Park: The Environmental History of an American Treasure* in 2013.

Libby Robin is an environmental historian at the Fenner School of Environment and Society, Australian National University and the National Museum of Australia. She is a guest professor at the KTH Royal Institute of Technology, Stockholm. She has authored 12 books, including several that have won major prizes in history, literature and zoology. She also has many published papers on the environmental history and conservation thinking and science.

Lise Sedrez (PhD in Latin American History) is an environmental historian at Universidade Federal do Rio de Janeiro, where she is the editor of the academic journal *Topoi*. She has worked and published in the United States and Brazil, and is the co-editor of the series Latin American Landscapes, by University of Arizona Press. Professor Sedrez's research interests include urban environmental history and history of disasters, and she is the author of a forthcoming book on the environmental history of Guanabara Bay, Rio de Janeiro.

Phia Steyn teaches African political and environmental history at the University of Stirling, Scotland. Her research and publications have focused mainly on Nigerian oil industry, apartheid and the environment in South Africa, cattle plague and other environmental crises in the Orange Free State republic in the 1890s and the food ways of Southern African communities. She is currently writing on the environmental impact of war and conflict in Southern Africa in the 1970s and 1980s, South African participation in international environmental initiatives in the 1970s and cattle plague remedies and the diffusion of scientific knowledge in Southern Africa in the 1890s. Recent publications include 'Changing times, changing palates: The dietary impacts of Basutho adaptation to new rulers, crops, and markets, 1830s–1966' in Christina Folke Ax et al. (eds), *Cultivating the Colonies: Colonial States and Their Environmental Legacies* (2011).

Hein-Anton van der Heijden is a senior lecturer in political science at the University of Amsterdam. His current topics of interest include environmental movements, international environmental politics and political discourse analysis. He has widely published about these topics in journals like *Environmental Politics*, *Environmental Values*, *Organization and Environment*, *International Political Science Review* and the (Dutch) *Yearbook for Ecological History*. He was one of the contributors of Flam, H. (ed.) 1994, *States and Anti-Nuclear Movements*. His most recent (2010) book is *Social Movements, Public Spheres and the European Politics of the Environment. Green Power Europe?*

Mei Xueqin is a historian of modern world history at Tsinghua University. Her research interests are nineteenth- and twentieth-century history, with a particular interest in British industrialization, urbanization and their impacts on the environment within Britain and abroad. She is investigating how modern British people have incorporated nature and the environment into their productive fields and their everyday life, the problems and solutions encountered during these processes and how countries such as contemporary China could learn from Great Britain's history of modernization. Before coming to Tsinghua University, she taught at Beijing Normal University, having received a PhD from Nanjing University in 1994.

Stephen Zavestoski is an associate professor of sociology and a co-chair of the Environmental Studies Program at the University of San Francisco. He is currently labouring over his book titled *Toxic Evolution in Bhopal: How a Social Movement Became Global*, which draws on his research examining the mobilization of transnational social movement networks in response to the increased risk of industrial hazards brought on by globalization. He is also the co-editor, with Phil Brown, of *Social Movements in Health* (2005), and, with Phil Brown and Rachel Morello-Frosch, of *Contested Illnesses: Citizens, Science, and Health Social Movements* (2012). His research areas include environmental sociology, social movements and sociology of health and illness.

Frank Zelko is an associate professor at the University of Vermont. Zelko's research focuses on the history of environmental movements. He has published work on environmental activism in the United States, Canada, Germany and Australia. His book on the history of the international environmental organization, Greenpeace, was published in 2013.

INTRODUCTION

Marco Armiero and Lise Fernanda Sedrez

Local versus global

'Think globally, act locally'—few slogans have been more fortunate than this one. It has been so popular that it is even difficult to trace its history.[1] Indeed, the slogan embodies some of most significant beliefs environmentalists shared, despite all the differences among them. It not only implies a strong connection linking the local and the global, but it also suggests that any environmentalist action must be understood from the ground-up, first and foremost from the local viewpoint.

Looking at Selborne in England or Walden in New England, environmentalists learnt of the world around them; Gilbert White in the eighteenth century and Henry David Thoreau in the nineteenth century prefigure this ecological awareness of place. As Donald Worster wrote regarding Gilbert White's account of Selborne, apart from the meticulous exploration of local nature, the acknowledgement of the ecological connection between species and places was the main contribution of that kind of studies.[2] In contrast with those who believe they may live detached from nature, environmentalists recognize that they are part of a community made of multiple relationships—both biotic and abiotic. This is an ecological concept; ecology explains that all organisms are connected in a network which makes what is called an ecosystem. Interconnection is a touchstone of ecology; everything that occurs in any given part of an ecosystem will affect the rest, many times in unexpected ways.

According to the environmentalist and physicist Barry Commoner, the principle that 'everything is connected to everything else' must be considered the first basic law of ecology. While it may be more intuitive to trace those connections at the local scale, they are not less strong and real at the global level. For instance, the way of producing, consuming and living in Europe or North America has historically affected faraway places and even the entire Earth, as in the case of global climate change. Fluxes of energy, materials, people, animals, germs, viruses and toxic substances criss-cross the planet and connect places and cultures. The awareness of these connections has always been at the core of environmentalism, even where there are different perceptions of the scale of these ties. Realizing we are part of an interconnected community can be a place-based experience or a global one. As this book shows, the former does not preclude the latter.

Connections are more than a matter of scale; the quality of those links and the ways in which they are perceived also matter. Ordinarily, people do not envision themselves as part of an ecosystem. Rather, we belong in places and communities. The ties binding people to socio-natural environments are not made only of energy and materials. They are not just *scientific* facts understandable through *scientific* knowledge. They are also made of feelings and attachments. People believe they belong to specific places to which they are connected not by laws of biology or flows of energy, but through stories, memories and feelings. Rob Nixon has defined those places 'vernacular landscapes' in which generations of people have carved their intimate maps on the geologies and ecologies of space.[3] Raymond Williams wrote that people are born into placeable relations[4] that shape what he and David Harvey called 'militant particularism',[5] that is the militant 'place-bound politics' that blends particular struggles in particular places.[6]

At the roots of several environmentalist struggles, we might recognize such a 'sense of place', that is a special bond connecting people to specific pieces of nature. Nonetheless, our understanding of the 'sense of place' is not merely a matter of individual taste but rather an evolving social process involving the collective cultures and practices through which the environment is represented, perceived and shaped. This was the case in the Lake District in England, the Yosemite Valley in California, the Marmora Falls in Italy and the Little Desert in Australia. Indeed, recognizing one's local, specific community is a common experience shared by environmentalists around the world. Historically, this bonding has worked mainly in a positive way, establishing connections linking *notable* places (such as Yosemite) to *notable* people (such as John Muir). As in the few examples we have mentioned, the connection has often implied the identification of people and places with specific landmarks or portions of landscapes which have become symbolic in the construction of their identity. The history of the national parks can be framed in this way. Nevertheless, the special bond linking some people to some places, which turns a geographical fact into a personal/collective experience, or, in simpler words, into a home, is not just a cultural construction deeply marked by post-materialistic values which will inevitably lead towards a real or dreamed natural park; instead, the connection is often made of work linking people and nature in a productive rather than a contemplative or recreational way, as, for instance, in the case of rubber tappers in the Amazon forest.

Everywhere indigenous communities identify themselves with *special* places and resources as they fight to protect them from rapacious exploitation. In some indigenous cultures, the identification with nature may be extremely deep, deriving from and constructing religious beliefs and driving the organization of daily life. Nonetheless, these bonds do not require a separation of environment and society, nor do these communities intend to save nature from humans (or maybe just from *some* humans); in these cases, to protect nature means to protect the sources of the communities' livelihood. This is what Joan Martínez Alier and Ramachandra Guha have called the environmentalism of the poor.[7] As we will see later, their work has undermined the basic assumption of a large portion of political and sociological theory, that is the idea that environmentalism is the product of affluence—only rich people could afford the luxury of being 'green'.

The special bonds connecting local people and their environment do not necessarily result from non-material values; people might connect to nature through their work, subsistence, families and, of course, through their bodies. From this point of view, the connection with the local environment might be even deeper; the ties enter into the body blending external and internal nature. It may be the contamination coming from oil extraction and passing from water and soil to animals and people; it may be toxic waste dumped near poor communities around the world; it may be exposure to polluting substances in the work and living milieu. To bond with a specific environment does not always bring the special and positive feeling of belonging to a place; sometimes it might become a frightening experience, a trap from which one wants only to be freed.

In the last decades, these experiences of contamination and loss have increasingly shaped the 'local' aspects in the environmental movements. Everywhere, in the global North as well as in the South, local communities have begun to oppose unwanted factories, infrastructures and waste facilities, fighting to protect the health of people and the ecosystem. Those are local struggles and yet they are connected to a global network of resistance and awareness. Often the connection between humans and the environment becomes so close that the boundaries between them may be considered a hybrid form.[8] Those local environments are not separated from people's daily lives; as the US environmental justice activists say, nature is where they work, study, play and pray.[9] When the local environment is at risk, the communities are also at risk. A sense of place drives communities to recognize the hidden hazards in the environment they know. It also enables them to trace and understand the multiple and unpredictable ways in which environmental damage moves between nature and human bodies. This has been the challenge of the environmental justice movement (EJM), a new wave of environmentalism raised in the United States and especially in the African American communities in the last three decades. Chapter 8 (Armiero) will retrace the story of that movement. In the EJM struggles, the defence of the local—meaning both the community and the environment—has been so forceful that local activists have been accused of being selfish, caring only for their own interests. The acronym NIMBY—Not In My Back Yard—summarizes the main critique against this kind of environmentalist mobilization; according to that narrative, the bond linking local people and their environment may produce an irrational and sturdy opposition to the introduction of any novelty, privileging the community's well-being over the general good. In a NIMBY scenario, it would be enough moving an unwanted infrastructure, for instance an incinerator, to any other community, merely protecting the space where one lives.

Indeed, people in Afton, North Carolina, or in Love Canal, New York, did not ask to have toxic waste in their backyards. However, theirs were more than NIMBY battles. Those struggles flared a wider movement for environmental justice which went far beyond Afton and Love Canal, exposing the racial arrangement of the US society, the social injustice embodied in unequal distribution of environmental hazards and the constituencies of what we define science, progress and welfare. As Henri Acselrad has stated,

> Far from having a 'not in my back yard' attitude, the actors who began to unite behind this movement were fighting for the politicization of environmental racism and inequality, denouncing the perceived predominant attitude of 'always in the poor people's backyard'.[10]

Besides the relevance of the local, which, by the way, needs to be better defined, the environmentalist cultures also often include a strong sense of the whole. Scholars have pointed out how the emergence of the modern environmentalism was linked to a new understanding of the Earth as a global system. While the images of the Blue Planet from the space demonstrated this sense of global unity,[11] new environmental threats, including desertification, atomic fallout and climate change, have proved that the fight for nature needs a global frame. Nobody and no place can be environmentally safe separated from the whole. Environmentalism exists in this delicate balance between local and global. It must be local and global at the same time.

At first sight, it seems a simple matter of scale: as at the local scale everything is connected, bringing all to a global scale makes the local a part of the whole. Yet, things are more complicated than that. At closer examination, we realize that the scale we choose to adopt changes the way in which we understand problems and frame solutions. Let's consider, for instance, certain severe environmental regulations which, applied in rich countries, have simply produced the shift of dangerous productions to poor countries with weaker environmental laws, in what is called 'environmental dumping'.[12] Likewise, polluting substances which are banned in the North are often still allowed in the global South. The traffic of toxic waste from the 'developed' world to the South represents another aspect of this problem of scale. While at the local level (nation) it is enough to dispose of what is dangerous and unwanted in poor neighbourhoods, on a global scale, poor countries have been transformed into planetary dump. Thus, these might seem good solutions only if the nation is the scale; for business as usual, nothing is more convenient than a remote continent, invisible to public opinion, to implement a strategy based on 'remove and forget'.

Scale is never merely a geographical matter; it also has inherent political content. To consider the environment only at the national scale keeps the decision-making processes also at national level, responding to the national public opinion or, more precisely, to voters. The politicization of scale also affects the geometries of distances and proximities; sometimes neighbouring countries seem much farther apart than their distance in miles suggests, as in the cases of Mexico and the United States or of Western Europe and some former socialist countries in the East. From this perspective, distance and proximity derive not only from geography but also from power. Places, or countries, are not only distributed on a flat map, but they are also arranged on a hierarchic pyramid implying that some have more power to decide over their future—or over the future of others. Lawrence Summers' infamous 1991 memo on the convenience of relocating polluting activities in Africa well exemplifies the consequences for the environment of this power inequality at global level.[13]

The politicization of scale, however, goes beyond the mere—and obvious—hierarchical arrangement among countries; the very framing of places and issues in global or local terms is political. As Steven Yearley has argued, while the Amazon forest has been transformed into a global place, a theme for international debate, the mass consumption of sports utility vehicles (SUVs) in the North has received a very different treatment, for example, and is perceived as a local matter, or even a private right.[14] Likewise, megalopolises in the global North, which might have become global places for their impact on the planet, remained rather comfortably framed within their national borders. As with places, global environmental discourse has turned iconic animals, the so-called mega fauna, into a global matter, as heritage of humanity, while the protection of seeds or the free access to water has never acquired the same global status. Environmentalists have pointed out for many years how wealthy countries, while eager to discuss in global arenas how to manage Brazilian forests or African large mammals, are less willing to accept interferences regarding their internal affairs or the regulation of the global market economy.

Recently, climate change has become the most significant global environmental issue; actually, it may be considered the symbol of the common destiny of the planet. Undoubtedly, climate change is a global problem that calls for collective actions; by definition, it must be framed in a planetary scale because it affects everyplace and everybody on Earth. Nevertheless, a purely global perspective for climate change may hide the unequal effects it has on different countries, classes and ethnic groups. While climate change is indeed a global issue, it does not follow that all humans are responsible or affected in the same way. Indeed, responsibility may be far from impact. While much mainstream rhetoric on climate change is formulated in terms of a singular common battle against a common enemy, environmental justice demands that the voices of those who shoulder a disproportionate share of the impact should be heard more clearly. In other words, rather than a claim for a generic universal cooperation, climate justice needs confrontation, recognition and resistance.

Local and global perspectives blend in the history and practices of environmentalism, as well as in the pages of this book. The stories we have gathered are deeply rooted in specific places; yet these local stories taken together inform a transnational and comparative, even global, perspective. This is a collection of paradigmatic stories that, read together, illustrate diverse and plural environmentalist movements. They draw on a variety of geographical areas, historical times, environmental concerns and social actors. The approaches of the writers are also diverse.

Some authors, for instance, have chosen to focus on certain environmental movements in the context of the 'new social movements' with their emphasis on post-materialist rather than on materialist values. Others, instead, have selected case studies in which the continuity with more traditional social movements highlights the material aspects of those struggles. Some writers identify with political science or social theory; others are environmental historians. Despite these differences, there is a common thread that connects the chapters of the book: each story has an environmental conflict at its core. From the struggles for the creation of national parks in the United States and in Australia to the anti-atomic mobilization in Germany, from the quest for justice in Bhopal to the waste crisis in Naples, Italy, from Chico Mendes and rubber tappers in the Amazon to the battles for the protection of the antelope in China, from the Ogoni's resistance against Shell to Greenpeace's campaign to save the seals, these stories are stories of conflicts. Beyond their narrative value, we believe the focus on conflict is itself instrumental in better understanding the relationships between humans and nature. Environmental conflicts can offer windows through which we can observe the transformation of cultural perceptions, ways of production and consuming and ecological and social changes.[15]

The story of environmentalism

The history of environmentalism has generated a diverse and significant literature. Many of these works have often centred on nations, and as a result, there are many 'histories of environmentalism' as it has developed in certain countries and cultures. Some writers focus on specific institutions or, more recently, on individual biographies.[16] Political ecologists have accumulated a rich collection of studies on environmental conflicts throughout the world, giving particular emphasis to specific places. In this book, we borrow from both approaches and combine their insights together. The book compares and contrasts paradigmatic stories of environmental struggles in different places and times which, taken together, contribute to a stronger transnational sense of what a global history of environmentalism might look like.

'Environmentalism' is an all-encompassing word, covering different ideas of nature and society, as well as different forms of activism. 'Environmentalism' is not a monolithic movement, and to reduce it to this is misleading, even imperial. Our historical perspective ensures that it is considered pluralistically. In this book, however, the questions we sought to bring to our readership are largely influenced by the US literature on the environmental justice movement and, more broadly, on subaltern environmentalism. Namely, Robert Bullard, Andrew Hurley, Robert Gottlieb, Chad Montrie, David Pellow and Laura Pulido have contributed to uncover different paths of environmentalism and deeply affected our ways of thinking about the history of environmentalism.[17] While their scholarship focused mostly, but not exclusively, on the US experience, on a global scale we acknowledge our debt to the work of Joan Martínez Alier and Rob Nixon.[18] These authors have developed the concept of environmentalism of the poor which is crucial to this book.

So far, Joan Martínez Alier and Ramachandra Guha have provided the most effective global account of the 'varieties of environmentalism'. They contrast three main branches, which they describe, respectively, as the cult of wilderness, the gospel of eco-efficiency and the environmentalism of the poor. The cult of wilderness, for instance, embodies the most traditional approach to environmentalism, that is the emphasis on 'untouched' nature and its protection through parks and environmental laws. A corollary to the wilderness approach is a strong dichotomy between the spaces of nature and humans; environmental concerns are only related to the former, which should be preserved by human intervention. At least for a long time, mainstream environmentalist organizations have basically avoided the social justice dimensions of ecological problems. As David Peterson del Mar has pointed out, the majority of Sierra Club members in 1972 (at this time mostly from the dominant, wealthier communities who enjoyed hiking in remote areas) explicitly opposed engaging with environmental problems concerning urban poor and ethnic minorities.[19] Giovanna DiChiro, as well, wrote of how the coalition of Latino women fighting against the construction of an incinerator in East Los Angeles found no support from well-established environmental organizations because, according to them, theirs was not an 'environmentalist' struggle.[20] A frequent criticism of the cult of wilderness is that it not only neglects urban and domestic spaces as environmental spaces, but it also harbours misconceptions of what 'counts' as wilderness. In particular, a concept of wilderness as 'untouched nature' denies the agency of indigenous communities in shaping the environment.[21] It also tends to privilege recreational uses for the elites and regards subsistence practices of subaltern groups as undesirable.[22] Even so, several aspects of the cult of wilderness are groundbreaking. It encouraged the consideration of nature for its own value, and on its own terms. Deep ecology and animated debates on the reasons to protect nature in the political arena emerged from its crucible. In an age obsessed by economic growth where nature was often unappreciated, fighting to protect some parts of it from the worst ravages of the market economy was in its time, visionary.

While the cult of wilderness aims at the protection of nature, or more precisely of selected parts of nature, somehow saving from exploitation, the 'gospel of eco-efficiency' goes in the opposite direction. Building upon Samuel P. Hays's expression 'gospel of efficiency', Guha and Martínez Alier identify a 'gospel of eco-efficiency', which has the declared objective of using nature in a rational or, as formulated later, sustainable way.[23] In some versions, the origins of such environmentalist culture can be traced to eighteenth-century German forestry, which aimed at exploiting forests without destroying them. Instead of contemplating nature as it is (or as it is perceived), the gospel of eco-efficiency envisions the environment as a space for wise human intervention. Better and more modern technology offers the solution for nature, in contrast with wasteful, obsolete uses of natural resources; humans have the right to use natural resources while science provides the tools to exercise this right wisely. While the cult of wilderness has produced national parks and laws for the protection of species and habitats, the gospel of eco-efficiency has pushed towards including nature into the economy. Rather than protecting the environment, it seems to focus on reproducing economic growth without damaging world's natural capital. Probably, the most significant and resilient product of the eco-efficiency discourse has been the concept of sustainable development, as the basic idea of sustainability is precisely the possibility to use nature in a rational way, within the planet's carrying capacity. Not by chance, advocates of eco-efficiency often use economic-driven metaphors, likening sustainable development to prudent human beings who live off the interests from their trust funds without diminishing the main capital. This model of environmentalism has also been subject to several criticisms, among which are its utilitarian view of nature, its faith on the ability of science to regulate the environment and its frequent disregard of social inequalities when considering the best use for the environment. Despite its limits, however, the gospel of eco-efficiency has contributed to a better management of natural resources and waste, and at least has fostered a globalizing debate on these themes. In fact, by focusing on the concept of 'carrying capacity', it introduces the ecological idea of limits and directly opposes the economic model of nature as an infinite reserve of resources and an unlimited dump for waste.

The third form of environmentalism as suggested by Martínez Alier and Guha goes against the conventional wisdom according to which environmentalism is a 'full-belly' movement, or that only rich (well-fed) people care about nature. To understand Martínez Alier and Guha's proposition and how it breaks with traditional perceptions of environmentalism, we must first analyse these perceptions in their more sophisticated formulation. Many scholars have argued that the best defence for the environment will come from strong economic growth. Thus, it would be possible to understand the evolution of environmental concerns following Kuznets curve; the raising of citizens' complaints about environmental problems would be correlated with income levels rather than with actual environmental problems.[24] On this argument, the richer a country became, the greener would be its policies. This is the reassuring mantra of the priests of the market. A correlation between wealth and environmentalism has been explained in technological and sociological terms. On the one hand, richer countries can invest in improving the efficiency of their economic system, saving energy and raw materials, reducing pollution and paying for natural protection; on the other hand, in these countries the social structure has profoundly changed, reducing the number of people working in large and highly polluting factories, while transferring the labour force towards white-collar professions. Thus, newly empowered social groups have become the main actors of the environmentalist movement. In this sense, environmentalism has been included in the so-called new social movements whose main characteristic is to be centred on values and cultural identities rather than on class identities and economic claims. Indeed, these movements have departed markedly from the traditional labour unions, who mobilize on the basis of economic interests and class identities.[25] This kind of narrative, some governments from the global South claim, gives them a right to override environmental concerns in the hope of achieving economic growth in the first instance. However, this mainstream interpretation of environmentalism as a values-based, post-materialistic phenomenon, championed by Ronald Inglehart,[26] has been challenged on the ground by the myriad of struggles connecting social and environmental issues, and at the theory level by the emergence of environmentalism of the poor[27] and the environmental justice movement.[28] Unlike the cult of wilderness, subaltern environmentalism does not divide the space of work and daily life from that of nature; actually, it does not separate body and nature, but chooses to focus on urban and work environment and, more precisely, on the connections between economic production and public health. A necessary corollary to this notion is the concept of 'slow violence', elaborated by Rob Nixon; as he has written, the violence against ecosystems and communities is not always fast and immediately visible, but it may extend over time leaving its imprint over generations.

> For if the past of slow violence is never past—Nixon argues—, so too the post is never fully post: industrial particulates and effluents live on in the environmental elements we inhabit and in our very bodies, which epidemiologically and ecologically are never our simple contemporaries.[29]

The issue of visibility versus invisibility and the causal connections between environmental damages and health problems are at the core of so many environmental struggles, which, therefore, engage with the very construction and legitimacy of scientific knowledge.[30] In contrast to the gospel of eco-efficiency and its trust in technology and science, subaltern environmentalism proposes democratic control for both technology and science, as well as more a critical vision about the possibilities to solve the ecological crisis through technocratic solutions. The basic assumption of subaltern environmentalism is that ecological problems and hazards are not equally distributed among classes, races and genders; poor, minorities and women pay a higher price in terms of contamination and exposure to environmental risks. Beyond this basic assumption, however, environmentalism of the poor varies widely, shaped by the environmental and social realities of the people concerned. Some are quite aware of the planetary implications of their struggle; others are more deeply involved in local issues of survival and subsistence. There is no single template.

It is tempting to place those three branches of environmentalism on a chronological scale, maybe an evolutionary scheme, and to affirm that in the beginning it was the wilderness, then eco-efficiency came and finally the age of justice arrived. Some historians have told the story of environmentalism in this way. This is not the case of Robert Gottlieb, one of the most innovative scholars working on this issue, who has indicated the 1970s as a major shift in the environmentalist movement, marking the passage from a focus on wilderness protection to a wider interest on urban and industrial problems.[31] Others have argued that the publication of *Silent Spring*[32] in 1962 should be considered the trigger for the development of environmentalism. We suggest, on the contrary, that the history of environmentalism is much more diverse and with more multiple origins than a chronological, evolutionary narrative may convey.

In fact, Joan Martínez Alier had already argued that a subaltern environmentalism had a much longer and independent history, citing the struggles over mining activities in Ashio, Japan, in 1907 and Andalusia in the 1880s,[33] and recently Chad Montrie has explicitly challenged the 'standard periodization' of the movement, considerably backdating the beginning of a working-class environmentalism at least to the 1940s but even earlier in the nineteenth century.[34] Thus, the varieties of environmentalism are not sequential or evolutionary models, but parallel and sometimes competing ways to see, to experience and to care for the environment.

We interpret those concerns about periodization as a challenge to tell a more complex story of environmentalism—a story that includes well-known landmarks, such as the publication of *Silent Spring*, the celebration of Earth Day in 1970[35] or the nuclear accident of Three Mile Island in 1979,[36] but which also includes longer processes, lost in mainstream narratives and linear evolution constructions. This approach suggests that the environmentalist movement has not passed through a succession of mutually exclusive stages. While wilderness protection is still very relevant for global biodiversity, and discourses on sustainable development and ecological modernization remain high on the contemporary political agenda, struggles that connect social and environmental justice have a deeper common history than previously thought. It would be possible to argue, for instance, that resistance to enclosures in England since the sixteenth century had both an environmental and a social content.[37] Revisionist periodization notwithstanding, however, most authors agree that the number and the intensity of environmental struggles connecting social and ecological issues dramatically increased from the 1970s.

By writing this history of the environmentalism, then, we argue that the cult of wilderness, the gospel of eco-efficiency and the environmentalism of the poor are extremely useful ideal types that help us to understand the main ideological roots for environmental movements. In less abstract examples, however, these roots are often intertwined. Environmental conflicts arise in very concrete circumstances and the social actors negotiate their own strategies and movements in these concrete circumstances. Sometimes they are successful, other times less successful and often they generate new experiences and qualitatively different sorts of environmentalism. For instance, local communities, while fighting for access to local resources or against contamination, which would be good examples of the 'environmentalism of the poor', often need to establish international coalitions with groups that differ greatly from their own grassroots origins. They may incorporate discourses of sustainability or economic advantage (e.g. that health costs are a future cost to society); they may seek for access to more efficient tools or machines in their relation with their own environment, without losing track of their own interests and goals.

Likewise, eco-efficiency or wilderness advocates often find themselves in a conundrum when they discuss global commons and the needs of different groups around the world. Faced with the need to bring different partners to the table, environmentalists are forced to define their environmental scope pragmatically. Sometimes they discover that their fight is much deeper than any hypothetical idea of nature would allow.

By focusing on these more complex networks of environmental conflicts, we highlight the rich diversity of environmentalist experiences. There is not a right or a wrong environmentalism, but narratives and practices of environmentalism which are historically produced. As we bring them together to weave a transnational history of environmentalism, we find that these narratives and practices are dynamic, and they themselves keep changing in response to a globally changing world.

Local struggles for global stories

From China to Brazil, from the seals to working-class people, from national parks to atomic power plants, from the Ogoni to the Australian scientists—this book offers a variety of snapshots of environmentalist cultures and activism. Each chapter presents real, down-to-earth experiences of environmentalism, including the feelings of the actors themselves. The main tenets of Guha and Martínez Alier are intermixed in these stories. We have sought to cover different geographical areas, as well as the variety of actors and visions, without claiming to be exhaustive. Many themes and critical struggles are missing from this picture; nevertheless, we hope that the stories gathered in this book can together contribute to a wider debate on the history and trajectories of environmentalism.

There is a common thread in the stories: what is nature, or the environment? A question intimately connected to the theories and practices of conservation, it permeates the entire book, intersecting the protection of particular species—as, for instance, the Tibetan antelope or the harp seal, or the creation of natural parks. In Jerry Frank's chapter on the history of the US national parks, he addresses precisely the construction of 'nature' as a *place* worth of protection. Frank points out how the making of national parks required both a narrative about nature and concrete policies and practices to shape it on the ground. Transforming a piece of nature into a national park implied the eradication of the memory of indigenous people living there, as well as the suppression of what did not fit in the new human-made 'pristine' landscape, including predators and forest fires. Indeed, the story of what has been called 'America's best idea'[38] contains two conflicts: on the one hand, the struggles against economic interests to create national parks and, on the other, the battles over meanings and memory in making space for the parks and in telling their history.

Nature and conservation are also the keywords in Libby Robin's chapter. In particular, she introduces the role of scientists in providing the 'voice of nature'—the creation of the concept of biological diversity was a way to define nature, and also who had the right to speak for it. Activists and experts in the environmental struggles grappled with how to use the ecological definition for a social outcome. As Robin states, 'The Little Desert case study provided a political moment when the collaboration between environmental sciences and public policy was on show.' According to Robin, conservation was mainly a matter for negotiation and, therefore, intrinsically political; nonetheless, science had to inform that negotiation. The making of science, the relationships linking academics, activists and decision makers and the interactions between official and informal experts are some of the most provoking themes present in this chapter. They can be found far beyond Australia and the Little Desert, as central pieces in so many other stories of environmental conflicts.

The conservation of biological diversity—natural parks—and the protection of endangered species are, as mentioned earlier, at the heart of classic narratives of environmentalism; therefore, Tibetan antelopes and harp seals are also among the figures evoked in this book. Nevertheless, as Mao Da and Mei Xueqin, and Frank Zelko demonstrate in their chapters, there are several ways in which environmentalism can embrace the protection of wild animals. The relationships between environmental organizations and governmental bodies, the clash with workers interested in using rather than protecting nature, the connections with the global public opinion are topics common to both chapters. Mao Da and Mei Xueqin focus mainly on government/civil society dialectic in the strategies for the protection of the Tibetan antelope, an animal highly targeted for the market value of its wool. The authors do not indulge in a celebration of the conservationist endeavour. Rather, they analyse the limits of both environmentalist organizations and the Chinese state. On the one hand, environmentalists needed to be sensitive to the region's economic development needs, even though it could eventually lead to the destruction of the antelope, in the case of Tibet. On the other hand, governmental bodies showed a 'nationalistic' approach to the antelope protection, in which they carried on a harsh denounce of Western consumerism while also downplayed and dismissed other transnational environmental elements of the antelope trade, namely those related to the defence of the Indian tiger. Frank Zelko's chapter takes a very different direction, although he also analyses the protection of wild animals. In this case, the protagonist is not a local activist group, but rather one of the most influential global environmentalist organizations, Greenpeace. Therefore, the story of its anti-sealing campaign is an excellent case study to reflect on the environmentalism of an NGO, its strategy and main tenets. Zelko offers a thoughtful approach to the vexed question of work versus environment. Seeking to save seals from being killed on the ice of Newfoundland, Greenpeace activists confronted the staunch resistance of local hunters defending their source of income. Zelko illustrates the conflagration between environmentalists from metropolitan cultures and local dwellers, deeply rooted in their rural world. In the Great North as well as in the Amazon, in the US Northwest forests or in the industrial towns everywhere, movements to protect nature often clash with work needs and the demands for jobs. Conflict is part of this complicated relationship, but not the only part. The focus on the binary opposition of nature protection and job protection hides another part of the story which is made also of cooperation, shared campaigns and coalitions.[39] In the case analysed by Frank Zelko, different groups seek a compromise between the defence of the seals and the interests of the workers. Thus, Greenpeace opted to target the large capitalist companies involved in the hunting while sparing the local people who were also killing the animals. The compromise eventually failed, and Zelko proceeds to a careful analyses of its dynamics, its limits and the causes of its collapse. If the fight for jobs and the protection of nature are not necessarily in diametric opposition, neither constitute an easy, natural alliance.

Stephen Zavestoski's and Marco Armiero's chapters refuse the mainstream narrative in which work and the environment are in an irreconcilable conflict, or more in general, in which environmentalism and subaltern movements are necessarily opposed to each other. Both authors deal with the raising of a different branch of environmentalism that is not centred on the traditional nature conservation, but on urban dilemmas. Not endangered species or special places rich in biodiversity but working-class people and human health are the main objects of this environmental mobilization. Zavestoski addresses one of the world's most tragic industrial disasters in the city of Bhopal, India, and its legacy. The chemical contamination that followed the explosion in the Union Carbide factory in Bhopal in December 1984 killed an uncertain numbers of victims, from 3,800 of the official statistics up to 15,000, according to non-governmental agencies. However, Zavestoski does not focus on the event *per se*, but mainly on its legacy in terms of social mobilization for justice, decontamination and recognition. In Bhopal, as in every industrial disaster, the border between the unpredictable accident and the deliberate undervaluation of safety procedures to maximize profits were controversial; furthermore, the identification of who the victims are may be questionable. Even more contested was the scientific correlation between specific health conditions and the industrial accident, which had massive legal implications. Finally, setting a monetary value to the damages and the punishment for those eventually found responsible brought in question the unequal power of the parts involved and could only be settled through legislation and legal battles. By exploring the history of those conflicts, Stephen Zavestoski focuses mainly on the intersection between global and local. As graffiti on the wall of the Union Carbide factory states, *Bhopal is the real face of globalization*, because it reveals the violence inherent in global capitalism and its imposition of a profit regime over any precautionary measure. The unknown street artist's graffiti also demonstrates how such environmental struggles and social movements are painfully aware of their global connections.

While Bhopal embodies the exceptional disaster, the waste crisis in Naples, Italy, is an icon for day-by-day capitalist imposition of environmental injustice in an urban setting. Blending local stories and global references, Armiero draws the contours of the subaltern environmentalism and what it has meant for the environmentalist movement. Although unusual as a case study in environmental injustice, the case of Naples contains the main characteristics of that story. In Italy as in the United States, poor and marginalized communities suffered unequal distribution of environmental burdens. While the entire region of Campania became the dump of the factories from the Italian north, on the local scale, government and corporate powers sought to impose waste facilities onto the poorest and already contaminated communities, following the path of least resistance. This assumption proved wrong; those marginalized communities resisted their fate, by proposing a different vision of environmentalism. Armiero analyses what this implies in terms of relationships between scientific knowledge and activism, a combination always central in the environmental mobilization, as shown in this book by Libby Robin.

Subaltern environmentalism is also at the centre of Phia Steyn's chapter on oil extraction and ethnic resistance in the Niger Delta. There, the defence of a fragile ecosystem coincides with the protection of the health and the very survival of ethnic minorities living in the area. Also in that case, as in Bhopal, not only the oil corporations are multinational but also the struggles for compensation, justice and decontamination of water and soil have become transnational. In particular, the brutal execution of Ken Saro Wiwa, the leader of the Ogoni people, brought the conflicts to the wider world, ensuring, as Steyn argues, 'public scrutiny of the role of multinational oil companies in the marginalisation of ethnic minority groups'. The Niger Delta case demonstrates that only the resistance of local communities has been able to uncover the social and environmental injustice imposed by oil corporations on poor people and ethnic minorities. Petro-conflicts are powerful case studies to reflect on the interconnections between ecology and power at both local and global scale. Power is embodied into the contaminated ecology of the Niger Delta as well as in the global regimes of truth imposed by corporations and international agencies. In fact, as Steyn points out, according to mainstream reports, the blame for contamination and spilling was to be placed on the communities' shoulders, guilty of sabotaging the oil infrastructures.

Likewise, Lise Sedrez's chapter also focuses on a community's struggle for survival in the heart of the Amazon. The rubber tappers' struggle in the 1980s became a celebrated symbol for the environmentalism of the poor. Their often told success story, which culminated with the adoption of the concept of extractive reserves in the Amazon and elsewhere, should not obliterate the price paid by poor communities throughout the work for their defence of their own environment and livelihood. Violence is not an occasional or unexpected by-product of environmental conflicts, but an intrinsic part of the daily challenges faced by these endangered communities. The murder of Chico Mendes and many other rubber tappers before and after him are grim reminders of these challenges. At the same time, by analysing the community's strategies of confrontation at local level, and the careful negotiation of international networks in support of the rubber tapper struggles, Sedrez highlights the connections of the local and global dimensions which are so much part of the history of environmentalism.

However, the alternative to the traditional environmentalism based on conservation of wild nature is not only the subaltern environmentalism which is significantly represented in our book; other aspects and even an alternative vision is offered by Hein-Anton van der Heijden in his chapter on the anti-nuclear movement in Europe. This movement has been extremely influential in the making of the new environmentalism. As van der Heijden states, the protest against atomic energy has challenged not only a strategic technology of post-war modernity but 'the very institutional features of modernity itself: capitalism, industrialism, surveillance, and military power'. According to the author, the anti-atomic movement is part of the so-called new social movements with a strong contiguity with other countercultures, and therefore based on post-materialistic values and identities rather than on class or economic interests. His approach to the evolution of the environmentalist movements and cultures completes and enriches the book. It is important to note that van der Heijden does not propose universal paradigms that work equally at all latitudes; instead, he argues that the forms of mobilization and their outcomes are not independent from the political structures—the Political Opportunity Structure—of each country.

***

Under ash-grey skies, before oil-coloured black seas, in a city shaken by hurricanes or drowning in waste, in messianic world conferences to negotiate CO2 emissions in exchange of development and wealth: wherever we are, nature has never been so close, so present and so significant. Two great social historians, Eric Hobsbawm and E.P. Thompson, once said that environmental issues would be the greatest challenge of the twenty-first century. Hobsbawm and Thompson, however, looked to the new millennium from their twentieth-century viewpoint, suggesting the idea that the environment is a realm of the future rather than that of the past. Predictions or prophecies, dreams or nightmares are not the usual bread-and-butter of historical work. There are other more common oracular sources in this arena of predicting the future. Climate scientists and economists, engineers and biologists, a former candidate to the White House and Nobel Prize winner and Hollywood stars all offer prognoses for the future condition of nature. Yet we believe that to understand this planet and our relationship with it, history does help. This book offers a collection of stories from planet Earth—nine meaningful histories of struggles and resistances in different places, each fought in the name of Nature. Together it is these people who are building a global history of environmentalism and, in this process, transforming the relations between humans and the environment on a planetary scale.

NOTES

1 A very useful account on the history of this slogan is actually available in Wikipedia. Available at: http://en.wikipedia.org/wiki/Think_globally,_act_locally#Origin_in_town_planning (accessed on 4 May 2013).
2 Donald Worster, *Nature's Economy. The Roots of Ecology* (San Francisco, CA: Sierra Club Books, 1977), 7.
3 Rob Nixon, *Slow Violence and the Environmentalism of the Poor* (Cambridge, MA: Harvard University Press, 2011), 17.
4 Raymond Williams, *Towards 2000* (London: Chatto & Windus, 1982), 180.
5 David Harvey, 'Militant particularism and global ambition: The conceptual politics of place, space, and environment in the work of Raymond Williams', *Social Text* 42 (1995), 69–98.

6 On this, see David Featherstone, 'Spatialities of transnational resistance to globalization: The maps of grievance of the inter-continental caravan',*Transactions of the Institute of British Geographers* 28:4 (2003), 404–421.

7 Joan Martínez Alier and Ramachandra Guha, *Varieties of Environmentalism: Essays North and South* (London: Earthscan Publications, 1997).

8 Paul S. Sutter, 'The world with us: The state of American environmental history', *Journal of American History* 100:1 (4 June 2013), 94–119, doi:10.1093/jahist/jat095.

9 Patrick Novotny, *Where We Live, Work, and Play: The Environmental Justice Movement and the Struggle for a New Environmentalism* (Westport, CT: Praeger, 2000).

10 Henri Acselrad, 'Grassroots reframing of environmental struggles in Brazil', in David V. Carruthers (ed.), *Environmental Justice in Latin America: Problems, Promise, and Practice* (Cambridge, MA: The MIT Press, 2008), 90.

11 On this issue, see Denis E. Cosgrove, 'Contested global visions: One-world, whole-earth, and the Apollo space photographs', *Annals of the Association of American Geographers* 84:2 (1994), 270–294.

12 On this issue, see Jennifer Clapp, 'The toxic waste trade with less-industrialised countries: Economic linkages and political alliances',*Third World Quarterly* 15:3 (1994), 505–518; David Naguib Pellow, *Resisting Global Toxics: Transnational Movements for Environmental Justice* (Cambridge: The MIT Press, 2007).

13 Lawrence Summers to distribution, 'GEP', Unpublished memo. World Bank, 12 December 1991. Available at: http://www.whirledbank.org/ourwords/summers.html (accessed on 8 May 2013).

14 Steven Yearley, *Cultures of Environmentalism. Empirical Studies in Environmental Sociology* (New York: Palgrave Macmillan, 2005), 47.

15 Marco Armiero, 'Seeing like a protester: Nature, power, and environmental struggles', *Left History* 13:1 (2008), 59–67.

16 Although it would be impossible to include here the enormous amount of literature produced on the history of environmental movements, a few examples are Keith Thomas, *Man and the Natural World: A History of the Modern Sensibility* (New York: Pantheon Books, 1983); Robert Gottlieb, *Forcing the Spring: The Transformation of the American Environmental Movement* (Washington, DC: Island Press, 1993); Philip Shabecoff, *A Fierce Green Fire: The American Environmental Movement* (Washington, DC: Island Press, 2003); David Peterson del Mar, *Environmentalism* (New York: Pearson/Longman, 2006); Christof Mauch, Nathan Stoltzfus and Douglas R. Weiner (eds), *Shades of Green: Environmental Activism Around the Globe* (Lanham, MD: Rowman & Littlefield Publishers, 2006); Michael Egan, *Barry Commoner and the Science of Survival: The Remaking of American Environmentalism* (Cambridge, MA: The MIT Press, 2007); Mark H. Lytle, *The Gentle Subversive: Rachel Carson, Silent Spring, and the Rise of the Environmental Movement* (New York: Oxford University Press, 2007); Donald Worster, *A Passion for Nature. The Life of John Muir* (New York: Oxford University Press, 2008); Chad Montrie, *A People's History of Environmentalism in the United States* (London: Continuum, 2011).

17 Robert Bullard, *Dumping in Dixie: Race, Class, and Environmental Quality* (Boulder, CO: Westview Press, 1999); Gottlieb, *Forcing the Spring*; Robert Gottlieb, *Environmentalism Unbound: Exploring New Pathways for Change* (Cambridge, MA: The MIT Press, 2003); Andrew Hurley, *Environmental Inequalities. Class, Race, and Industrial Pollution in Gary, Indiana, 1945–1980* (Chapel Hill: University of North Carolina Press, 1995); Montrie, *A People's History of Environmentalism*; David Pellow, *Garbage Wars: The Struggle for Environmental Justice in Chicago* (Cambridge, MA: MIT Press, 2002); Laura Pulido, *Environmentalism and Economic Justice: Two Chicano Struggles in the Southwest* (Tucson: University of Arizona Press, 1996).

18 Guha and Martínez Alier, *Varieties of Environmentalism: Essays North and South*; Joan Martínez Alier, *The Environmentalism of the Poor: A Study of Ecological Conflicts and Valuation* (New Delhi: Oxford University Press, 2005); Nixon, *Slow Violence*.

19 Peterson del Mar, *Environmentalism*, 163.

20 Giovanna DiChiro, 'Nature as community: The convergence of environment and social justice', in William Cronon (ed.), *Uncommon Ground: Rethinking the Human Place in Nature* (New York: W. W. Norton, 1996), 299.

21 On the idea of wilderness as cultural construction, see the classic William Cronon, 'The trouble with wilderness; or, getting back to the wrong nature', in Cronon (ed.), *Uncommon Ground*, 69–90. On the obliteration of local people's activities, see Roderick P. Neumann, *Imposing Wilderness. Struggles over Livelihood and Nature Preservation in Africa* (Berkeley: University of California Press, 1998).

22 Karl Jacoby, *Crimes Against Nature: Squatters, Poachers, Thieves, and the Hidden History of American Conservation* (Berkeley: University of California Press, 2001).

23 Samuel Hays, *Conservatism and the Gospel of Efficiency* (Cambridge, MA: Harvard University Press, 1959).

24 Shannon O'Lear, 'Oil wealth, environment, and equity in Azerbaijan', in Julian Agyeman and Yelena Ogneva-Himmelberger (eds), *Environmental Justice and Sustainability in the Former Soviet Union* (Cambridge, MA: The MIT Press, 2009), 98–99.

25 Brian K. Obach, *Labor and the Environmental Movement: The Quest for Common Ground* (Cambridge, MA: The MIT Press, 2004), 17.

26 Ronald Inglehart, 'Post-materialism in an environment of insecurity', *The American Political Science Review* 75:4 (1981), 880–900; 'Public support for environmental protection: Objective problems and subjective values in 43 societies', *PS: Political Science and Politics* 28:1 (1995), 57–72.

27 Martínez Alier, *The Environmentalism of the Poor*.

28 Bullard, *Dumping in Dixie* (Boulder, CO: Westview Press, 1990).

29 Nixon, *Slow Violence*, 8.

30 Nixon, *Slow Violence*, 47.

31 Robert Gottlieb, 'Beyond NEPA and Earth Day: Reconstructing the past and envisioning a future for environmentalism: Presented as the plenary address to the Biennial Meeting of the American Society for Environmental History, Las Vegas, Nevada, March 8, 1995', *Environmental History Review* 19:4 (1995), 1–14.

32 In 1961, the US biologist Rachel Carson published *Silent Spring*, a powerful critique of the modern chemical industry and its effects on health and ecosystem. The book, translated into over thirty languages, became a classic in the environmentalist culture. See the online exhibition on *Silent Spring*, edited by Mark Stoll, and http://www.environmentandsociety.org/exhibitions/silent-spring/overview.

33 Martínez Alier, *The Environmentalism of the Poor*, 55–57; 59–62.

34 Montrie, *A People's History of Environmentalism*, 3–6.

35 The first Earth Day occurred on 22 April 1970; the democrat senator Gaylord Nelson proposed it as a nationwide teach-in series of events to raise attention on environmental problems. With about 20 million people involved in the event, 1970 Earth Day is considered the largest demonstration in history. Denis Hayes, 'Earth day', in Shepard Krech III, J. R. McNeill and Carolyn Merchant (eds), *Encyclopedia of World Environmental History* (New York: Routledge, 2004), 355–356.

36 On 28 March 1979, there was a nuclear accident in the Three Mile Island atomic plant in Pennsylvania; according to the Nuclear Regulatory Commission, this was the most serious nuclear accident occurred on the US soil. Thomas A. Birkland, 'The Three Mile Island accident', in Paul Robbins (ed.), *Encyclopedia of Environment and Society* (Los Angeles: Sage, 2007),1729–1730.

37 See, for instance, Edward Palmer Thompson, *Whigs and Hunters: The Origin of the Black Act* (London: Allen Lane, 1975).

38 Roderick Nash, *Wilderness and the American Mind* (New Haven, CT: Yale University Press, 1967).

39 Stefania Barca, Robert Gottlieb, Chad Montrie, Brian Obach and Christopher Sellers and Joseph Melling, for instance, have contributed to unveil these often neglected narratives and to demonstrate that coalitions linking workers and environmentalists are not only possible but became sometimes historical realities. See Stefania Barca, 'Laboring the earth: Transnational reflections on the environmental history of work', *Environmental History*, 19:1(2014), 3–27. Gottlieb, *Forcing the Spring*; Chad Montrie, *Making a Living: Work and Environment in the United States* (Chapel Hill: University of North Carolina Press, 2008); Montrie, *A People's History of Environmentalism*; Obach, *Labor and the Environmental Movement*; Christopher Sellers and Joseph Melling, *Dangerous Trade: Histories of Industrial Hazard Across a Globalizing World* (Philadelphia, PA: Temple University Press, 2012).

1

Preservation, Parks and Place: Rethinking America's 'Best Idea'

Jerry J. Frank

Introduction

National parks are fascinating. They provide an alluring look at the relationship between humans, nature and history. Some have gone so far as to posit that America's national parks—and the ethos of preservation they embody—represent one of our nation's greatest contributions to the modern world. Ken Burns's recent documentary, *The National Parks: America's Best Idea*, argues as much. Placing the national park system on such a high pedestal, however, is dangerous business.

For more than a century, historians and film-makers like Burns have used the terms 'preservation' and 'conservation' as tools to explain the growth and development of national parks. If we have learned anything at all from postmodern approaches to historical inquiry, however, it is that words matter. To some extent, our words shape perceptions of reality, which, in turn, shape behaviour among and between people and the non-human world. To historians who are largely interested in discerning truth from the murky world of yesteryear, the words we use to frame our heuristics and to advance our arguments are also of the utmost importance. Select the wrong word or employ a poorly framed research question and months—even years—of research can yield results that are far less than satisfying.

In this sense, linking national parks so tightly to 'preservation' and 'conservation' paints us into a corner that is difficult to escape. Both of these words, as it turns out, come with significant ideological freight.

They assume both a pristine past and a protection of that perfect heritage into some unknown point in the distant future. Both also hint at resource management that is largely passive. Park boundaries, as these words imply, offer a sort of force field between a hurly-burly world of change outside and a static, timeless and serene one within. Thus, if we begin our probing into the creation of the national park system as a reflection only of such ideologies, we have ceded too much ground before we have even begun. As wonderful and important as our national parks are, they are not so-called 'virgin' landscapes, nor have they functioned solely to protect that virginity from the groping hands of change.

Rather, major Western national parks like Yellowstone, Yosemite and Rocky Mountain have complicated human histories that stretch deep into the past, just as they are places of significant change that has occurred under the watch—even at the command—of those intent upon protecting them. This does not diminish the importance of national parks. Instead, it makes them more interesting and positions us to see more clearly what parks are, and what they reveal about attitudes regarding the natural world.

Geographer Yi-Fu Tuan has given us an elegant framework with which to approach the relationship between people and the ground they trod: space plus culture equals place.[1] As a historian, I might tweak the equation but a bit to include the passage of time: space plus culture plus time equals place. In other words, *places* are produced (socially constructed) through the application of culture over time in a given location. As humans inhabit—or in some cases, imagine—certain *spaces*, they imbue them with meaning and significance, and thus *spaces* (expanses bereft of cultural meaning) are transformed into *places*, which hold some level of cultural significance.

Tuan's framework works well to understand national parks on two levels. First, we can use it to discern the processes through which indigenous peoples created *places* in those areas that later became national parks. Peering into the indigenous histories of national parks, in turn, reveals that many of our most cherished parks had important human histories well before the moniker of national park was attached. Thus, the common assumption that parks were vacant 'pristine' land is not only wrong, but also quite instructive. It reveals a great deal about what park creators told themselves they were doing, just as it tells us something important about their attitudes towards Native Americans.

Second, we can apply the same equation to the processes that led to the formation of the National Park Service (NPS) and its early management directives. More than any government agency, the NPS was founded with the aim of creating *places* with very specific cultural meaning. In its organic legislation, for example, the NPS's charge was to 'conserve the scenery and the natural and historic objects and the wildlife therein and to provide for the enjoyment of the same in such manner and by such means as will leave them unimpaired for the enjoyment of future generations'.[2] From its birthday forward, the NPS has been mandated—by law—to create specific types of *places* that meet evolving definitions of all the key terms. Conserving. Natural. Historic. Wildlife. Enjoyment. Unimpaired. At the location of each would-be national park (i.e. *space*), the NPS has had to manage for a range of often contradictory values (i.e. *culture*) in their efforts to create parks imbued with cultural meaning and significance (i.e. *places*). Making matters more complicated still is the fact that NPS' philosophies towards exactly what sort of *places* parks should be has been fluid as concepts regarding 'conserving', 'natural', etc., are not historically static, but have shifted with changes in science and popular demand.

National parks are filled with the ironies, contradictions and conflicts that make history so engaging. Rather than view them as reflections of either pure preservation or conservation, we can learn still more about parks, about nature and about the past by analysing the ways in which parks have been constructed and reconstructed over time. In the earliest days of parks like Yellowstone, Indians were written out of park narratives and physically removed from the region in an effort to construct a pristine *space*—one that fits comfortably within the imaginations of tourists.

Once parks like Yellowstone were recast as vacant *spaces*, administrators embarked upon a continual process of transforming parks into what they and the broader public imagined nature perfected to look like. The exclusion of fire and predators from national parks, both of which have had widespread ecological consequences, offers glimpses into this process. The removal of historic structures tells us still more about the complicated human history within parks that often challenges the pristine façade that the NPS has long needed and wanted to present to the touring public. In all of these ways we see that national parks, and the national parks concept, were not born in the sense that historians and the NPS often mean. Rather, parks are very much *places*—both real and imagined—that have been made and remade through successive generations of interaction between humans, human ideas and the non-human world.

Contested place

The American West has produced a panoply of complicated, contested and contradictory stories. On one hand, the novels of Zane Grey, films like *Little Big Man* or *Dances with Wolves* and a small mountain of Western historiography reveal an American West of yesteryear replete with Native Americans. Although the depictions of Indians vary widely from one work to the next, the message is clear—historians and even film producers understand that the American West holds a rich and deep human history that predated the arrival of whites by millennia. With this in mind, it is an odd wonder that so many of our Western national parks have sought to obscure, even hide, their early human histories.

Yellowstone National Park, for example, has a human history that stretches back at least 11,000 years. In what is now an iconic national park, human beings long ago hunted Pleistocene mega fauna including wooly mammoths and giant bison.[3] Millennia ago, many of the giant animals Palaeo-Indians hunted had gone extinct bringing about a shift in human subsistence patterns towards the gathering of plants and the 'hunting of smaller game animals'.[4] Beyond harvesting the plants and animals of the region, indigenous peoples also quarried and traded impressive amounts of Yellowstone obsidian, and they used fire to alter the landscapes around themselves.[5] In these ways, we glimpse the material significance of the Yellowstone region to the Native Peoples who lived there, as well as to those who traded with them.

Just as indigenous peoples transformed the wilds of Yellowstone into *places* through their hunting, gathering and burning, they also made spiritual connections to the land. The sulphurous, bubbling, spitting and hissing geysers and hot pots—features that wowed nineteenth-century Anglo explorers—have also long been of interest and importance to the region's Native Americans. According to historian Mark Spence, '[m]any native peoples no doubt believed that Yellowstone's thermal features possessed spiritual powers, and contemporary Indians from surrounding reservations continue to attribute special healing properties to the hot mineral waters'.[6] Likewise, many of the region's mountaintops also served as vision quest sites and possible locations for fasting beds.[7] To the Indian groups that spent time in the Yellowstone region, including the Bannock, Shoshone and the Mountain Crow, Yellowstone was a materially and spiritually significant *place*. It had been made so through countless generations of hunting, gathering, burning and questing.

The nineteenth century brought with it new and ominous waves of human migrants that broke across the American West. Not unlike the indigenous peoples that were there before them, the white settlers, military men and eventually tourists who spilled into the Yellowstone also brought with them ideas about what the region was and what it should be. They, in other words, also sought to make Yellowstone a *place*. As we shall see, however, the *place* they came to envision was far different from the one created by the Shoshone, Crow and Bannock.

As legend would have it, the idea for the creation of America's first national park was born into the cool night air in September 1870. Sitting beside a crackling fire, the men of the Washburn–Langford–Doane expedition recounted their journey through the fantastic Yellowstone country. Realizing the incredible rarity of what they had seen, and recognizing that the teeth of development would soon chew up the natural wonders for personal profit, Cornelius Hedges proposed that the men 'should work to have it all set aside as a national Park'.[8] The other members of the party quickly agreed. This story, which did not become public until 1905, has been a touchstone of environmental remembrance ever since, forever linked to our national stories about the birth of American preservation: one man and one idea so powerful that Congress quickly followed his lead and created Yellowstone National Park in 1872.[9]

Although generations of Americans and NPS personnel have held fast to this romantic rendering of the origins of our first national park, most scholars have long believed that the story is more than a little dubious. Rather than a single individual hoping to save irreplaceable natural wonders from the hands of profiteers, historians now understand that a wide range of cultural and economic factors were at play, including tight connections between the Yellowstone region and the Northern Pacific Railroad's desire to increase passenger traffic on its lines.[10]

This is not to say, however, that the romantic tale about Hedges's campfire vision—and the tenacity to which many have clung to it—is not instructive. Quite the opposite. The so-called 'Firehole' tale of the birth of America's 'best idea' might well stand as the first attempt on the part of white Americans to create the *place* that is now Yellowstone. The telling and retelling of the 'Firehole' story stands as an early example of Anglo Americans transforming the wilds of Yellowstone into a *place* by anchoring the birth of preservation in the landscape itself. In intriguing ways, then, the national park ideal was thus not born that crisp September night, but has been born and born again through the telling of stories about that night. But there was a problem. Yellowstone was not pristine, and it was not vacant land. It was not the *space* Hedges and his followers imagined. That *space* would have to be created before the *place* could fully take shape.[11]

Empty space

In January 1872, as members of Congress debated the wisdom of creating a great 'pleasuring ground' for the American people, Senator Trumbull—who favoured creation of the park and whose son had been a member of the Washburn–Langford–Doane expedition—made a telling statement regarding the proposed reservation. To allay fears that the park would encompass private property, the senator stated that the area was 'uninhabited'. Further, he went on to say that 'nobody lives there; it was never trod by civilized man' until recently.[12] Trumbull's sentiment tells us much about his attitudes regarding Indians as uncivilized as it does about the process of transforming a cultured landscape into vacant *space* so it could be re-appropriated without guilt or explanation.[13]

Efforts to create the park were successful and in 1872 the United States held up the very first national park for the world to admire. But more was needed to erase Indians from Yellowstone and its narratives, and many were happy to oblige. In furtherance of removing Indians from the Yellowstone narrative, park superintendent Philetus Norris repeated what would become a popular refrain regarding Indians and the park's many natural curiosities.

In his first annual report, he claimed that the 'isolation of the park ... and the superstitious awe of the roaring cataracts, sulphur pools, and spouting geysers' kept the 'pagan Indians' from visiting Yellowstone.[14] Charles Gibson, an early concessionaire at Yellowstone, was also all too happy to inform a *New York World* reporter that there were no Indians in the park and that they thought it was 'the abode of evil spirits and don't like to go there'. They were so fearful, claimed Gibson, that they 'will not even talk about it'.[15]

Casting Indians as simple and fearful pagans who avoided Yellowstone was a powerful rhetorical strategy. At once it denied the reality that Indian groups had long made the region a *place*, it instilled confidence that Yellowstone was a safe tourist destination, and it obscured the messy realities of Indian removal that creation of this national park entailed. If the land belonged to no one, then it had been taken from no one. This sentiment, so early and deeply rooted in the narratives about Yellowstone, persisted well into the twentieth century. A tourist brochure published in 1982, for example, continued to claim that Indians feared the natural curiosities of the park and thus stayed away, thereby ensuring that the 'majority of the park is in its natural state, exactly as it was before man arrived'.[16] In this way, denying the Indian pasts of Yellowstone also became a fulcrum in leveraging a mythic past of environmental purity for which modern tourists clamoured. But just because Indians were being written out of the Yellowstone narrative did not mean that they were actually disappearing from the landscape. That took a little more doing.

Treaty negotiations between the US government and many of the Indian groups of the region began the long process of moving and concentrating Indian populations in specific areas. Although portions of what would later be Yellowstone National Park were initially ceded to the Shoshone, Crow and Blackfeet through treaties, those cessions would not long stand.[17] In addition to growing pressure for the timber, mineral and grazing resources of the area, concerns over the safety of tourists in and around Yellowstone were also central to creating pressure to push the Indians out. The Nez Perce War, violence at the Fort Hall Reservation, the Sheep Eater War and other conflicts raised the spectre of visitor safety and generated further political will to forever separate Indians from the national park—a feat pretty well accomplished by the 1890s.[18]

By the turn of the century, Indians of the Yellowstone region had been removed from the Yellowstone region just as they were assiduously written out of its narratives. Thus, Yellowstone National Park was remade in the minds of Americans as a blank slate. As historian Mark Spence has demonstrated, many of our most iconic Western national parks witnessed similar processes. Writing Indians out of park narratives and physically removing them from the landscape were key elements of remaking would-be and newly created national parks into empty *spaces*. What remained to be done, however, was transforming them into *places* befitting the name of national park.

Institutionalized

Well before there was a single agency to manage what was turning out to be a park system, Congress had carved out several iconic parks including Yellowstone, Yosemite, Mt. Rainer, Glacier and Rocky Mountain, among others. But the ideas and ideals that many Americans attached to parks were still quite protean. To many, including the much-heralded 'father' of Rocky Mountain National Park Enos Mills, the distinctions between America's national forests and national parks remained somewhat unclear during the earliest years of the twentieth century. The earthquake that struck San Francisco in 1906—and the fantastic damage it brought to the slap-trap city—initiated events that would give shape and force to the national park idea and help bring about the creation of its parenting agency.

San Francisco, like all major metropolitan areas of the Golden State, has a rich history tied directly to the quest for water. Beginning in the 1880s, the city 'had begun scouring the High Sierra to find a suitable source for a permanent fresh-water supply'.[19] It looked jealously towards the deeply carved valleys of Yosemite National Park, and in 1901 San Francisco petitioned to dam the Tuolumne River and transform the Hetch Hetchy Valley, which had been added to Yosemite National Park in 1890, into a reservoir for the city.[20] The petition, though it initially failed, raised serious questions about the meaning of parks and the inviolability of their protecting legislation. Even if many people were still ambivalent about the deeper meanings of words like 'natural' and 'preservation' attached to national parks, park proponents like John Muir and his growing cadre of influential men and women were certain that the concept of a national park precluded the construction of major human elements such as the proposed dam.

Then, on 18 April 1906, a fantastic earthquake hit San Francisco, destroying nearly 30,000 buildings and delivering its citizens into the arms of chaos.[21] Fires consumed large portions of the city by the bay and amid the pandemonium, the 'city's water supply system broke apart' and its 'cast-iron pipes cracked at the joints and the water jetted uselessly into the air'.[22] Rather than a failure of planning and leadership, the citizens of San Francisco believed that they had been unwitting victims of a natural disaster, and they set out to find a natural solution.[23] A short six weeks following the levelling of the city, head of the National Forest Service Gifford Pinchot began encouraging the city to again push for the acquisition of water from Yosemite National Park.[24]

Pinchot, and his United States Forest Service (USFS), had recently gained control of one-third of the original land of the park through a series of boundary adjustments in 1905 and 1906, thereby opening those regions to mining, grazing and logging.[25] With the blessing and support of the USFS—a conservation agency that was quickly coming into its own—San Francisco's bid for the Hetch Hetchy was granted in 1908. To Muir, who came to understand Yosemite National Park as a sacred *place*, these were troubling developments, indeed.[26] Battling ill health and a flagging spirit, the aging Muir rallied a portion of the Sierra Club, which was riven by the debate, and other allies to block construction of the dam.[27] After long and exhausting years of fighting, their efforts came to naught as President Wilson signed into law legislation effectively giving the valley to San Francisco in 1913.[28]

The failure of Yosemite National Park to protect one of its iconic valleys from inundation cast a dark pall on the future of all national parks. The *places* that Enos Mills, John Muir and many members of the Sierra Club imagined parks to be—great pleasuring grounds forever spared the threat of resource development—were drawn sharply into question. President of the American Civic Association J. Horace McFarland and others had spent years trying to generate the political will to create an agency whose sole purpose it was to administer, champion and protect national parks.[29] The loss of Hetch Hetchy invigorated their efforts and gave them still more momentum.

In the wake of the final ruling on Hetch Hetchy, Secretary of the Interior Frank Lane named Stephen T. Mather to the position of Assistant to the Secretary to look after parks and continue to drum up support for national park service legislation. This 'energetic, backslapping, high-minded extrovert with a fondness for mountain climbing' tirelessly 'buttonhole[ed] Congressmen' and garnered the votes needed to create a parks agency. Working in concert with men like McFarland, and surrounding himself with talented people like Horace Albright and Bob Marshall, Mather enlisted the help of Robert Sterling Yard and others to publicize the parks, generate widespread public support and jam a parks bill through Congress.[30] Their efforts, which included a whirlwind two-week camping tour attended by a wide array of influential policy makers, journalists and others, finally won the day in August 1916 when the president of the United States signed the bill that created the National Park Service.[31]

(Re)Making place

With the stroke of President Wilson's pen, the national park system was institutionalized and set within an agency whose primary job was to create and protect *places* worthy of the name National Park. Although several parks existed before 1916, the uncoordinated and grossly underfunded nature of their existence meant that there was still a great deal to be done to transform parks into America's best ideas. The creation of the National Park Service marks a moment when a community of like-minded individuals coalesced with a passion for protecting, promoting and creating some of the most striking *places* in the United States. From the first director of the NPS, Stephen T. Mather, to rangers scattered across far-flung posts, the dedicated members of the budding NPS community responded to popular notions of both what nature was and was not, just as they became significant agents in shaping those very same attitudes through the parks themselves.

At the core of the new agency was the institutional need and desire to draw visitors to the parks. More visitors, park administrators and others wagered, would translate into increased public support, which would build political protection and more robust Congressional appropriations. Thus, when Stephen Mather, Horace Albright and a long chain of NPS directors read the enabling legislation of the NPS and crafted agency policy to meet those management directives, they put themselves in the position to discern both what the parks were and what they thought middle- and upper-class Americans wanted them to be. They were, in other words, squarely in the business of imaging just what sort of *places* parks should be. But when they read in the organic act that it was their duty to 'conserve the scenery and the natural and historic objects and the wildlife therein and to provide for the enjoyment of the same in such manner and by such means as will leave them unimpaired for the enjoyment of future generations', they did so from a very specific moment in time.[32] What constituted scenery? What was natural? What was historical? What was wildlife? How should people enjoy such areas and what exactly did unimpaired imply? These were all serious questions, the answers to which helped shape national parks as culturally significant *places* in the minds of the hundreds of millions of Americans that have visited them since.

How national parks appear to the naked, untrained eye of would-be pleasure seekers has always been of fundamental importance to the national park concept. The impulse to protect natural curiosities and glorious mountaintops—so-called monumental scenery—was crucial to the process of creating all early Western national parks. In intriguing ways, the giant sequoia of California and the geysers of Yellowstone and the fantastic peaks of Glacier gave Americans something for which they had longed—a sense of national greatness.[33] Lacking the deep human history and cultural institutions of Europe (and unwilling to recognize our indigenous history as such), many Americans of the nineteenth century insecurely cast about for something that elevated the United States above their European brethren and their dismissive attitudes about the upstart nation. In the end, the great mountains and valleys of the West provided just that.

Protecting the great scenic wonders of the United States—and by extension our nation's great natural heritage—was thus a chief concern of the newly created National Park Service. But the desire to protect scenic wonders raised still more questions about exactly what would be protected, and from what. With the creation of the NPS in 1916, it seemed that parks were pretty well safe from the ravages of grazing, just as they were to be spared forever the sting of the prospector's pick and the grating teeth of the lumberman's saw. But other threats still loomed. From the top of the NPS to its most junior ranger, early employees of the NPS understood that fire posed a grave threat to their living museums and the scenic beauty that they sought to preserve. Keeping the licking flames far from parks was a difficult, expensive and dangerous task, but one that the NPS and its supporters undertook with fervour.

The US Army, which had fiduciary responsibility for many major Western parks before the establishment of the NPS, had earlier began a long tradition of fire suppression and exclusion of fire in national parks.[34] Following suit, members of the newly created NPS viewed fire as an enemy and as 'a threat to everything they cherished'. Uncontrolled fires 'destroyed more than mere vistas. Fire killed people, demolished property, and upended social organization. It was to be fought at all costs'.[35] But the National Park Service did not have the men, the money or the expertise to build anything approaching a systematic fire suppression team. Lacking available options, Director of the NPS Stephen T. Mather early relied upon partnerships with concessionaires and citizens of nearby towns to pitch in when lightning struck or a campfire escaped the confines of the fire ring. More importantly, the NPS turned to other federal agencies like the Forest Service, which had been at the business of fire suppression for some time.[36] But abrogating fire suppression to agencies like the USFS meant that Forest Service practices and ideas about fire also became part of NPS philosophy and management.

It would be decades before the NPS began to question its fire suppression efforts and distance itself from the fire philosophies of the USFS, and still longer until they began flirting with the idea of letting some fires—those that did not threaten life or property—burn within parks.[37] In the meantime, the near exclusion of fire from parks at the hands of the NPS had significant ecological consequences. As the NPS would eventually learn, fire is a critical component of all of the ecosystems of the American West. Although the timing and intensity of fires vary according to a range of factors including available fuels, weather, aspect, elevation and humidity, fires had forever shaped the natural West. The removal of Native Americans initiated the first disturbance in the many of the region's established fire regimes by reducing the frequency of fires burning in any given year. The establishment of two agencies (the USFS and the NPS) bent on protecting the West from the ravages of fire marked a second major disturbance in the region's fire regimes.

Absent periodic fires, significant changes in forest composition occur as some tree species, such as the Ponderosa pine, are often less able to reproduce.[38] A marked decline in fire frequency in a given location can also foster conditions that make it easier for non-native weeds, such as cheat grass, to proliferate.[39] Moreover, in some forest ecosystems, full-scale fire suppression practiced over long intervals has led to the accumulation of large stores of forest 'fuels', thereby ensuring that when fires do strike they are large, intense and often wholly destructive. Reducing the frequency of fires in many areas also often replaces patchwork forests—ones that are characterized by a variety of different tree types of different ages—with

stands of trees that are more homogenous in age and species. Under such circumstances, major tree-born insect infestations are more likely to occur, and are more widespread when they do.

By excluding fire from national parks, the forests that appeared to be 'primeval' or 'pristine' or 'natural', all words that contemporaries used to describe early Western parks, were not exactly what visitors imagined. Rather, these parks and their forests were reflections of specific human ideas about nature, national parks and beauty. They may have looked pristine—they may have looked like an Albert Bierstadt painting—but the removal of fire and Indians from these forests brought them firmly into the cultural realm.

Fire was not the only unwelcome guest in national parks. Predators, including mountain lions, bobcats, lynx, wolves and a host of others were also deemed threats to national parks. They were not, in other words, part of the natural world that fit within the definition of such *places* held by many early park employees and visitors. In this sense, the killing of predators across Western national parks was a reflection of broader public sentiment that regarded predators as inherently 'bad'. This sentiment, which grew out of stock raisers' need to protect their herds from depredation, was combined with the early efforts of the NPS to 'present to the public an idealized setting of tranquil pastoral scenes with wild animals grazing in beautiful forests and meadows bounded by towering mountain peaks and deep canyons'.[40] According to Stephen T. Mather, anything that posed a threat to copious herds of game animals threatened the concept of the national park and should be destroyed.[41]

The parks of the American West, however, contained a great number of predators and killing sufficient numbers of them to protect desirable 'game' animals was a major undertaking. Although deciding which animals should die and how was often left up to the individual park superintendents, the NPS incentivized predator killing by allowing employees to cash in on some percentage of the animals they killed. Like the case of fire management, the NPS also turned to another of its institutional cousins to aid them in clearing the parks of bloodthirsty animals. The Biological Survey, which was deeply involved in ridding the West of its carnivorous animals, was a frequent partner in such endeavours as the NPS used them as hired guns to hunt, trap and poison predators out of the parks.[42]

Rocky Mountain National Park (RMNP), founded in 1915, was profoundly shaped by the predator control efforts of the NPS. In their first year of predator reduction in 1917, for example, the NPS killed five foxes, at least four coyotes and seven martens.[43] Far more disconcerting than the presence of marten and fox in the park was the skulking, lengthy and furtive mountain lion. More than any predator that remained in the park, the mountain lion was directly implicated in a wide range of elk, deer and bighorn sheep killings—all animals that visitors wanted to see. The perceived villainy of the big cats is revealed in tone of newspaper articles and NPS monthly and annual reports, which were often written like police reports where mountain lions committed 'homicides' and 'murders' and were promptly 'executed' for their 'crime'.[44]

Given what we know now about the crucial relationship between predators and prey, the first-hand accounts of predator removal read a bit like a bad horror movie. Beginning in 1922, for example, after receiving numerous complaints from landowners about dammed streams and damaged property, the NPS retained a trapper to capture beaver in and around the park. In all, he trapped some forty-six beaver, with the hides apparently taken as payment for his services.[45] Not yet making any apparent connections between extensive predator control and booming populations of beaver, the NPS forged ahead. In the winter of 1921–1922, they had killed a total of six mountain lions, twenty bobcats and various other unwelcome animals. In all, they exterminated forty-seven predators from the park in that single year.[46] Later that season, alarmed park personnel reported that the 'Wyoming ground squirrel is getting to be a great pest in the Park'. Although 'it was not known in this region until a few years ago' it was 'increasing so rapidly that much destruction [had] been done to crops, meadow lands, and gardens'.[47] In just a few years, the elk herds of Rocky Mountain National Park and Yellowstone—now effectively released from predation—also grew at a near geometric rate. As early as the 1930s, both parks began showing range degradation and overgrazing by elk and deer—a direct result of the success of their predator removal programmes.

Predator control, and the cascade of environmental consequences that flowed from it, offers us still another example of the relationship between the sort of *places* managers and visitors imagined parks to be and the *places* they created. Although no one would argue that wolves, mountain lions, coyotes and a host of other predators were not native to the American West, they clearly did not fit within the early *places* that parks were becoming. Armed with guns, traps and poison, park employees and hired guns played a key role in shaping parks by removing from them animals that visitors did not want to see and those that preyed upon the 'game animals' than they did.

Glimpsing the processes involved in place-making focuses our attention upon what was and was not allowed within parks. For the first many decades of the NPS, indigenous peoples, fire and predators were all—to the degree possible—excluded from parks. But creating the type of national parks that Mather, Albright and others envisioned required still more action. Like many Western parks, a handful of privately owned lodges and guest ranches provided quaint accommodations during the early years of Rocky Mountain National Park. While lodging at the Sprague Ranch or the Stead's Guest Ranch, vacationers could ride horses, while away rainy afternoons under the protection of open porches or discuss with fellow travellers the day's events while sitting beside a crackling fire. As tourists cast a lazy gaze from the cozy porch at Stead's or Sprague's, they likely saw any one of dozens of small cabins and other rustic buildings that dotted the landscape. Lodges and cabins both constituted an honest, if not entirely desirable, admission that this park had a natural history that was inseparable from its human history. The existence of cabins, roads and other pre-park structures thus raised uncomfortable questions about the 'pristine' park that the NPS had long laboured to create.

During the 1960s, the NPS launched Mission 66, which amounted to a major rebuilding programme for the parks and their flagging buildings and roads. Through the largess of this programme, Rocky Mountain National Park was able to purchase a large percentage of the remaining privately owned property within the park. According to the park's planning document, Mission 66 was designed to 'restore to their original condition any natural features that have been disturbed by man'.[48] As such, removal of most human structures within the park received top priority.

Through the land acquisition programme, RMNP sought to purchase all remaining privately owned cabins. Many of these had been long abandoned, their greying walls sagging under the weight of collapsing roofs and heavy winter snows. Others were used seasonally and still in good repair. The desire on the part of NPS officials to buy such properties raises the question of why? If it was evident that no commercial development was either proposed or had taken place, why spend the hundreds of thousands of dollars to acquire such properties?

The answer is clearly reflected in a land acquisition report completed in 1956. This report, which offers a complete list of all property the NPS intended to purchase in the park, was presented in tabular form, broken into eight categories, including priority, name of owner, tract number, description, explanation, method of acquisition, acreage and cost. Under the column dedicated to 'explanation', a long list of 'cabins' were slated for purchase because they were 'an eye-sore along Moraine Park Road', or they 'spoil[ed] scenic view from Bear Lake Road', or 'spoiled scenic view from Moraine Park Road' or 'spoil[ed] scenic view from Trail Ridge Road'. In all, some $422,800 was set aside to purchase and destroy these 'eye-sores'—a figure that represents roughly 10 per cent of the overall Mission 66 budget for land acquisition.[49]

To Rocky Mountain National Park superintendent James Lloyd and others, such obvious reminders of human history complicated and detracted from the park experience. Here again, the sentiment that RMNP was best understood as a 'natural museum' is instructive. In their natural museum, anything that reflected a human past or present became an 'eye-sore', needing to be destroyed. In the words of Lloyd himself, 'an increased sense of the wilderness character will accompany the elimination of manmade intrusions' including hotels, lodges and cabins.[50] To the management of RMNP at least, there existed distinct lines between nature, culture and history.

Conclusion

The conservation and preservation impulses—as complicated and sometimes convoluted as they are—are important elements of the history of national parks. But there is much more to be learned from parks than either of those words can offer. Rather than seeking to understand the ways in which parks preserved or conserved the natural world, we can learn still more about parks by probing those elements of them that required acts of creation or re-creation. This tack illustrates the powerful forces at work in creating *places* of national significance and the sometimes drastic changes that managing for such values have entailed.

Within the boundaries of national parks like Yellowstone, Yosemite and Rocky Mountain, we see fluid attitudes about nature, humans and history echoed across the landscape itself. The attitudes are reflected in how we include or exclude indigenous peoples from the parks and the origin stories about our nation's best idea; in the changes in forest composition that flowed from decades of fire suppression; in the troublesome populations of deer and elk that were long ago released from predation and that continue to threaten the ecological integrity of many Western parks; and in those instances where the NPS has scrubbed historic structures from the parkscape in an effort to unmoor these magnificent *places* from their human histories.

Notes

1 Yi-Fu Tuan, *Space and Place: The Perspective of Experience* (Minneapolis: University of Minnesota Press, 1977), 4–6, 136, 179.

2 Several historians have rightly pointed out the difficulty—some say, impossibility—of meeting a mandate that at once requires conserving the scenery and providing the enjoyment of the scenery in a fashion that is 'unimpaired'. See Alfred Runte, *National Parks: The American Experience*. 2nd ed. (Lincoln: University of Nebraska Press, 1987), 160.

3 Alston Chase, *Playing God in Yellowstone: The Destruction of America's First National Park* (New York: The Atlantic Monthly Press, 1986), 92.

4 Mark David Spence, *Dispossessing the Wilderness: Indian Removal and the Making of the National Parks* (New York: Oxford University Press, 1999), 43. The debate over the exact cause of the extinctions continues to be a matter of contention. For a good introduction to all facets of the debate, see Paul Martin and H. E. Wright (eds), *Pleistocene Extinctions: The Search for a Cause* (New Haven, CT: Yale University Press, 1967). For more recent coverage of the debate, see chapter one, 'Pleistocene extinctions', in Shepard Krech, *The Ecological Indian: Myth and History* (New York: W. W. Norton & Company, 1999). See also '(Over) Hunting large game', Michael Harkin and David Rich Lewis (eds), *Native Americans and the Environment: Perspectives on the Ecological Indian* (Lincoln: University of Nebraska Press, 2007).

5 Spence, *Dispossessing*, 43–44. There is still a good deal of debate among scholars regarding the intensity of Indian fire use in pre-contact North America, but there is no doubt that Indians employed fire as a tool to shape the world around them. Charles Mann's recent book, *1491: New Revelations About the Americas Before Columbus* (New York: Vintage Books 2005), essentially claims that all of North America was a garden prior to the arrival of Europeans that had been extensively shaped by the hands of Indians. Historian Stephen Pyne, who pioneered much of the history of fire and humans, holds essentially the same position in *Fire in America: A Cultural History of Wildland and Rural Fire* (Seattle: University of Washington Press). More sceptical of the widespread use of fire to alter landscapes are ecologists like William Baker who contends that the data does not exist from the fire record to support such intense claims. See William Baker, *Fire Ecology in Rocky Mountain Landscapes* (Washington, DC: Island Press, 2009), 364–366.

6 Spence, *Dispossessing*, 43.

7 Spence, *Dispossessing*, 44.

8 Paul Schullery and Lee Whittlesey, 'Yellowstone's creation myth: Can we live with our own legends', *Montana: The Magazine of Western History* 53:1 (2003), 2.

9 Schullery and Whittlesey, 'Yellowstone's creation myth', 2. Chris Magoc, *Yellowstone, The Creation and Selling of an American Landscape, 1870–1903* (Albuquerque: The University of New Mexico Press, 1999), 12.

10 Magoc, *Yellowstone*. See especially chapters 1–3.

11 Spence, *Dispossessing*, 43. According to Spence, one of the members of the Washburn party specifically described the Yellowstone region as 'a primeval wilderness "never trodden by human footsteps" '.

12 Aubrey L. Haines, *Yellowstone National Park: It's Exploration and Establishment* (Washington, DC: US Department of the Interior, National Park Service, 1974). Available at: http://www.cr.nps.gov/history/online_books/haines1/iee3b.htm.

13 For a good introduction to this process, which was common in the intercourse between Indians and their colonizers, see chapter 4, 'Bounding the land', in William Cronon, *Changes in the Land: Indians, Colonists, and the Ecology of New England* (New York: Hill and Wang, 1983).

14 Philetus Norris, *Report upon the Yellowstone National Park to the Secretary of the Interior* (Washington, DC: Government Printing Office 1877), 10; as cited in Spence, *Dispossessing*, 59–60.

15 'The nation's great park', *New York World*, 8 March 1887, 3; as cited in Magoc, *Yellowstone*, 141–142.

16 Michael D. Yandell (ed.), *National Parkways Comprehensive Guide to Yellowstone National Park*, 7, 70; as cited in Chase, *Playing God*, 107.

17 Spence, *Dispossessing*, 49–50.

18 Spence, *Dispossessing*, 60–70.

19 Alfred Runte, *Yosemite: The Embattled Wilderness* (Lincoln: University of Nebraska Press, 1990), 80.

20 Runte, *Yosemite*, 81.

21 Donald Worster, *A Passion for Nature: The Life of John Muir* (New York: Oxford University Press, 2008), 396–397.

22 Worster, *Passion*, 397.

23 Ted Steinberg, *Acts of God: The Unnatural History of Natural Disaster in America* (New York: Oxford University Press, 2000). See chapter two, 'Disaster as archetype'.
24 Steinberg, *Acts of God*, 400.
25 Runte, *Yosemite*, 79.
26 Worster, *Passion*, 425.
27 Worster, *Passion*, 428–453.
28 Runte, *Yosemite*, 81.
29 Horace Albright as told to Robert Cahn, *The Birth of the National Park Service: The Founding Years, 1913–1933* (Salt Lake City, UT: Howe Brothers, 1985), 7.
30 Donald C. Swain, 'The passage of the National Park Service Act of 1916', *The Wisconsin Magazine of History* 50:1 (1966), 6–7.
31 Swain, 'The passage of the National Park Service Act of 1916', 9–13.
32 Lary Dilsaver, *America's National Park System: The Critical Documents* (New York: Rowman & Littlefield Publishers, 1994). Available at: http://www.cr.nps.gov/history/online_books/anps/anps_1i.htm [accessed 20 November 2013].
33 Runte, *National Parks*, chapters 1 and 2.
34 Hal Rothman, *Blazing Heritage: A History of Wildland Fire in the National Parks* (New York: Oxford University Press, 2007), see chapter 1, 'Fighting fire on horseback: The military in the national parks, 1872–1916'.
35 Rothman, *Blazing Heritage*, 4.
36 Rothman, *Blazing Heritage*, 35.
37 Rothman, *Blazing Heritage*, chapters 5–7.
38 Baker, *Fire Ecology in Rocky Mountain Landscapes*, 257.
39 Baker, *Fire Ecology in Rocky Mountain Landscapes*, 263.
40 Richard West Sellars, *Preserving Nature in the National Parks: A History* (New Haven, CT: Yale University Press, 1997), 70–71.
41 Sellars, *Preserving Nature in the National Parks*, 70.
42 Sellars, *Preserving Nature in the National Parks*, 71–73.
43 Rocky Mountain National Park, Superintendent's Annual Report, 1917; Rocky Mountain National Park, Superintendent's Monthly Report, February 1917.
44 Rocky Mountain National Park, Superintendent's Monthly Report, April 1917.
45 Rocky Mountain National Park, Superintendent's Monthly Report, April 1917.
46 Rocky Mountain National Park, Superintendent's Monthly Report, April 1917.
47 Rocky Mountain National Park, Superintendent's Monthly Report, June 1922.
48 'Master Plan for the Preservation and Use of Rocky Mountain National Park Mission 66 Edition', National Archives Record Group 79 Numerical Subject Files 1953–1965, Box 2, 8NS-079–97–437, file folder 'Protection of Areas of Public Enjoyment', 8.
49 'Proposed Land Acquisitions', 30 January 1956, National Archives Kansas City Record Group 79 Box A98, 3–8–55 to 2–8–56, file folder 'Mission 66', 1–17.
50 James Lloyd to Frank Cooper, 23 October 1956, National Archives Kansas City Record Group 79, Box A98, 3–8–55 to 2–8–56, file folder 'Mission 66'.

Further reading

Baker, William. 2009. *Fire Ecology in Rocky Mountain Landscapes*. Washington, DC: Island Press.

Frank, Jerry J. 2013. *Making Rocky Mountain National Park: The Environmental History of an American Treasure*. Lawrence: University Press of Kansas.

Nash, Roderick. 1982. *Wilderness and the American Mind*. 3rd ed. New Haven, CT: Yale University Press.

Schullery, Paul and Whittlesey, Lee. 2003. *Myth and History in the Creation of Yellowstone National Park*. Lincoln: University of Nebraska Press.

Tuan, Yi-Fu. 1974. *Topophilia: A Study of Environmental Perception, Attitudes, and Values*. New York: Columbia University Press.

Border between South Australia (right) and Victoria (left) – 1969
(Photographer: Peter Attiwill, courtesy)

2

Biological Diversity as a Political Force in Australia

Libby Robin

Biodiversity and crisis management

The 1980s were marked by a sense of crisis in species loss on a planetary scale. Michael Soulé described conservation biology as 'a science of crisis'.[1] The task of conservation biologists, in Soulé's words, was to study 'the dynamics and problems of perturbed species, communities, and ecosystems'.[2] Soulé wanted to situate conservation biology as a science useful to policy makers at a time when he saw the world's accelerating extinctions demanding both action and good science. He and many other ecologists were concerned that while not everything could be 'saved', there was a rational basis for making decisions among options. Conservation biology focused on the long-term viability of whole systems. Its key tool for measurement and comparison was biological diversity. 'BioDiversity' emerged in this era as a media-friendly variant of this concept at a well-publicized Smithsonian Institution teleconference in 1986, featuring prominent North American ecologists Thomas Lovejoy, E. O. Wilson and Paul Ehrlich.

Historian Timothy Farnham, in his book *Saving Nature's Legacy*, argued that biodiversity became 'a new name for nature' following this meeting.[3] Farnham documented the rise of the terms 'biological diversity' and 'biodiversity', using the North American Institute for Scientific Information database, where there were zero references to biodiversity in 1980 and 1981 and just seven in 1982, but by the twenty-first century there were thousands—over 4,000 references in 2004.[4] His analysis charts the rapid rise in international currency of the term, via North American scientific publications. There is no doubt that biodiversity became a tool and a *raison d'être* for green groups, such as Conservation International, which was established in 1987, on the heels of the Smithsonian conference. It offered a comparative way to measure responses by governments and others responsible for the conservation of species. It was also adopted at this time by more established conservation authorities, like the International Union for the Conservation of Nature (IUCN) (founded in 1948), as the world's first 'global environmental organization'.[5] The earlier history in different conservation movements and the role of the science of ecology itself may be lost in this globalizing discourse.

Farnham and others promulgate an 'origins' story rather than a nuanced sense of what drives the global concept of biodiversity, and its uses today.[6] While there is no doubt that a 'global environmentalist story' accelerates from the 1980s, it is useful to document its roots in actual places, in case histories. Local stories lay the ground for the later widespread uptake of global phenomena. The environmental movement of the Earth Day (1970) era fanned anxiety about species loss in the 1980s, but it built on earlier conservation movements that had been supported by nature lovers, hunters, hikers and national parks activists for more than a century.[7] This chapter documents an explicitly political use of the idea of biological diversity in 1969 by nature conservationists, significantly before the emergence of green political parties. Australia was not the only place where local stories and individual histories of the idea of biological diversity feature different sorts of actors from the later 1980s movement. America itself has its 'gospel of efficiency' conservationists predating the environmentalists.[8] The shift from 'conservation' to 'environmentalism' is striking, yet has been little studied.[9] The Australian case of the Little Desert controversy straddled that shift, and thus it offers a local historical window on changing global ideas, a way to 'slice' through earlier and later stories. Environmentalism changed the world views of some, and alienated others. But none denied that 'something had happened'.

Natural history for conservation

Natural history was the chief motivation for conservation, in Australia and in many other places in the 1960s.[10] Jenny Beckman has traced the power of field naturalists to arouse political support to 'save species' in Sweden, for example.[11] In Australia, like Sweden, 'activists' for national parks in the same period tended to be middle-class retirees who were interested in birds or plants, and loved walking and the bush. These serious, older people valued biological expertise. When they needed to fight against developers for their special patches of nature, they asked ecologists to evaluate their case.

Naturalists and bushwalkers joined forces with unlikely allies, including agricultural economists and ecologists, to oppose an agricultural development in an area known as the Little Desert, on the south-eastern edge of the arid centre of Australia. They wanted to save 'thein' bushland from becoming wheat and sheep farms, a project dear to the heart of the Minister for Lands, Sir William McDonald. His idea of beauty was 'grass as far as the eye can see'—and this was his electorate, where the economy was struggling and the local high school was about to close down because of low numbers. He was astonished to find opposition in people who thought this 'wasteland' aesthetically pleasing and important for animals and plants. Perhaps he was even more surprised that so many of them drove from Melbourne, a big city seven hours drive away from the region, to appreciate the bush there.

The Little Desert dispute was, in a sense, one of the last of an era in conservation lobbying before Australia (and the rest of the world) turned 'green'. The Little Desert was disputed in an atmosphere where the political preferences of the activists were outside the campaign. There was little shared political ground between them. Little Desert campaigners ranged from 'card-carrying communists' to members of the Melbourne Club, the city's most conservative and exclusive gentlemen's club.

The 'environmentalists' of the 1970s could be characterized as young, left-voting and politically articulate. By contrast, there were very few young activists in the 1960s Save Our Bushlands Action Committee, the activist group concerned about the Little Desert.[12] The protagonists did not vote alike. What they shared was a love of nature. Many of these earlier activists became very uncomfortable with the overt left-leaning politics of the greens, and bemused that the environment had fostered an 'ism', or social movement.

Green political movements

The first green party in the world was the United Tasmania Group in 1972. In May of the same year, New Zealand's Values Party became the first national political party with a 'green' remit and a manifesto 'Blueprint for New Zealand—An Alternative Future'. The name 'Green' was originally fostered by the Builders Labourers Federation in Australia, who, in partnership with the local residents (mostly women, conservative and older), instigated 'Green Bans' protesting to work on sites of cultural and environmental significance in Kellys Bush, an exclusive, leafy suburb of Sydney.[13] The Green movement expanded internationally later in 1972 with the Popular Movement for the Environment in Neuchâtel, Switzerland. In 1980, *Die Grünen* made 'Green' a major political force in Germany, with a brief to oppose pollution and nuclear power. Increasing partnerships between socialist and environmentalist principles (e.g. Germany's 'red-green' alliance) emerged in these years.[14] The Finnish Green Party became the first European Green party to be part of a national Cabinet in 1995. In 2012, there were Green political groups in about 90 countries.[15]

When I came to write about the Little Desert dispute in the 1990s, just as the green movement was on the rise, many of the former activists opposed the new green politics. They felt underappreciated as pioneering activists for biodiversity, and for national parks and reserves. This conservation work created the niche for policy structures that enabled environmentalists of the 1970s to talk to politicians, but they themselves felt excluded from the 1990s environmentalist discourse. Most of all they regretted that although the Little Desert dispute had established structures for people with environmental concerns to speak directly to governments, governments 'only listen to the greenies'.[16] Many of them, including some ecologists, were concerned that the science was by 1990s distanced from campaigning. Over the years in between, ecologists had inspired and supported other environmentalist campaigns. Canadian Neil Evernden commented wryly that the public interest in the environment:

> engendered, in bureaucratic circles, a craving for experts.... It was to the universities, citadels of expertise and scientific management, that the bureaucrats turned. And there, as if waiting for discovery, was an obscure biological specialty called 'ecology', which was to become a household word.[17]

Ecology was an important expertise for bureaucrats, but it did not always support the moral positions of the environmental movement, and this was a source of discomfort for some conservationists whose actions were grounded in natural history and science.

Experts for the environment

On 14 October 1969, The Honourable J. W. Galbally moved in the Legislative Council (the Upper House of the Victorian Parliament) that a Select Committee be appointed to inquire into and report upon the proposal to open the Little Desert to agricultural settlement. The Committee was required to have special regard for the suitability of the land, the economics of the proposed farm units and 'the value of the area as a sanctuary for native flora and fauna'.[18]

The Little Desert Settlement Committee (LDSC) was a political exercise, instigated by left-leaning, opposition politicians who held a useful majority in the Legislative Council (upper house), but not enough seats in the lower house to win government. Although Jack Galbally (the Chair) was a barrister, and its style was legalistic, the LDSC was never intended to be a 'balanced' inquiry. Conservative members of parliament, including Sir William McDonald, the Minister for Lands, declined to be witnesses for the development scheme. This left the unenviable task of explaining the Minister's development scheme to a hostile inquiry to Alan Judge Holt, the Secretary of Lands, his most senior public servant.[19]

Galbally, who was not himself a nature enthusiast, used the drama of the inquiry to discredit on the government and its development scheme. The inquiry also set new standards of public accountability and transparency for agricultural development in the state. Galbally suggested that the public craved 'solid evidence'. Even in 1969, there was growing 'trust in numbers', to use Theodore Porter's phrase, so ecological descriptions of the place and measures of changes that would be wrought by the farming scheme were crucial.[20] Ecologists were enthusiastic about applying their science to 'public' purposes, although they were not particularly looking for the political outcomes that drove Galbally. In addition, two senior agricultural economists were prepared to testify that the scheme was not viable economically. An earlier proposal had been abandoned by a commercial developer, and since this time (1963) commodity prices of wheat and wool had fallen sharply, and there had been a major drought in all of south-eastern Australia in 1967–1968, one of the worst in the century. Thus the 'numbers' came not just from ecology, but also economics, and together they lent extraordinary support to the nature-lovers' cause.

Two ecologists gave formal evidence: Peter Attiwill, a forest ecologist, and Malcolm Calder, a pollination ecologist and reproductive biologist. Both came from the University of Melbourne's Botany School. This Botany School participated significantly in public intellectual life and natural resource management under the leadership of Professor John S. Turner, who was head from 1939 until 1973. If he had not been in England on sabbatical at the time of the Galbally inquiry, he would probably have given evidence himself. The younger scientists were confident that their appearance at the inquiry would be endorsed by the 'Prof.'

Botanists taught and controlled aspects of the curriculum for foresters and agricultural scientists and had cooperative research ventures with a number of government departments. John Turner arrived in Melbourne from Cambridge England in January 1939, just as Victoria was devastated by the massive Black Friday bushfires.[21] Turner later said that he regretted that he had not had sufficient background to seize that opportunity to study 'forest fire ecology'.[22] The fires caused massive soil erosion, and made soil conservation a vital concern for the state authorities managing water and electricity. Detailed research into the ecology of the high country was undertaken by Maisie Fawcett from the Melbourne Botany School, with support from the Soil Conservation Board.[23] In the years from 1941 until 1948, Maisie Fawcett worked in various alpine catchment areas. Early in 1945, at Fawcett's request, the State Electricity Commission fenced a 7.7 ha area at Rocky Valley to begin an ecological survey of the Kiewa catchment. Fawcett compared grazed areas with the closed area by pegging out various plots of matching size and similar vegetation. She was thus enabled to evaluate accurately the effects of cattle on the vegetation. The major scientific description of the work, 'The Ecology of the Bogong High Plains', was finally published in 1959, some fifteen years later.[24]

The concept of an enclosure (or what later became known as an 'exclosure') was not new to ecological science, but was new in Australia. It was adapted from the work of Cambridge ecologist, A. S. Watt, who taught Turner and visited Australia.[25] The high country plots became the centre for annual fieldwork excursions by Melbourne Botany School teams every summer for a decade from the mid-1940s to the mid-1950s, and on a less frequent basis until the 1990s. In the summer of 1949–1950, over one thousand sites were sampled.[26] David Ashton, one of Melbourne's most eminent forest ecologists, based his own work on techniques tested in the high plains. The historian and botanist Linden Gillbank described the convivial atmosphere of the annual alpine research and noted that the work 'provided an important cohesive force for research students and staff in Turner's department'.[27]

Before 1969, neither Attiwill nor Calder was particularly acquainted with the Little Desert area. Both were recent appointments to the University staff. Calder was an agricultural biologist originally from New Zealand, who came via the Welsh Plant Breeding Station at the University of Aberystwyth. Attiwill, who had grown up in Melbourne, had trained initially as a forester then later had completed a doctorate in soil fertility and plant nutrition. From 1964 to 1966, he was a visiting fellow and visiting assistant professor at Cornell University, Ithaca, New York, where, among other things, he first heard about measuring 'biological diversity'.[28] Calder and Attiwill taught the Agricultural Botany courses for final year agriculture students together. Both were impressed by Professor Turner and committed to 'practical science for the state'.

The central ecological research on the Little Desert was undertaken in a single, week-long field trip, an educational exercise for agricultural botany students, held in August 1969. Both Attiwill and Calder were leaders of this trip.[29] Attiwill chose the destination because of the ongoing controversy, which offered a topical botanical task for students. The Little Desert was more 'relevant' than the department's coastal field station at Wilsons Promontory, where there was little of *agricultural* interest. The agricultural applications were also supported by a third staff member, Tom Neales, a plant physiologist. The 'point quadrat' method for examining plant communities was a standard international procedure, but it was a particularly apt choice for the Little Desert work. D. W. Goodall, a Cambridge biostatistician internationally well known for his work on quadrats in the 1950s, had visited Turner's department and introduced this method to the Fawcett high plains plots work, in an endeavour to reduce the labour and time needed.[30]

The method for surveying the Little Desert built on the idea of quadrats (temporary enclosures) and statistical sampling, both frameworks developed by the Botany School in the high plains and tested over many years. Students outlined the structure of plant communities in the Little Desert in general terms by listing the flora of selected plots. The task was not to make an exhaustive list of species in the Little Desert, something that would be impossible in a week's fieldwork (not least, because not all species flower at once). They studied how plants coexist in a range of physically contrasting environments. General areas were identified for the students with assistance from enthusiastic local amateur naturalists, Alex Hicks, P. L. Williams, Avelyn Coutts and Keith Hateley, all of whom were active in opposing the Little Desert Scheme. The actual plot sites were random within these areas. The students were encouraged to think about whether it would be possible to develop part of the Little Desert for agriculture whilst not losing too many plant communities. It was a practical pedagogical exercise in 'development versus conservation' at the time it was undertaken. Later, with the Galbally inquiry, the students' data assumed a new public importance.

Ecology and the general public

How did ecology gain a space in the public arena? It was known to scientists from around the turn of the century, but did not really emerge as a discipline until the 1920s.[31] Ecology entered public consciousness through reforms to the science curriculum in secondary schools in Australia and through increasing concerns about the vulnerability of habitat fostered through field naturalists' clubs. Ecological studies undertaken for the purposes of soil conservation alerted public servants to the value of ecological science. The Turner Botany School had left a mark on these developments, and Turner himself 'networked' between the public service, the educational establishments (secondary and tertiary—he was on the Examinations Boards of both) and the national and international science community. He was also personally interested in landscape conservation and aesthetics (he was a very good artist).

In the mid-1940s, the science educator F. G. Elford wrote in a popular journal about understanding the 'web of life'—or the interdependence of natural systems—something familiar to ecologists but a new concept for the general public.[32] Ecology became important in the new postwar subject of General Science. The teaching of science in Australian schools underwent massive changes in response to the decision in 1935 that biology should be taught in secondary schools. It was part of what the educational historian Rod Fawns described as the 'scientific restructuring of the culture'.[33] Turner demanded high standards to meet the needs of the new scientific age:

> The young inquisitive mind is disappointed with an advanced nature study course when the magic words Physics, Chemistry, Astronomy, Biology, Geology and so on beckon. In this scientific age, General Science should be science and not merely popular science.[34]

If science were indeed 'an essential humanity', then it became natural for this new generation to express its humanity in scientific terms.

Crosbie Morrison's *Argus* articles of the 1930s, his magazine *Wild Life* (1938–1954) and his radio broadcasts of the same name were part of this genre.[35] Writers from the nineteenth and early twentieth century, such as Donald Macdonald and Charles Barrett, had established very successful nature study columns in newspapers and magazines.[36] Morrison, with his MSc in Zoology, however, introduced a new, consciously scientific note into nature study writings and broadcasts. By the 1950s, the science of ecology was regarded, for example, by Edna Walling, a well-known Melbourne landscape gardener, as an 'essential adjunct' to conservation and landscape design.[37]

In the 1960s, science writers began to move away from selling the virtues of scientific progress towards writing material that was critical of technology and development. The most internationally significant work in this new genre of popular scientific literature was Rachel Carson's *Silent Spring*, published in 1962.[38] In Australia, A. J. Marshall's popularly written *The Great Extermination* marked the beginning of scientists as 'whistle-blowers'. Marshall, a fine writer, was foundation professor of zoology at Melbourne's new Monash University. While technology supported development, increasingly sciences like ecology came to oppose it.

Ecology was increasingly used in field naturalists' circles in arguments for the conservation of the 'the web of life' and, a little later, the preservation of habitat. Ecology was the science that justified nature conservation, but the moral purpose grew out of natural history and nature study.

In the early 1960s, the International Council of Scientific Unions launched an International Biological Program (IBP) to promote the science of ecology, and to put it on a more quantitative basis. Turner was one of the two representatives sent by Australia to the IBP's preliminary meeting in Paris in mid-1964, the other being (Sir) Otto Frankel, world-renowned genetic conservationist. Always alert to public applications, they suggested that the Australian contribution to IBP should support urgent conservation objectives. Ecologists were frequently hampered in responding to conservation concerns, as they all felt the need for 'a big general survey' that it seemed no one had time to do. Turner nominated R. L. Specht, a member of his own department (and then President of the Victorian National Parks Association), as the Australian coordinator for the IBP programme at the Paris meeting. IBP gave Australia a new reason to undertake detailed surveys of its plant communities, and they set about mapping each state's vegetation in a format that conformed with international standards.[39]

The interconnectedness, yet separateness, of ecology and conservation was a difficulty that each scientist resolved differently. Ecologist David Ashton put it thus:

> Ecology is the study of why plants and animals are where they are... Conservation is an appreciation of what we have and want.... You can't conserve scientifically unless you know something of the 'why'.[40]

He saw conservation as overlapping with science, but involving something else, captured in the words 'appreciation' and 'want'. Conservation was a matter of negotiation rather than an absolute science. There was, however, unanimity among conservationists, scientists and natural resource managers that science, especially ecological science, was and should be a guiding principle in its negotiation. By 1969, even politicians had noticed ecology. There was no question of the relevance of ecological testimony to the Galbally inquiry into the Little Desert.

The evidence

Jack Galbally was a barrister, experienced at presenting evidence before a court. His opening question to each scientist was about formal qualifications. He carefully orchestrated it so that each testimony began with a statement revealing academic qualifications including a PhD and distinguished international research experience.[41] This served to suggest to the LDSC that ecologists Peter Attiwill and Malcolm Calder both represented 'pure science', despite the fact that Calder was officially nominated as representative of the activist group Save Our Bushlands Action Committee at the inquiry.

Attiwill's testimony centred on a scientific argument for the preservation of the *biological diversity* of the region. 'Biodiversity' is such a familiar term now that this seems unsurprising, but in 1969 it was a new concept. Attiwill explained it carefully. He described a technical definition of 'diversity' as the probability of finding particular species in ten plots placed randomly throughout a plant community. The plots were evaluated using the technique of 'minimal area quadrats'. Quadrats (plots) were of increasing size: 1, 2, 4, 8, 16 and 64 sq. m. The principle of the method is that when the number of species in each quadrat is counted, vegetational diversity can be evaluated by graphing the number of species versus size of plot. If there is great diversity, the graphs show increasing numbers of species. In a vegetationally uniform area, the species per plot graph flattens out.[42] Attiwill reported that he had established that many species were found at only one or two of the ten plots examined. This indicated that the Little Desert was not just biologically rich but also *diverse*.

Although the plots were random in an area, the areas themselves were spread throughout the whole area under consideration for development. This diversity meant that whatever the area chosen, some species would, statistically speaking, almost certainly be lost, even if a development was undertaken in only part of the area, and a substantial part of the Little

Desert was retained as bushland. On the evidence of the agricultural botany students' 1968 survey, Attiwill could state that species did not occur throughout the region. Rather, they were found only in certain parts of the Little Desert area. Because the survey had been so brief, he was not able to state categorically which species would be lost in any particular place, only that it was statistically likely that some would be lost. This was a clever argument, for it carried the implication that time-consuming and detailed research would be needed before any alienations (land developments) could 'safely' occur. In summing up, Attiwill called for the preservation of all remaining unalienated areas in the Little Desert. The basis for his summary argument moved away from his specific expertise to what he called 'a new morality':

> [The] recognition of the need for conservation is part of a world-wide movement which, in essence, appears to be related to the problem of over-population and greatly increased mobility. We now recognise that a finite world can support a finite population. The goal of 'the greatest good for the greatest number' is simply not possible—we cannot maximise two variables at the same time. I believe we must maximise 'goodness', or the quality of life. It is the desire to maximise the quality of life—to make the world a fit place in which to live—that has brought to our attention problems of pollution, of contamination, and of conservation. The need to control the quality of our environment is, I consider, part of a new morality which is now man's urgent responsibility.[43]

Malcolm Calder (although he had also supervised the Botany School field trip) focused on the aims of the Save Our Bushlands Action Committee, who wanted to 'express their concern over the failure of the government to recognise the social, scientific and even moral responsibility they have to conserve large areas of our natural environment'.[44] Calder emphasized the growing awareness that 'land is a finite resource', and that it therefore needed 'a far-sighted policy on land use, taking into consideration the needs of the rural industries and primary producers as well as the needs of society for national parks and wildlife reserves, housing, roads and communications, recreation areas and industry'. He urged that 'the Little Desert can only be considered in relation to other areas and within such a comprehensive policy of land use'.[45] Calder boldly proposed an 'alternative development scheme'. The Little Desert was ideally suited to 'the establishment of a National Park in association with a field study centre along the lines of the Field Study Centres operating so successfully in Britain'. Calder argued that field studies like those he and Attiwill had recently undertaken with the agricultural botany students to develop the practical skills used by ecologists were of value to the whole population. Such skills provided 'a cultural and aesthetic discipline,... bringing an increasingly urbanised population into closer touch with natural phenomena and rural life'.[46] Such a centre could be financed by the government redirecting priorities away from a 'high level of investment in doubtful primary production' towards a field centre which would offer the general public greater knowledge and respect for the environment and would 'assist to a similar level the policy of decentralization'.[47] Galbally commented that this was 'a most interesting and arresting suggestion'.[48]

The ecologists showed themselves in 1969 to be so confident of the credibility of their science that they felt free to speak beyond their disciplinary expertise. Their arguments for a national park in the Little Desert appealed to all the conservationist and resource management traditions of their time, in addition to their ecological recommendations. Attiwill's 'quality control' had utilitarian overtones, whilst Calder appealed to a more populist and romantic sense of loss of wild nature felt by the urban population, a sentiment more often expressed by heritage groups. Both ecologists were conscious that non-scientific arguments would appeal to parliamentarians and the media.

It was, perhaps, easier for ecologists to accept social responsibility for their actions than it was for other scientists at the time—for instance, nuclear physicists. But they were conscious of the professional risk, not so much for their reputations as for the time spent away from their scientific work doing advocacy. American sociologist Dorothy Nelkin argued from a study of the professional association of American ecologists, a largely academic group at the time, that by the early 1970s American ecologists preferred to return to the isolation of their laboratories, rather than to try to keep up with the mountain of socially responsible work that was accumulating for the few trained specialists in the field.[49] This was certainly the view of Australian ecologists that I interviewed. The level of demand placed on qualified scientists to speak about environmental issues increased so sharply by the end of the 1960s that they just could not cope with the workload. In 1971, Turner wrote to a citizen seeking support for a campaign against development in the south-eastern growth corridor of Melbourne:

> I am now getting several letters a week requesting the assistance of my department on some conservation matter or another.… [T]he time has come when I simply cannot take any more work of this kind. I fully sympathise with the case you propose to present, and I know that you will have difficulty in finding people with sufficient ecological knowledge to speak in that field. However, everything is progressing so quickly that the burden on the few ecologists in the State is becoming almost intolerable.[50]

The social responsibility of ecologists was something each worked out according to his or her own lights. Australian ecologists never had the vast resources for basic research that university ecologists did in the United

States, but they perhaps felt less the burden of defending a discipline. The lower degree of professionalization, and the nature of opportunities to study ecology in Australia, meant the notion of ecology as 'management tool' was more readily accepted in Australia than in North America.[51]

Conclusions: Biodiversity as nature?

The invention of 'the environment' as a holistic concept in the 1940s and 1950s led to the naming of a new interdisciplinary field of study: 'environmental science' in 1962.[52] Collaboration across sciences such as soil science (pedology), pasture science (agrostology), forestry, agricultural economics and ecology (including rangelands science) increased from the 1960s onwards. The Little Desert case study provided a political moment when the collaboration between environmental sciences and public policy was on show. The deliberations of the Galbally inquiry directly influenced public outcomes for managing land, natural resources and public open space in Australia.

The new integrated science and politics of environmental understanding successfully used 'biological diversity' as a tool to change the policies of government. The incoming government of 1970 saw that it had a new obligation to nature: voters had dumped Sir William McDonald, the architect of the Little Desert development scheme, from his long-held seat in parliament. This was not quite a 'mandate': the dispute did not change the governing political party.[53] But it was a wake-up call. (Sir) Rupert Hamer, Victoria's new premier in 1970, recognized the need for a change in policies with respect to managing land that people valued as nature. While the previous premier, Henry Bolte, had regarded the Little Desert as wasteland that would have been better developed, he listened to the activists, some of whom were personal friends, and was persuaded by them. He decided to retire, and to make way for a new, younger premier, with a different, more transparent method for land management. Hamer was personally sympathetic to nature conservation, and when in 1970, he created the Land Conservation Council as an independent authority, he included representatives of conservation interests in its membership. The dispute also changed the way that conservation groups themselves made claims. The Conservation Council of Victoria (CCV) was established as a 'peak body' that had a seat on the Land Conservation Council.[54] The CCV represented the interests of a wide range of self-identifying conservation societies. The concept of 'biological diversity' contributed importantly to achieving conservation aims by turning nature ('bushland') into a measured space, measured for 'diversity', rather than area. This changed the framework of the political inquiry in 1969, and the pattern of policy making and national parks management thereafter.

Biological diversity did not create a green movement. Nor was it associated with a particular political party. It was used by scientists and activists to change policy, not to change governments. The later BioDiversity movement of 1986 was not directly responsible for a political party in the United States either, but increasingly became part of the global conservation effort. Biodiversity has now become part of the discourse of powerful international environmental lobby groups, such as Conservation International and Greenpeace. It is commonly used in green political arguments at the national and sub-national level around national parks and land and sea management, perhaps particularly by green parties where these parties are influential.

The fact that biodiversity can be measured is more important to its scientific and policy credibility than to its influence in green politics or environmentalism. Policy makers and science alike trust *numbers*: they rely on them for making 'objective' decisions between competing claims.[55] Thus, biodiversity has become a major tool of scientifically credible global organizations, such as IUCN, that seek out forms of discourse that work across languages and cultures. Biodiversity thereby frames much of global governance of nature. It certainly did not mean 'nature' in the 1960s. However, through its history of use in governance, and in political moments like the Little Desert dispute and many others, it has emerged as the measure of nature in the twenty-first century.

Notes

1 Michael E. Soulé, 'What is conservation biology?' *Bioscience* 35:11 (1985), 727–734. Libby Robin, 'The rise of the idea of biodiversity: Crises, responses and expertise', *Quaderni* (Journal of l'Institut des Sciences Humaines et Sociales du CNRS); Special Issue: *Les promesses de la biodiversité* 76:1 (2011), 25–38.

2 Soulé, 'What is conservation biology?' 727.

3 Timothy Farnham, *Saving Nature's Legacy: The Origins of the Idea of Biodiversity* (New Haven, CT: Yale University Press, 2007), 2.

4 Farnham, *Saving Nature's Legacy*, 1–3.

5 IUCN website 2012: http://www.iucn.org/about/. See also: CI 2012—website: http://www.conservation.org/about/pages/history.aspx.

6 Farnham's work is not alone on this point. E. O. Wilson himself writes of his role in the biodiversity moment as 'pioneering' (e.g. E. O. Wilson, *The Diversity of Life*, New York: Springer, 1992). Radkau also follows the American story as a counterpoint to the German one, without recognizing the non-political, more general scientific trajectory found elsewhere. Joachim Radkau, *Nature and Power: A Global History of the Environment* [original German 2002] (Cambridge, MA: Cambridge University Press, 2008).

7 Samuel P. Hays, *Conservation and the Gospel of Efficiency* (Cambridge, MA: Harvard University Press, 1959); Samuel P. Hays, *Beauty, Health and Permanence: Environmental Politics in the United States 1955–1985* (New York: Cambridge University Press, 1987); Roderick Nash, *Wilderness and the American Mind* (New Haven, CT: Yale University Press, 1987 [1967]). Beyond the United States: Melissa Harper, *The Ways of the Bushwalker* (Sydney: University of New South Wales Press, 2007); Kirstie Ross, *Going Bush* (Auckland: Auckland University Press, 2008); John Sheail, *Nature in Trust: The History of Nature Conservation in Britain* (Glasgow: Blackie, 1976); Jane Carruthers, *The Kruger National Park* (Pietermaritzburg: University of Natal Press, 1996); Claes Grundsten, *National Parks in Sweden: Europe's Last Wilderness* (Stockholm: National Environmental Protection Board, Information Division, 1987).

8 Hays, *Conservation and the Gospel of Efficiency* and *Beauty, Health and Permanence*.

9 George Sessions, 'Shallow and deep ecology: A review of the philosophical literature', in Robert C. Schultz and J. Donald Hughes (eds), *Ecological Consciousness* (Washington, DC: University Press of America, 1981), 422.

10 Tom Griffiths, ' "The *Natural History of Melbourne*": The culture of nature writing in Victoria, 1880–1945', *Australian Historical Studies* 93 (1989), 339–365.

11 Jenny Beckman, 'Biodiversity as species protection: ArtDatabanken and its histories', in Steven Hartman, Anna Storm and Sverker Sörlin (eds), *The Environmental Humanities* (The Sigtuna Symposium). Routledge Environmental Humanities Series. (London: Routledge 2015, forthcoming).

12 The Little Desert dispute also became linked with another campaign against a dairying development at Kentbruck Heath, near Portland, at the same time. The two development proposals, both in western Victoria, initiated by the same Minister for Lands, were natural companion-causes. Young activists did join later environmental campaigns, but not this one. At this time, they were fighting conscription or the Vietnam War itself. Conscription was abolished in Australia in 1972, and this freed the Vietnam generation to join (and shape) 'environmentalism'.

13 Tim Bonyhady, *Places Worth Keeping: Conservationists, Politics and Law* (St Leonards: Allen & Unwin, 1993).

14 In the twenty-first century, there is now another sort of environmentalism allied with far right groups, see Madeleine Hurd 2012. 'The nation, the *Volk* and the *Heimat*: Understanding ecofascist iconographies of space and nature'. Paper read at Nordic Network for Interdisciplinary Environmental Studies (NIES) Annual Symposium, Oslo, 28 September 2012. 10 pp.

15 Cassandra Pybus and Richard Flanagan (eds), *The Rest of the World is Watching* (Sydney: Sun, 1990). Elim Papadakis, *The Green Movement in West Germany* (London: St Martin's Press, 1984). Radkau, *Nature and Power*. See also http://en.wikipedia.org/wiki/Green_party for a useful summary.

16 Interview with Bill Middleton, forester and Little Desert campaigner, 9 February 1990. On the outcomes, see Libby Robin, *Defending the Little*

Desert: The Rise of Environmental Consciousness in Australia (Carlton: Melbourne University Press, 1998).

17 Neil Evernden, *The Natural Alien* (Toronto: University of Toronto Press, 1985), 5.

18 Little Desert Settlement Committee (LDSC), *Report upon the Proposal to Open the Little Desert to Settlement (Together with Appendices)*, Legislative Council, Melbourne, 17 March 1970 (includes relevant extracts from the Minutes of the Proceedings of the Legislative Council), 2.

19 Transcript of evidence given before the Little Desert Settlement Committee (LDSC Transcript, hereafter), 23 December 1969, records the invitation issued to McDonald on 22 October, and his reply, on 15 December, declining to appear. Alan Holt recalled that Galbally had apologized for placing him in an invidious position [Interview with Libby Robin, 18 November 1991].

20 Theodore M. Porter, *Trust in Numbers: The Pursuit of Objectivity in Science and Public Life* (Princeton, NJ: Princeton University Press, 1995).

21 The 1939 Black Friday fires were the greatest in Victoria's history until the Black Saturday fires of 2009. The devastation of Black Friday fires shaped forestry, soil conservation and land management practices throughout the postwar years.

22 Turner, transcript of interview with Libby Robin, 28 January 1991, p. 3. 'Fire ecology' is possibly a term used with the hindsight of the 1990s. The interview was held at the height of the fire season. Turner strongly encouraged his staff (including David Ashton and Peter Attiwill) to undertake ecological studies of *Eucalyptus regnans* (Mountain ash) affected by the 1939 fires from the 1940s. See Tom Griffiths, *Forests of Ash: An Environmental History* (Port Melbourne: Cambridge University Press, 2001).

23 Linden Gillbank, *The Biological Heritage of Victoria's Alps: An Historical Exploration*. Report prepared for the Historic Places Section (Melbourne: Department of Conservation and Environment, 1991), 26–38.

24 Stella G. M. Carr (née Fawcett) and J. S. Turner 'The ecology of the Bogong high plains', (Parts I and II) *Journal of Australian Botany* 7:1 (1959), 12–63.

25 A. S. Watt, 'On the ecology of British beechwoods with special reference to their regeneration', Part II Sections II and III, *Journal of Ecology* 13:1 (1925), 27–73.

26 David Ashton, *Personal Communication*, 12 March 1993.

27 Gillbank, *The Biological Heritage of Victoria's Alps*, 30.

28 Peter Attiwill, interview with Libby Robin, 21 October 1991.

29 It was also supported by good advice from local Kaniva contacts, particularly P. L. Williams, Alex Hicks and Avelyn Coutts. Attiwill and Calder both returned to the Little Desert later in the year to add to the student work, and to recheck details for the report to the Galbally Committee. [Calder, LDSC Transcript, p. 193].

30 For the history of 'metre plots' (quadrats) and 'exclosures' in the United States, see Ronald C. Tobey, *Saving the Prairies* (Berkeley: University of California Press, 1981), 204–207.

31 Donald Worster, *Nature's Economy: The Roots of Ecology* (Cambridge: Cambridge University Press, 1991 [first published 1977]).

32 'Ped' (F. G. Elford), 'Ecology in general science', *Wild Life*, 7 November 1945, 351.
33 Roderick Alan Fawns, 'The maintenance and transformation of school science', PhD diss., Monash University, Clayton, 1987, 2.
34 Turner's 'Preface' for the 1954 edition of James and Rowney's *New General Science*, as quoted by Fawns, 'The maintenance and transformation of school science', 20.
35 Libby Robin, 'The professor and the journalist: Scientists in popular conservation campaigns', *Victorian Historical Journal* October (1994), 154–168.
36 Griffiths, 'The *Natural History of Melbourne*'.
37 Edna Walling, *The Australian Roadside* (1952), republished as *Country Roads: The Australian Roadside* (Lilydale, Pioneer Design Studio, 1985), 16–18.
38 Rachel Carson, *Silent Spring* (New York: Ballantyne, 1962).
39 R. L. Specht, author's interview, 29 May 1991. IBP occupied Specht's time for two decades, long after he had moved to take the Chair of Botany at the University of Queensland in 1966. On IBP, see also Libby Robin, 'Nature conservation as a national concern: The role of the Australian Academy of Science', *Historical Records of Australian Science* 10:1 (1994), 1–24.
40 David Ashton, *Personal Communication*, 24 March 1993.
41 LDSC Transcript, p. 71 (Attiwill) and p. 188 (Calder).
42 Peter Attiwill, *Personal Communication*, 18 September 1991.
43 Attiwill, LDSC Transcript, 75.
44 Calder, LDSC Transcript, 190.
45 Calder, LDSC Transcript, 190A.
46 Calder, LDSC Transcript, 190B.
47 Calder, LDSC Transcript, 192.
48 The suggestion was not taken up by governments, but by a private entrepreneur, Whimpy Reichheldt, whose successful Little Desert Lodge business continues in the twenty-first century (see Robin, *Defending the Little Desert*).
49 Dorothy Nelkin, 'Scientists and professional responsibility: The experience of American ecologists', *Social Studies of Science* 7 (1977), 75–95.
50 Turner to W. J. (Bill) Kilpatrick of Hawthorn, 17 June 1971. Turner Collection Box 20 (Conservation), University of Melbourne Archives.
51 Libby Robin, 'Radical ecology and conservation science: An Australian perspective', *Environment and History* 4:2 (1998), 191–208.
52 Libby Robin, Sverker Sörlin and Paul Warde (eds), *The Future of Nature: Documents of Global Change* (New Haven, CT: Yale University Press, 2013).
53 'Mandate' became a key word in the language of Australian politics from December 1972, in the rhetoric of reformist Prime Minister, Gough Whitlam, who was appointed after his left-wing party had been in opposition for 23 years.
54 The deliberations of this body continued for two decades. The Little Desert was not formally declared a national park until 1988, but was protected from development while the discussions continued.
55 Porter, *Trust in Numbers*, 1995.

Further reading

Bonyhady, Tim. 1993. *Places Worth Keeping*. Sydney: Allen and Unwin.
Dovers, Stephen. 2000. *Environmental History and Policy: Still Settling Australia*. Melbourne: Oxford University Press.
Doyle, Timothy. 2005. *Environmental Movements in Minority and Majority Worlds: A Global Perspective*. New Brunswick, NJ: Rutgers University Press.
Doyle, Timothy and Doug McEachern. 2001. *Environment and Politics*. London: Routledge.
Flannery, Tim. 1995. *The Future Eaters: An Ecological History of the Australasian Lands and People*. New York: G. Braziller.
Griffiths, Tom. 1996. *Hunters and Collectors: The Antiquarian Imagination in Australia*. Port Melbourne: Cambridge University Press.
Pybus, Cassandra and Richard Flanagan (eds). 1990. *The Rest of the World is Watching*. Sydney: Sun.
Robin, Libby. 1998. *Defending the Little Desert: The Rise of Environmental Consciousness in Australia*. Carlton: Melbourne University Press.
Robin, Libby, Sverker Sörlin, and Paul Warde (eds). 2013. *The Future of Nature: Documents of Global Change*. New Haven, CT: Yale University Press.
Ross, Kirstie. 2008. *Going Bush: New Zealanders and Nature in the Twentieth Century*. Auckland: Auckland University Press.
Smith, Mike. 2013. *The Archaeology of Australia's Deserts*. New York: Cambridge.

3

Oil, Ethnic Minority Groups and Environmental Struggles Against Multinational Oil Companies and the Federal Government in the Nigerian Niger Delta since the 1990s

Phia Steyn

Introduction

In a public lecture on the impact of oil on the Nigerian economy in 1980, P. C. Asiodu, a former Federal Permanent Secretary in the Ministry of Mines and Power, acknowledged that the oil-producing communities in Nigeria lagged behind in terms of development when compared to other non-oil-producing communities, and that the Nigerian government was still a long way from meeting the developmental expectations of the oil-producing regions. However, importantly, the government apparently saw no real threat in the discontent of the oil-producing communities, with Asiodu remarking that 'given ... the small size and population of the oil producing areas, it is not cynical to observe that even if the resentments of the oil producing states continue they cannot threaten the stability of the country nor affect its continued economic development'.[1]

The Ogoni struggle, led by Ken Saro-Wiwa and the Movement for the Survival of the Ogoni People (MOSOP), against the multinational oil company, Royal Dutch/Shell (hereafter Shell International), Shell Nigeria,[2] and the Nigerian government would prove Asiodu wrong in the course of the 1990s. Uniquely for one of the estimated 247 ethnic minority groups within Nigerian society that is dominated by only three ethnic majority groups, the Ogoni succeeded not only in bringing an end to Shell Nigeria's oil production in their traditional territory, but more importantly their struggle triggered the explosion of popular discontent among most of the other oil-producing ethnic minority communities residing in the Niger Delta, which discontent had plunged the whole region into political instability in recent years, thereby threatening the very basis of the Nigerian economy. This in itself is no small achievement for an ethnic minority group which, despite political, economic, social and environmental marginalization dating back decades, took the political initiative to confront the powerful oil industry and their country's despotic military rulers.

The gist of oil-related ethnic minority struggles in Nigeria since the 1990s revolves around their environmental marginalization due to oil developments in their traditional territories which they have inhabited for centuries. Because these communities live on top of the wealth that has sustained their countries economically, oil-producing ethnic minorities have had to bear the direct brunt of the adverse environmental impacts that are present at every stage of oil exploration, exploitation and the eventual decommissioning and abandonment of oil wells and structures once the crude oil deposits have been exhausted.[3] The environmental marginalization of oil-producing ethnic minority groups is closely related to their political and economic marginalization within present-day Nigeria. Due to their historical lack of political power, their lack of control over local and national economic development and the nature of Nigerian political and economic processes, ethnic minority groups in the Niger Delta were relatively powerless, until the 1990s, to take the necessary precautionary measures to lessen the intensity and spread of environmental degradation that is an inherent part of oil developments, let alone stop all oil-related activities within their homelands. The political mobilization of these minority groups from the early 1990s onwards, and their agitation against their national governments and the multinational oil companies active in their territories, however, changed the parameters of what constituted acceptable environmental practices in minority oil-producing regions in Nigeria.

Aided by international human rights and environmental organizations many of these groups succeeded in internationalizing their struggles which ensured support for these minority groups on a global scale as they started to make demands to multinational oil companies and national governments in the course of the 1990s. While the internationalization of oil-related environmental struggles proved remarkably beneficial for oil-producing communities, the same cannot be said of the multinational oil companies that constantly found themselves on the wrong end of bad publicity and civil action in the developed and developing worlds. The accusations of environmental and human rights abuses by the oil industry cast doubts not only on the real environmental and social management practices of multinational oil companies in the developing world, but also on the relationship and cooperation between these oil companies and their host governments, especially those with authoritarian political tendencies and bad human rights practices.

Using the Nigerian Niger Delta as case study, this chapter explores the complexity of environmental, political, economic and social issues involved in oil production in the African tropics. Readers should note that independent Nigeria suffers from what has since 1993 came to be known as the 'resource curse'. This entails three interrelated phenomenon: firstly, the spectacular growth of the Nigerian oil industry since the 1960s has directly contributed to a drastic decline in all other economic sectors, in particular agriculture on which an estimated 70 per cent of the Nigerian population depend for their livelihood. The only real growth period in the latter industry during the independence era was experienced between 1987 and 1992 when agricultural output grew at an annual rate of 3.5 per cent as a direct result of the unpopular structural adjustment policies pursued by the Gen Ibrahim Babangida regime.[4] Secondly, the unstable oil price has since the 1973 Oil Crisis created a great deal of revenue volatility which in turn placed severe restrictions on annual budgeting and longer term development planning. And thirdly, as a typical petro-state, successive Nigerian governments accrued the normal rents, royalties and taxes associated with oil production and exportation without the need to be actively involved in this industry. The enormous wealth generated by these rents, royalties and taxes in turn has led to massive corruption, waste, competition among political elite for control over this wealth and its distribution in the wider Nigerian society (it is not for nothing that the country has been subjected to six military coups d'état since independence in 1960), political instability and conflict.[5]

This chapter focuses in particular on the three main role players involved in oil-related environmentalist struggles in Nigeria, namely oil-producing ethnic minority groups residing in the Nigerian oil fields, the Nigerian federal government and the multinational oil companies responsible for oil production in the country. The chapter will conclude with an analysis of the five most important and contested contemporary issues in terms of the Nigerian oil industry and its relationships with host communities. Two issues in particular are highlighted in this chapter: firstly, that the narrative of oil production in contemporary Nigeria is not simply a narrative of local inhabitants being subjected to environmental injustice at the hands of multinational oil companies. Rather, local resistance to the oil industry and the federal government has in recent years often morphed into criminal activity by militia groups who has succeeded to a large extent in drowning out the legitimate complaints of actual oil-producing communities with the aid of heavy weapons and its corresponding political and security instability. As such, this case study underscores the reality that the history of environmentalism in contemporary Africa is often more complex than it tends to be portrayed in the Western press. Secondly, that there is very limited consensus on what the roles and responsibilities should be of multinational oil companies operating in the Nigerian Niger Delta, even within the context of Corporate Social Responsibility (CSR).

Oil, society and the environment in the Niger Delta

Oil production in Nigeria started in the late 1950s following the discovery of commercially viable oil deposits at Oloibiri in 1956. Since 1956, the Nigerian oil industry has expanded tremendously and increased from the production of an average of 5,000 barrels per day (b p/d) in 1958 to an average of 2,530,000 b p/d by 2011. The following table provides statistical evidence for the massive expansion of the oil industry between 1958 and 2011 (Table 3.1).

Table 3.1 Daily oil production in Nigeria, 1958–2011 (selected dates only)[65]

Year	Average daily oil production (in barrels per day)
1958	5,000
1962	70,000
1966	420,000
1969	540,000
1970	1,085,000
1974	2,260,000
1979	2,300,000
1987	1,325,000
1990	1,810,000
1995	2,000,000
2000	2,165,000
2005	2,630,000
2011	2,530,000

As is the case with many other oil producing and exporting countries, over time oil came to dominate the Nigerian economy providing over 95 per cent of the country's foreign export earnings and between 80 and 85 per cent of all government revenue, and approximately 32 per cent of GDP since the 1970s. This in turn ensured that political processes in the country mostly revolve around competition between the major ethnic groups over access to and the distribution of oil revenues in a complex patronage system that pervades the whole society.[7]

Oil in Nigeria is produced onshore in the oil-rich Niger Delta and offshore in shallow, deep and ultra-deep water in the Bights of Benin and Bonny, and the Gulf of Guinea. Deep and ultra-deep exploration and production have in particular become popular since the late 1990s owing to the violence and political instability prevalent in the Niger Delta, from which violence also spilled over to shallow offshore production facilities as oil bunkering, piracy and militancy increased after 2000.[8] The Niger Delta, where the bulk of Nigeria's onshore oil is produced, is a unique ecosystem, and the Delta is one of the world's largest wetlands, encompassing nearly 26,000 km^2. The defining characteristic of the Niger Delta ecosystem is the dynamic equilibrium between flooding, erosion and sediment deposition that has shaped and reshaped the Delta throughout its existence, and which has ensured fertile soil for agricultural production through the ages.[9]

Socially the Nigerian Niger Delta comprises a diversity of ethnic groups who account for nearly 25 per cent of the total Nigerian population of an estimated 162.5 million people (2012 World Bank estimate). About 70 per cent of the population live in rural communities, making a living from fishing or subsistence farming, supplementing both their diet and income with a variety of forest products. Land, especially arable land, is very scarce in the densely populated Delta with land scarcity exacerbated by declining crop yields and soil pollution that renders vast tracts of land unusable. The oil-producing regions of the Niger Delta are mostly inhabited by ethnic minority groups such as the Ijaw, Abriba, Andoni, Effiks, Isekiri, Kalabari and Ogoni, and these and other oil-producing communities have largely been excluded from the benefits of oil production in their traditional territories where poor infrastructure, poor housing and lack of water supply, electricity and sanitation prevail. Poverty levels in the Niger Delta are exacerbated by high levels of unemployment and high rates of male outmigration to the urban areas. As a result, women play a key role in Niger Delta communities. In addition to infant and child care, women are responsible for at least 50 per cent of agricultural labour, operate most of the retail sector and process nearly all fish catches, while also providing the much-needed continuity within the community and social structures.[10]

The environmental impact of the oil industries in the Niger Delta and their inhabitants has been far-reaching in all the phases of oil and gas development, from exploration, development through to production and transportation of crude oil and gas.

In Nigeria, 'normal' environmental problems associated with an oil industry, such as widespread oil, water, soil and air pollution (from gas flaring and oil spills to name but two), are greatly complicated and exacerbated by a general lack of enforcing environmental standards, poor regulation of its oil industry, substandard equipment and operational practices by oil companies and a general lack of regard for both the natural and human environments by the oil industry and the Nigerian federal and state governments. As a result, the Nigerian oil industry has over time become synonymous with widespread water, air and soil pollution, which result from oil spills, gas flaring and the discharge of industrial effluents into water courses, which has caused serious damage to the Niger Delta ecosystems and the health of local oil-producing communities.[11]

Ken Saro-Wiwa and Ogoni struggle against Shell Nigeria and the Nigerian federal government

We have woken up to find our lands devastated by agents of death called oil companies. Our atmosphere has been totally polluted, our lands degraded, our waters contaminated, our trees poisoned, so much so that our flora and fauna have virtually disappeared. We are asking for the restoration of our environment, we are asking for the basic necessities of life—water, electricity, education; but above all we are asking for the right to self determination so that we can be responsible for our resources and our environment.

DR GARY LETON[12]

What Shell and Chevron have done to Ogoni people, land, streams, creeks and the atmosphere amount to genocide. The soul of the Ogoni people is dying and I am witness to the fact.

KEN SARO-WIWA[13]

Back in 1958 when oil of commercial quantity and quality was first discovered in Ogoniland by the Shell-BP Petroleum Development Company of Nigeria, Ltd (renamed Shell Nigeria in 1979), the Ogoni did not envision that they would one day wake up to find their lands, water, fauna and flora degraded. Like too many other oil-producing communities in the developing world, the Ogoni were tricked into believing that the oil wealth would transform their own communities and enable this ethnic minority group in Nigeria to realize their developmental aspirations. Instead, the oil wealth was transported to areas with no oil and dominated by the three majority ethnic groups, especially the Hausa-Fulani in the north and the Ogoni, along with the other oil-producing ethnic minority groups in the Niger Delta, were neglected and marginalized in the name of national development.[14]

Decades of neglect spilled over in the early 1990s and resulted in the founding of the Movement for the Survival of the Ogoni People (MOSOP) in 1990 to address the environmental, political, economic and social marginalization of the Ogoni people at the hands of the Nigerian federal government and Shell Nigeria. Their well-known oil-related struggle in the first half of the 1990s succeeded in focusing global attention on the human and environmental rights abuses associated with the Nigerian oil industry. But their struggle also eventually robbed this ethnic minority group of their political and charismatic leader, Ken Saro-Wiwa, who, along with eight other Ogoni, were executed by the Gen. Sani Abacha regime on 11 November 1995 under strong international protest and on dubious legal grounds. While the shock of Saro-Wiwa's death initially impacted negatively on MOSOP's activities and the Ogoni struggle as a whole (it took a few years for MOSOP to organize properly again), their struggle succeeded in triggering popular discontent among most of the other oil-producing ethnic minority groups residing in the Niger Delta. This discontent gradually plunged the whole region into political instability and chaos in recent years, thereby threatening the very basis of the Nigerian economy.[15]

Wider impact of the Ogoni struggle on oil-producing ethnic minority groups in the Niger Delta

International interest concerning the state and the future of the oil-producing regions in the Niger Delta had a significant impact on the grievances of these communities, and their agitation against the Nigerian federal government has, since 1995, become the most important repercussion of the brutal suppression of the Ogoni struggle and the execution of the Ogoni 9. The campaign and strategies of MOSOP presented other oil-producing minority groups, with similar grievances, with a 'blueprint' on how to articulate their grievances to both the federal government and the oil company that operates in their territory. Consequently, in the aftermath of the executions, the Niger Delta descended into a cycle of activism, militancy and repression as oil-producing ethnic minority groups mobilized against multinational oil companies and the federal government. Voicing similar complaints of ethnic, political, social, economic and environmental marginalization as did the Ogoni, these groups have plunged the Niger Delta into a perpetual state of political instability by storming oil installations, shutting down flow stations, blockading roads, taking foreign staff of the oil companies hostage and forcing oil companies to relocate their operational headquarters from

Warri to Port Harcourt owing to the fact that political instability in Warri has reached alarmingly high proportions.[16]

In the wake of Saro-Wiwa's execution, numerous ethnic-based organizations have come forward to demand environmental justice from the Nigerian federal government and the oil industry, which include the Movement for the Survival of the Izon (Ijaw) Ethnic Nationality in the Niger Delta; the Movement for the Reparation of Ogbia; the Movement for the Survival of Itsekeri Ethnic Nationality; the Izon National Development and Welfare Association; the Isoko Community Oil Producing Forum and the Ijaw Youth Council. Governmental reaction to oil-related ethnic minority agitation in the Niger Delta has been harsh and violent as it has tried initially in vain to restore order in the country's most important economic zone and to restore oil production to 1995 levels.[17] Limited attempts by the government to address some of the grievances of the oil-producing ethnic minority groups followed after Obasanjo came to power in 1999, of which an increased allocation of oil revenues earmarked for the oil-producing regions and the establishment of the Oputa Panel were the most important.[18] Despite these and other attempts by the Obasanjo government to restore order to the Niger Delta, the violence and instability in the region continued unabated and further increased during the 2003 general elections campaign when candidates employed militant groups to intimidate and threaten their opponents in the Delta region.[19]

Probably the most significant development in the Niger Delta in the 2000s has been the emergence of ethnic militant groups who, according to Joab-Peterside, 'reject the authority and legitimacy of the federal and state government and operate outside the effective control of traditional governance institutions'.[20] Publicly these militant groups presented their grievances against the Nigerian federal government and multinational oil companies to a global audience packaged in a similar fashion as that of MOSOP and the Ijaw, claiming widespread environmental, political and economic marginalization within independent Nigeria. In reality, however, these militant groups rather emerged within the context of the new political space created by the Fourth Republic and the corresponding 13 per cent oil and gas revenues directly allocated to the federal states of origin from 1999 onwards to make use of the new economic opportunities by way of violence.[21] Paul Collier's 'new political economy of war' has served these groups such as the Movement for the Emancipation of the Niger Delta (MEND, founded in 2005) well as they set out to profit from the new opportunities to quick wealth in the form of oil bunkering, illegal refining, kidnapping for ransom and so forth, while simultaneously claiming to be actively working to better the lives of oil-producing communities in the Delta region.[22] As Cesarz et al. noted,

> [these militias] have brought to the confrontation new assets: rocket-propelled grenades, AK-47s, machine guns, satellite phones, and

> speedboats. They demonstrate a willingness, and ability, to kill Oil Company and Nigerian military personnel and credibly threaten oil sector infrastructure. Quickly, they proved their dominance of Delta waterways and ability to impede the passage of security agents.[23]

The federal government responded to these actions with even more violence that plunged the Delta region into political instability, which, in turn, seriously affected the local communities as well as the oil industry. By mid-2008, for example, the instability had resulted in almost half of the country's oil wells being shut down or shut in, which in turn greatly reduced the income of the Nigerian federal state. This instability only subsided in 2009 when President Umaru Musa Yar'adua offered amnesty to all militants who received cash payments and training in exchange for their weapons. By October 2009, more than 20,000 ex-militants had already accepted the government's offer and were participating in a disarmament, demobilization, reorientation and reintegration (DDRR) programme.[24] While levels of political violence and instability have subsided greatly since the amnesty, it still remains high enough for the United Kingdom's Foreign Office to advise against all travel to riverine areas and against all but essential travel to non-riverine areas of this region in January 2014.[25]

Wider impact of the Ogoni struggle on multinational oil companies operating in the Niger Delta

The Ogoni struggle not only motivated other oil-producing ethnic minority groups to mobilize but it also impacted greatly on Shell International and its subsidiary in Nigeria. Along with other oil and resource-related environmental struggles in the developing world, the Ogoni's struggle against Shell Nigeria would eventually contribute to a 'revolution' in the way in which multinationals view their role and responsibilities in the countries in which they operate and would force these companies to start with long overdue processes of change in corporate social responsibility, especially in the developing world. Whereas the powerful American Petroleum Institute could claim in the mid-1990s that American oil companies 'provide powerful support for humanitarian activities' wherever they operate in the world and could proceed to refer to the 'humanitarian' nature of Unocal's activities in the Yadana region in Myanmar (where forced labour was used to build the company's oil pipeline),[26] that same institute now publish numerous works relating to the environmental and human rights commitments of the industry.[27] In relation to health, safety and environment, the American Petroleum Institute currently professes that its members are

> dedicated to continuous efforts to improve the compatibility of our operations with the environment while economically developing energy resources and supplying high quality products and services to consumers. We recognize our responsibility to work with the public, the government, and others to develop and to use natural resources in an environmentally sound manner while protecting the health and safety of our employees and the public.[28]

A quick glance at the corporate websites of the major multinational oil companies confirm that the industry has undergone major changes in the years since Saro-Wiwa's death, with corporate social responsibility, human rights and sustainable development high on the agendas of them all. This would not have been possible if there never had been an Ogoni struggle. But, the oil industry is in essence a dirty industry that pollutes and degrades the immediate and distant environments in which production, transportation and refining takes place, especially if no provision had been made for proper environmental safeguards and pollution control mechanisms, as is the case in the Niger Delta. In addition, changes in corporate policies have too slowly filtered through to their activities on the ground, which ensured accusations that oil companies are not practicing what they preach. This state of affairs has ensured that the environmental impacts of multinational oil production in the Niger Delta remained a highly contested issue within the region since 1995. In addition, the brutal suppression of the Ogoni and other minority struggles in the region and the general lawlessness in some parts of the Delta ensured public scrutiny of the role multinational oil companies play in the marginalization of ethnic minority groups, the insecurity in the region and the violent governmental responses to oil-related agitation in the region.

This brings us to the question: what are the role and responsibilities of multinational oil companies in the Niger Delta? The burgeoning literature on corporate social responsibility in the Nigerian oil industry demands *inter alia* that oil companies behave ethically (and transparently) in their interaction with local communities, ensure that the developmental benefits of oil and gas production trickle down to host communities and that constructive and remedial attention be paid to the detrimental environmental impacts associated with oil and gas industry. Many authors view CSR as the main solution to the numerous problems associated with the oil industry in the Niger Delta.[29] Yet, according to Peter Newell, CSR is not necessarily *the* answer and at present all that supporters of CSR can claim is that 'CSR can work, for *some* people, in *some* places, on *some* issues, *some* of the time'.[30] Frynas highlights additional problems with CSR as it is currently conceptualized in the literature when he notes

> even if some developmental benefits can be derived from CSR, CSR does not address crucial questions of governance. The reason why companies such as Shell in Nigeria have been asked to build schools and hospitals is

> that the government has failed in its developmental role. When governance fails, local people often turn to oil companies to provide development projects, and this phenomenon can be seen in extreme form in Nigeria, where Shell has been regarded by many as a quasi-government.[31]

The role and responsibilities of multinational oil companies in the Nigerian Niger Delta remains highly contested, notwithstanding the adoption of CRS policies by all oil companies in the past decade and greater commitment from the oil industry to environmental stewardship. Five broad fields in particular remain controversial and are approached rather differently by the oil companies, the federal government and the oil-producing communities, which in turn ensure that conflict persists between the various parties, despite numerous attempts at reconciliation. These five broad fields include environmental management, oil spills, economic issues, community development and security which are discussed in more detail below.

1. Environmental management

Historically, the oil industry has been very slow to adopt green technology, which in no small part resulted from the fact that oil has fuelled the global economy in the post-1945 period. It is significant that this industry managed to escape the demands for better environmental management in the early 1990s because the first Gulf War ensured that governments around the world opted to overlook the obvious negative environmental impacts of the industry in favour of securing oil supplies.[32] But, it was not business as usual as the industry believed at the time, and the Ogoni struggle and that of a number of Indian nations in Amazonia in Latin America managed to bring the devastating environmental impacts of the industry to light. In the case of the Ogoni people, Shell Nigeria vehemently denied any wrongdoing and maintained that their oil activities had limited impact on the environment. A great number of studies and documentaries have proven them wrong and have focused attention on the discrepancies of corporate environmental management in the developing world when compared to that in the developed world.[33]

A key demand of oil-producing ethnic minority groups, local, national and international NGOs, and local leaders has been that multinational oil companies adhere to the same environmental standards in Nigeria as they do in their operations in the developed world. Oil companies have been slow to incorporate this demand into their environmental management strategies, claiming in particular that they comply with Nigerian environmental legislation, which are the only guidelines they accept for their operations in this country. In their view it is not their fault if successive Nigerian federal governments have failed to properly implement and police environmental legislation.

Their claims of complying with the law are not necessarily correct and the continued occurrence of gas flaring is a good case in point. Gas flaring was banned in terms of the Associated Gas Re-injection Act which required that all oil companies develop plans for gas re-injection projects by 1 April 1979. However, oil companies ignored the Act and lobbied government for its amendment. The result was the Associated Gas Re-injection (Amendment) Act of 1985 that also aimed at reducing wasteful gas flaring, but allowed for exemptions and insignificant fines. The Act was basically rendered useless when the government granted exemption to most of the operating oil wells in the country, while the 2 kobo fine per 28,317 m^3 flared gas proved an insignificant fee when compared to the cost of compliance with the gas re-injection act.[34] More recent attempts by the Nigerian government to end all gas flaring have continuously been renegotiated by oil companies such as the 'flares-down' date at the end of 2008, and more recently that of December 2012.[35] Indeed, promises to develop the necessary infrastructure to capture associated gas seem to have largely been made for publicity reasons and were seldom put in place. Shell Nigeria, for example, flared 30 per cent more gas in 2010 than it did in 2009, according to their own admission. The Italian oil company ENI, on the other hand, assured shareholders during their annual general meeting in June 2011 that there is zero gas flaring at their oil operations at Kwale in the Niger Delta. A fact finding mission led by the Prague-based CEE Bankwatch Network to the area in September 2011 documented gas flaring from at least five flare stacks at Kwale as well as ENI's Ebocha oil facility.[36] There literally does not seem to be an end to gas flaring in sight in Nigeria.

Currently, all the oil companies in Nigeria have detailed environmental policies. Total, for example, states that 'we are committed to safeguarding the environment and the prevention of pollution through the implementation of an effective Environmental Management System'[37] and proceeds to elaborate what this means to the company in nine areas, which includes a commitment to managing 'natural resources in a responsible way, to preserve biodiversity for future generations and promote sustainable development of our communities'.[38] Chevron, on the other hand, in 2005 claimed that their

> values, business strategies and field operations reflect the highest possible environmental standards. The company is committed to continually improving its processes for minimizing pollution and waste, conserving natural resources, responsibly stewarding our products and enhancing a broader understanding and management of the environmental aspects of its businesses.[39]

Whereas the company in 2005 set the goal to be 'recognized and admired everywhere for having a record of environmental excellence', by 2012 their position was slightly more modest and they now hold that

> We're committed to helping meet the world's need for energy in a safe and environmentally responsible manner. We believe that is the right thing to do and that it is critical to our success in a world in which energy sources should be compatible with an environment that's clean, safe and healthy. That's why we are continually working to improve our processes to reduce pollution and waste, conserve natural resources and reduce potentially negative environmental impacts of our activities and operations.[40]

Both companies, however, have struggled to make their operations more environmentally sound and safe as two events from 2012 illustrate. In January 2012, an offshore gas rig of Chevron exploded killing two expatriate workers. This explosion started a fire on the ocean surface that took 46 days of concerted action before it was extinguished. Total, on the other hand, took 54 days to stop a natural gas leak at its Obite natural gas field in the Rivers State in May 2012.[41] Clearly, while the environmental policies and initiatives of oil multinationals look very good on paper, they are still far from implementing proper environmental safeguards in their operations in the Niger Delta.

2. *Oil spills*

Multinationals also have the responsibility to address the abnormally high number of oil spills that occur in the Niger Delta. The World Bank estimates that there have been more than 4,000 oil spills since production started in 1958. Unfortunately, the fact that the Nigerian oil industry makes a distinction between three types of oil spills, namely equipment failure, human error and sabotage oil spills, has only complicated matters, especially since compensation for oil spills are only paid out when it is due to either equipment failure or human error. Oil companies have been very quick to attribute oil spills to sabotage since they do not pay for damages caused by sabotage as these are regarded by the industry as deliberate and malicious damage to oil pipelines and equipment by disgruntled people who either regard compensation paid for damage as inadequate or who want to increase compensation for damage already inflicted, or oil-producing communities who want to force oil companies to provide amenities for them.[42]

Shell Nigeria claimed in 2011 that just over a quarter of all oil spills associated with their facilities were due to operational causes, while 'Criminal activities including sabotage, oil theft and illegal refining... accounted for almost three-quarters of the oil that escaped from SPDC [Shell Nigeria] facilities.'[43] This controversial position of Shell Nigeria on the causes of oil spills at their Nigerian production facilities was affirmed by a recent much-awaited United Nations Environment Programme (UNEP) report on the environmental problems in Ogoniland that resulted from oil production. This report concluded that the Ogoni environment had been extensively contaminated by oil production between 1956 and 1993, but assigned only 10 per cent of the blame to equipment failures and negligence by Shell Nigeria. The remaining 90 per cent of blame were placed on Ogoni communities who, according to the report, steal, sabotage company pipelines and operate illegal oil refineries.[44] Needless to state that the UNEP report did not satisfy the environmental and human rights groups active in the Niger Delta with Nnimmo Bassey, chair of Friends of the Earth and director of Environmental Rights Action, stating that:

> It is incredible that the UN says that 90 per cent is caused by communities. The UNEP assessment is being paid for by Shell. Their conclusions may be tailored to satisfy their client. We monitor spills regularly and our observation is the direct opposite of what UNEP is planning to report.[45]

Multinationals in general are very slow to acknowledge the role their operations, their lack of equipment maintenance and their inferior standards play in the abnormally high levels of oil spills that occur in the Niger Delta when compared to that of other oil-producing regions in the developing world.[46] Companies are also quick to blame communities for holding up clean-up and restoration operations. The problems are exacerbated by the fact that few scientific studies have been conducted to determine the effectiveness of clean-up operations by multinational oil companies when they accept responsibility for oil spills. A recent study by Osam et al. found that 'containment measures carried out by the oil company at the time of [the Omoku old pipeline oil spill] was ineffective since four years after the spill and remedial action, there remained a "substantial amount of petroleum hydrocarbons" in the soil'.[47] Similarly, the recent UNEP environmental assessment of the impact of Shell Nigeria's oil production on Ogoniland found 'heavy contamination present 40 years after an oil spill occurred, despite repeated clean-up attempts' at Ejama-Ebubu.[48]

Oil spills are arguably one of the most controversial elements of oil production in the Niger Delta. Even communities such as the Ogoni that succeeded in halting Shell's operations in their territory are continuously reminded of the fallibility of the existing oil infrastructure through regular oil spills that have occurred since 1993. Oil-producing communities have a long list of complaints with regard to oil spills and the way in which these spills are managed, cleaned-up and compensated by the oil companies. Not only is there the demand that the oil companies acknowledge their role in the frequent oil spills (in terms of aging infrastructures, human failures, equipment failures, substandard operations and equipment), but also that they acknowledge how these oil spills contribute to the violence and insecurity, poverty, land loss, illness and even death in the region. It does not help that oil companies continue to hide behind legal loopholes that give them the power to decide the causes and consequences of oil spills, while leaving local communities waiting for company handouts in good old colonial fashion.

3. Economic issues

Compensating communities for oil spills and for land alienated by the oil industry tends to highlight the economic marginalization of oil-producing communities in that the companies control the compensation negotiations. Historically, oil companies have controlled negotiations with local communities with little outside involvement from the state despite the joint venture nature of oil production in the country. Consequently, it was left to the oil companies to place values on land and trees and crops destroyed in spills or alienated by oil developments. And, in many cases, compensation never reached the people directly affected by the spills, but often remained in the hands of the village elite who never passed the money on to the affected people. In this process, oil companies have made themselves guilty of widespread economic exploitation of the Niger Delta people and their environment.[49]

Monetary compensation for oil spills, oil-related damage, oil production, rents and royalties remain at the centre of many oil-related struggles in the Niger Delta. The Ogoni, for example, demand US$6 billion from Shell Nigeria in accumulated rents and royalties and a further US$4 billion for the environmental damages caused by oil production in Ogoniland.[50] The Nigerian senate entered this compensation debate in August 2004 when its members voted overwhelming in favour of a resolution in terms of which a US$1.5 billion payment is demanded from Shell Nigeria for compensation to oil-producing Niger Delta communities for environmental damages that resulted from oil production since production started in 1958.[51]

The Senate resolution is indicative of the real problem when dealing with the need to rehabilitate oil-polluted areas, namely the joint venture nature of oil developments in the country. Consequently, the state, through the NNPC is also being held responsible for the devastating environmental impacts of oil production in the country, and as the majority partner will have to make the majority contribution if ever such a resolution became law. However, the NNPC has showed little inclination towards implementing and adhering to minimum environmental standards while the Nigerian federal government continues to fail to enforce environmental legislation in place. In addition, they made no real effort in the past to regulate the industry, and the enormous environmental problems that plague the Nigerian oil industry in part can be attributed to the unwillingness of the NNPC to make infrastructural investments over the years. The prevailing dismal economic conditions since the 1980s also did not help and ensured that the state was and continues to be very reluctant to invest money into environmental safeguards for the oil industry.[52]

The equitable and fair distribution of the material benefits of oil production is a central issue in all the oil-related environmental struggles in the Niger Delta. And, unfortunately for the oil-producing communities, it is also a key political issue in independent Nigeria. As a typical petro-state, Nigeria is a rentier and distributive state in which political authority and economic control depend almost exclusively on the ability of the federal government to secure profits from the oil industry and to distribute these profits internally to those sectors of Nigerian society (i.e. the dominant ethnic groups) on whose survival the federal government depend. Over time, this state of affairs has ensured that oil windfalls in Nigeria were distributed to the dominant social and ethnic groups, to the detriment of the oil-producing ethnic minority groups.[53] It is difficult to envision multinational oil companies becoming very involved in the struggle between the federal state, on the one hand, and the oil-producing communities and their state governments, on the other, over resource ownership, rents and royalties. That demands for rents and royalties payments from local communities place multinationals in a difficult position cannot be denied, but the situation in Biafra in 1967 has taught the companies that it is better to remain outside this debate rather than be part of it.[54]

4. Community development

Financial compensation for oil-producing communities is an issue by virtue of the fact that most of these communities have not shared in the financial and modernizing benefits that went hand-in-hand with the modern oil industry in the country. While petro-dollars financed schools, roads, hospitals and so forth in the non-oil regions, the local communities that had to bear the environmental brunt of oil production are in general much less developed than non-oil-producing communities and regions, especially the North. And, ironically, oil-producing communities have had to content with shortages at the petrol pumps, leading to the emergence of the ubiquitous petrol queues in the Niger Delta. These shortages are almost never experienced outside the oil-producing regions where there is no need for motorists to compete for petrol at the pumps.[55]

Oil companies used to claim that they were already doing a great deal for local communities and were quick to point out scholarship schemes, the donation of school and hospital buildings, micro-schemes and so forth that had been in place for a very long time. But, in general, these companies resisted the call for greater company involvement in communities, stressing the fact that this is a state function and that the state should assume responsibility for the development of its communities. In addition, the companies are quick to point out that they were being targeted by oil-producing communities because these communities view them as surrogates for the Nigerian government who are more likely to react positively to community demands than the federal government. Oil companies have been very slow to link prevailing poverty levels, unemployment, lack of development and environmental damage to the violence prevalent in the region. Consequently, they have resisted claims by local communities that oil companies have the responsibility to develop these communities, to provide education and training opportunities for the youth, to provide employment for educated locals, that unskilled and skilled labour should be drawn from the catchment areas and that communities be consulted on all aspects of oil developments in their territories.[56]

An important consequence of minority agitation and the violence in the region was the fact that oil companies eventually come round to the fact that poverty and inequality is a major cause of instability in the region and that without addressing these issues, oil companies might as well pack up and go home. The result of this insight was the adoption of community development programmes by all the major oil companies operating in the Niger Delta. While in many cases, these development programmes entailed a mere extension of existing programmes in areas such as scholarship extensions, greater attention has been paid to skills transfers and local development. Total, for example, states that

> This commitment to local development is supported by a long-term program aimed at making a tangible, sustainable contribution to improving the quality of life of the 350,000 inhabitants of the communities of Rivers State and Akwa Ibom, the coastal states closest to the site. In our efforts to deploy initiatives tailored to community expectations, we teamed up with Pro-Natura, an NGO with extensive experience in the Niger Delta region. The NGO takes a participatory approach: rather than just simply providing financial or material aid, it helps communities to develop their own activities.[57]

While these programmes in general provided more opportunities for local communities, they are not always as successful as the companies would like us to believe. An internal review of Shell Nigeria's community projects in 2001, for example, highlighted the discrepancies between the actual performance of the community projects and the claims made by Shell Nigeria, with only 31 per cent of projects evaluated found to be successful. Included in the failed community projects was the provision of a motorized lawnmower to the Owaza community in the Abia State, which failed because there was no person with the necessary skills to operate the newly acquired lawnmower.[58] Shell's track record in community development spending in 2003 was of such a low quality that the auditing firm KPMG felt that they were 'unable to form a conclusion' about the spending and the projects.[59]

5. Security

It is well known that the security situation in the Niger Delta has deteriorated since 1999, and there has been a massive increase in general lawlessness, ethnic conflict, cult-related conflict, as well as oil-related conflict, which has made, among other things, the Niger Delta waterways some of the most dangerous in the world. Oil company response to the violence has been predictable in that they have tried to distance themselves from the activities of the security forces by claiming that they cannot interfere in the legitimate right of a government to maintain law and order. In their view, all matters relating to security and ensuring that human rights of local communities are recognized is the responsibility of the federal government and that they as companies cannot intervene in the processes.

Oil-producing communities, local communities, NGOs and other role players in the region, on the other hand, accuse the multinationals of direct complicity in the violence and the harsh repression by the federal government. In their view, oil companies share in the blame because they continue to do business with the government, they contract the supernumerary police force who protect the oil infrastructures, they are associated with the federal government because of the army that is deployed to protect the oil industry, they have failed to develop the region, which in turn has led to youth who has nothing to lose—these youths in general resort to violence because there is little else to do. Oil companies are also accused of fuelling violence by virtue of the fact that the industry represents the only wealth in the region. Consequently, the industry pitches neighbouring communities against each other as they compete for the modernizing impacts of oil developments. The wealth and developed nature of oil camps also contrasts greatly with the general underdevelopment in the region, which adds to the general discontent prevalent in Nigerian society.[60]

As in the past, it was once again a leaked internal document from Shell Nigeria that acknowledged oil company complicity in the violence and insecurity in the region. The confidential WAC Global Services report from 2003 concluded that Shell Nigeria's activities were partly responsible for the violence and insecurity in the region and the report stated that

> the SCIN [Shell Companies in Nigeria]-conflict links result rather from a quick-fix, reactive and divisible approach to community engagement expressed through different areas of policy, practice and corporate culture…
>
> There is no single policy, practice or element of corporate culture that, if addressed, will alone decrease company-community and communal conflict. Rather, it is the accumulation of many (seemingly small or isolated) practices that feed into conflict.[61]

The report proceeds to highlight the way in which Shell's activities result in conflict, from the way in which they negotiate with communities, incorporate communities in development plans and exclude other communities in the process, the practice of paying youths to not attack oil installations (the practice of giving protesters jobs is very unique to the Nigerian oil industry), paying gangs of youths to protect flow stations and installations, compensate communities for land acquisitions and for oil spills. The list is very long and encompasses almost every aspects of the oil industry.[62]

While Total and Shell have headed the call from the Niger Delta role players to start making public their security policies, all the oil companies refuse to make the security parts of their MOUs public. While their security rules outlines their commitment to use non-violent measures to deal with community agitation, they go out of their way to stress the fact that they are legally obliged to inform the government of threats to the oil industry. While some progress has been made in reaction to the leaked Shell report, the oil companies are still a long way from accepting that they share in the security responsibilities in the region, especially in terms of monitoring the activities of the security personnel and in investigating fully and disclosing the results of all accusations of violent government reactions to protesters and demonstrators. Due to the escalating conflict in the region, it is doubtful if Shell Nigeria, Chevron, Total and the other multinational oil companies will be able to escape the demand for greater transparency where it concerns security measures, and they will need to accept that they also have the responsibility to make sure that their activities do not further fuel violence and discontent in the region.

* * *

In 2009, Amnesty International UK published a briefing document *Shell Clean Up Your Act*, in which the environmental problems associated with Shell's activities in Nigeria were highlighted and consumers in the United Kingdom were asked to 'make sure that the company's management knows that people here [United Kingdom] are outraged by Shell's conduct in the Niger Delta and will not tolerate them putting profit before people. Tell them to clean up their act'.[63] If only the situation in the Nigerian oil industry was that simple, then the human and physical environments of the oil-producing communities in the Niger Delta would have improved some years ago. But perhaps in the final analysis, Frynas is on the right path when he identifies the lack of focus on governance issues as the most important limitation of current discourses on CSR and oil-producing communities.[64] It is, after all, ultimately the Nigerian federal government's responsibility to ensure that *all* its citizens share in the modernizing benefits of the oil industry. Until the federal government step up to the task, oil-producing ethnic minorities in the Niger Delta will continue to bear the brunt of the adverse environmental, social, economic and political impacts associated with the oil industry in Nigeria.

Notes

1 P. C. Asiodu, as quoted in G. N. Loolo, *A History of the Ogoni* (Port Harcourt: s.i., 1981), 45–46.

2 Shell Nigeria refers to the Shell Petroleum Development Company of Nigeria, which is a joint venture between Shell International (30 per cent), the Nigerian National Petroleum Company (NNPC, 55 per cent), ELF (10 per cent) and Agip (5 per cent). Shell Nigeria evolved out of the original Shell-British Petroleum (BP) joint venture, which was gradually nationalized in the course of the 1970s, and by 1979, on the eve of BP's nationalization, Shell International had a 20 per cent share, BP a 20 per cent share and the NNPC a 60 per cent stake in Shell-BP. Following the nationalization of BP in 1979, the NNPC held an 80 per cent share in Shell Nigeria, which was reduced to the current division in the early 1990s. Shell is the operator for Shell Nigeria.

3 For a short discussion of the environmental impacts of the oil industry, see Zighuo Gao, 'Environmental regulation of oil and gas in the twentieth century and beyond: An introduction and overview', in Zighuo Gao (ed.), *Environmental Regulation of Oil and Gas* (London: Kluwer Law, 1998), 4–8.

4 For more information, see, for example, Francis Theal, 'Domestic policies, external constraints and economic development in Nigeria since 1950', *African Affairs* 87:346 (1988), 69–82; Paul Mosely, 'Policy-making without facts: A note on the assessment of structural adjustment policies in Nigeria, 1985–1990', *African Affairs* 91:363 (1992), 227–240; Peter Lewis, 'From prebendalism to predation: The political economy of decline in Nigeria', *Journal of Modern African Studies* 34:1 (1996), 79–103; L. P. Frank, 'Two responses to the oil boom: Iranian and Nigerian politics after 1973', *Comparative Politics* 16 (1984), 295–314; Tina Wallace, 'The challenge of food: Nigeria's approach to agriculture 1975–1980', *Canadian Journal of African Studies/Revue Canadienne des Études Africaines* 15:2 (1981), 239–258; Olufemi A. Akinola, 'Reorganising the farmers, C. 1930–1992: Structural adjustment and agricultural politics in Ondo State, Southwestern Nigeria', *The Journal of Modern African Studies* 36:2 (1998), 237–264.

5 Nicholas Shaxson, 'The resource curse, of the paradox of poverty from plenty', *openDemocracy*, 23 September 2013. Available at: http://www.opendemocracy.net/ourkingdom/nicholas-shaxson/resource-curse-or-paradox-of-poverty-from-plenty [accessed 28 September 2013].

7 US Energy Information Administration, 'Nigeria', 16 October 2012.

8 US Energy Information Administration, 'Nigeria', 16 October 2012.

9 For more information on the Niger Delta ecology, see Nick Ashton-Jones, *The Human Ecosystems of the Niger Delta: An ERA Handbook* (Benin-City: ERA, 1998).

10 Augustine A. Ikein, *The Impact of Oil on a Developing Country: The Case of Nigeria* (New York: Praeger, 1990), 23, 28–29; Eno Okoko, 'Women and environmental change in the Niger Delta, Nigeria: Evidence from Ibeno', *Gender, Place and Culture* 6:4 (1999), 373–375; Elsbeth Robson, 'Commentaries on Eno Okoko's article, 'Women and environmental change in the Niger Delta, Nigeria: Evidence from Ibeno', *Gender, Place and Culture* 6:4 (1999), 379–381; The World Bank, *Defining an Environmental Development Strategy for the Niger Delta* I, (Washington, DC: The World Bank, 1995), 2–4.

11 Luis Esparza and Monica Wilson (eds), *Oil for Nothing: Multinational Corporations, Environmental Destruction, Death and Impunity in the Niger Delta*. Report of a US non-governmental delegation. (Washington, DC: Essential Action, 6–20 September 1999), 3–8; Onah R. Ogri, 'A review of the Nigerian petroleum industry and the associated environmental problems', *The Environmentalist* 21:1 (2001), 14–15.

12 Anon, 'Drilling fields', *Multinational Monitor* 17 (1995). Available at: http://multinationalmonitor.org/hyper/issues/1995/01/mm0195_06.html.

13 Ken Saro-Wiwa, *Genocide in Nigeria: The Ogoni Tragedy* (Port Harcourt: Saros International Publishers, 1992), 83.

14 As mentioned earlier, the oil-producing regions in the Niger Delta are mostly inhabited by ethnic minority groups who have largely been excluded from the benefits of oil production in their traditional territories where poor infrastructure, poor housing and lack of water supply, electricity and sanitation prevail. Ikein, *The Impact of Oil on a Developing Country*, 23, 28–29.

15 Maria Sophia Steyn, 'Oil politics in Ecuador and Nigeria: A perspective from environmental history on the struggles between ethnic minority groups, multinational oil companies and national governments', PhD diss., University of the Free State, South Africa, 2003, 373–378, 386–387.

16 Eghosa E. Osaghae, 'The Ogoni uprising, oil politics, minority agitation and the future of the Nigerian state', *African Affairs* 94 (1995), 343; Human Rights Watch, *The Price of Oil: Corporate Responsibility and Human Rights Violations in Nigeria's Oil Producing Communities* (New York: HRW, 1999), chapters 8 and 11; Lara Santoro, 'David and Goliath in Africa', *Christian Science Monitor* 90:248 (1998), 5; Cyril Obi, *Oil, Environmental Conflict and National Security in Nigeria: Ramifications for the Ecology-Security Nexus for Sub-Regional Peace*. ACDIS Occasional Paper (Urbana-Champaign: University of Illinois, 1997), 8–15; Ian Gary and Terry Lynn Karl, *Bottom of the Barrel: Africa's Oil Boom and the Poor*. Catholic Relief Services Report (Baltimore: CRS, 2003), 27; Jesper Strudsholm, 'The oil fields of Nigeria', *Africa Insight* 29:1/2 (1999), 36–39.

17 For more details on the violent repression of the Niger Delta struggles, see, for example, Human Rights Watch, 'Nigeria: Crackdown in the Niger Delta', *Human Rights Watch Report* 11 (1999), 2A; Human Rights Watch, *The Price of Oil*, chapter 8.

18 Ike Oguine, 'Nigeria's oil revenues and the oil-producing areas', *Journal of Energy and Natural Resources Law* 17:2 (1999), 114–119; Jedrzej Georg Frynas, *Oil in Nigeria: Conflict and Litigation between Oil Companies and Village Communities* (Hamburg: Lit Verlag, 2000), 49–50.

19 For more details, see Human Rights Watch, 'The Niger Delta: No democratic dividend', *Human Rights Watch Reports* 14 (2002), 7A, 1–37.

20 Sofiri Joab-Peterside, 'On the militarization of Nigeria's Niger Delta: The genesis of ethnic militia in Rivers State, Nigeria', *Niger Delta Economies of Violence Working Papers No. 21* (Berkeley: Institute of International Studies, University of California, 2007), 4.

21 According to Ruben Eberlein, these groups succeeded in 'appropriating social movements' discourse' to their own advantage. See Ruben Ebenlein, 'On the road to the state's perdition? Authority and sovereignty in the Niger Delta, Nigeria', *Journal of Modern African Studies* 44:4 (2006), 586.

22 The literature on the new political economy of war is very extensive. For a classical expression thereof, see Paul Collier, 'Doing well out or war: An economic perspective', in Mats Berdel and David Malone (eds), *Greed and Grievance: Economic Agendas in Civil Wars* (Boulder, CO: Lynne Rienner, 2000). This is by no means the only view on this matter, and some authors have attempted to 'explain' the militia actions in similar fashion as those campaigns of the ethnic minority groups, such as the Ogoni, against oil in their homeland. A representative example of this literature is Ukoha Ukiwo, 'From "pirates" to "militants": A historical perspective on anti-state and anti-oil company mobilization among the Ijaw of Warri, Western Niger Delta', *African Affairs* 106:425 (2007), 587–610.

23 Esther Cesarz, J. Stephen Morrison, and Jennifer Cooke 'Alienation and militancy in Nigeria's Niger Delta', *CSIS Africa Notes* 16 (2003), as quoted in Joab-Peterside, 'On the militarization of Nigeria's Niger Delta', 5:1–4. Available at: http://csis.org/files/media/csis/pubs/anotes_0305.pdf.

24 Paul Francis, Deirdre LaPin, and Paula Rossiasco, *Securing Development and Peace in the Niger Delta: A Social and Conflict Analysis for Change* (Washington, DC: Woodrow Wilson International Centre for Scholars, 2011), 6.

25 United Kingdom, Foreign Office, 'Travel advice for Nigeria'. Available at: https://www.gov.uk/foreign-travel-advice/nigeria. This point might seem insignificant to the reader, but it does mean that no UK-based academics or students can travel to this region on normal travel insurance, and in practice it has led to many students being advised to rather find different research topics to work on.

26 See Part 2 in Kenny Bruno (1999), Joshua Karliner and China Brotsky, 'Greenhouse gangsters vs climate justice'. Available at: http://www.wrm.org.uy/actors/CCC/greenhousegangsters.pdf; Project Underground (1997), 'Unocal: Betraying Burma'. Available at: http://www.moles.org/ProjectUnderground?motherlode/unocal.html.

27 See Health and Environment section of the American Petroleum Institute publication lists available at: http://api-ec.api.org/~/media/Files/Publications/Catalog/16_HES.ashx.

28 American Petroleum Institute, 'Environment, health & safety'. Available at: http://api-ec.api.org/environment-health-and-safety.aspx.

29 The literature on CSR in the Nigerian oil industry is very extensive. Some examples include Uwafiokun Idemudia and Uem E. Ite, 'Corporate-community relations in Nigeria's oil industry: Challenges and imperatives', *Corporate Social Responsibility and Environmental Management* 13 (2006), 194–206; Gabriel Eweje, 'Multinational oil companies' CSR initiatives in Nigeria: The scepticism of stakeholders in host communities', *Managerial Law* 49:5/6 (2007), 218–235; Felix M. Edoho, 'Oil transnational corporations: Corporate social responsibility and environmental sustainability', *Corporate Social Responsibility and Environmental Management* 15:4 (2008), 210–222.

30 Peter Newell, 'Citizenship, accountability and community: The limits of the CSR agenda', *International Affairs* 81 (2005), 556, as quoted in Jędrzej G. Frynas, 'Corporate social responsibility and international development: Critical assessment', *Corporate Governance* 16:4 (2008), 276.

31 Jędrzej G. Frynas, 'The false developmental promise of corporate social responsibility: Evidence from multinational oil companies', *International Affairs* 81:3 (2005), 596.
32 Joseph Stanislaw, *The New World Oil Order: Strategies for the 1990s*. Cambridge Energy Research Associates Private Report (Cambridge, MA: CERA, 1991), 1–22; Paul Aarts, 'Democracy, oil and the Gulf War', *Third World Quarterly* 13:3 (1992), 525–538; Chantale LaCasse and Andre Plourde, 'On the renewal of concern for the security of oil supply', *Energy Journal* 16:2 (1995), 1–23.
33 See, for example, Human Rights Watch, *The Price of Oil: Corporate Responsibility and Human Rights Violations in Nigeria's Oil Producing Communities* (New York: HRW, 1999); Catma Films, *The Drilling Fields*, a Catma Films production for Channel Four (UK), aired on 23 May 1994; Andrew Rowell, *Shell-Shocked: The Environmental and Social Costs of Living Next Door to Shell* (Amsterdam: Greenpeace International, 1994); Ike Okonta and Oronto Douglas, *Where Vultures Feast: Shell, Human Rights, and Oil in the Niger Delta* (San Francisco, CA: Sierra Club Books, 2001), 190–205.
34 Ashton-Jones, *The Human Ecosystems of the Niger Delta*, 144; Frynas, *Oil in Nigeria*, 87–89; Ikein, *The Impact of Oil on a Developing Country*, 42–43.
35 Shell Petroleum Development Corporation of Nigeria, *2004 People and the Environment Report: Annual Report* (Lagos: SPDC, 2005), 15; CEE Bankwatch Network et al., *The Reality Behind EU 'Energy Security'* (Prague: Bankwatch Network, 2011). Available at: http://bankwatch.org/sites/default/files/energy-security-nigeria.pdf.
36 Emeka Ugwuanyi, 'Shell records highest gas flaring in Nigeria, says report', *The Nation* 19 April 2011; CEE Bankwatch Network et al., *The Reality Behind EU 'Energy Security'*.
37 Guy Maurice, Total Nigeria Managing Director, 'Environmental policy', s.a., 2013. Available at: http://www.ng.total.com/03_total_nigeria_commitments/03020204_environmental_policy.htm.
38 Guy Maurice, Total Nigeria Managing Director, 'Environmental policy'.
39 Chevron, 'Environment', 2005. Available at: http://www.chevron.com/social_responsibility/environment/ [accessed 2 November 2005]; it is no longer available online, but the author possesses the print outs of these pages.
40 Chevron, 'Environment', 2012. Available at: http://www.chevron.com/globalissues/environment/.
41 Jon Gambrell, 'France's Total SA says it has stopped a major gas leak at a field in Nigeria after 45 days', *The Republic* (India), 13 May 2012; Drew Hinshaw, 'Chevron faces fire in Nigeria', *The Wall Street Journal*, 6 March 2012.
42 Innocent M. Aprioku, 'Collective response to oil spill hazards in the eastern Niger Delta of Nigeria', *Journal of Environmental Planning and Management* 42:3 (1999), 391–396; Steyn, 'Oil politics in Ecuador and Nigeria', 260–261.
43 Royal Dutch Shell, 'Oil leaks in Nigeria', 2011. Available at: http://www.shell.com/home/content/environment_society/society/nigeria/spills.
44 UNEP, *Environmental Assessment of Ogoniland* (Nairobi: UNEP, 2011).
45 John Vidal, 'Outrage at UN decision to exonerate Shell for oil pollution in Niger delta', *The Guardian* (UK), 22 August 2010.

46 Much has been written on this issue. See, for example, Ogri, 'A review of the Nigerian petroleum industry and the associated environmental problems', 17–18; Ashton-Jones, *The Human Ecosystems of the Niger Delta*, 151–153, 160; Aprioku, 'Collective response to oil spill hazards in the eastern Niger Delta of Nigeria', 392–395; Human Rights Watch, *The Price of Oil*, chapter 5.
47 Michale U. Osam, Matthew O. Wegwu and Augustine A. Uwakwe, 'The Omoku old pipeline oil spill: Total hydrocarbon content of affected soils and the impact on the nutritive value of food crops', *Archives of Applied Science Research* 3:3 (2011), 520.
48 UNEP, *Environmental Assessment of Ogoniland*, 9.
49 Royal Dutch Shell, 'Oil leaks in Nigeria'.
50 Osaghae, 'The Ogoni uprising', 336.
51 Sopuruchi Onwuka, 'Nigeria: $1.5bn compensation: Shell to Sue Senate', *Daily Champion*, 31 August 2004. Available at: http://allafrica.com/stories/200408310460.html a fee, and for free at http://shellnews.net/2004%20Documents/allafrica/allafrica1sept04.htm. The 2011 UNEP environmental study of Ogoniland estimated that it would take 25–30 years to rehabilitate the Ogoni environment, and would cost a minimum of US$1 billion for the first ten years. UNEP, *Environmental Assessment of Ogoniland*, 12–16.
52 For more details on the NNPC and the environment, see Steyn, 'Oil politics in Ecuador and Nigeria', 255–266.
53 For a detailed discussion on oil-producing communities and revenue allocation in independent Nigeria, see Steyn, 'Oil politics in Ecuador and Nigeria', 202–207. See also S. Egite Oyovbaire, 'The politics of revenue allocation', in K. Panter-Brick (ed.), *Soldiers and Oil: The Political Transformation of Nigeria* (London: Frank Cass, 1978), 224–249; Ike Oguine, 'Nigeria's oil revenues and the oil producing areas', 111–120; Michael Watts, 'The shock of modernity: Petroleum, protest, and fast capitalism in an industrialising society', in Stephen Daniels and Roger Lee (eds), *Exploring Human Geography: A Reader* (London: Arnold, 1996), 120–152; Terry Lynn Karl, *The Paradox of Plenty: Oil Booms and Petro-States* (Berkeley: University of California Press, 1997), 47–49.
54 For more information on oil companies during the Biafran war, see Phia Steyn, 'Shell-BP and the Nigerian civil war', in Toyin Falola and Matt Childs (eds), *The Changing Worlds of Atlantic Africa: Essays in Honor of Robin Law* (Durham: Carolina Academic Press, 2009), 393–411.
55 Oyovbaire, 'The politics of revenue allocation', 225–229; Oguine, 'Nigeria's oil revenues and the oil producing areas', 111–112; Watts, 'The shock of modernity', 124–125; Frynas, *Oil in Nigeria*, 42–44; Ikein, *The Impact of Oil on a Developing Country*, 28–29.
56 See, for example, Uwafiokun Idemudia, 'Community perceptions and expectations: Reinventing the wheels of corporate social responsibility practices in the Nigerian oil industry', *Business and Society Review* 112:3 (2007), 369–405; Idemudia and Ite, 'Corporate-community relations in Nigeria's oil industry: Challenges and imperatives'; David Wheeler, Heike Fabig, and Richard Boele, 'Paradoxes and dilemmas for stakeholder responsive firms in the extractive sector: Lessons from the case of Shell and the Ogoni', *Journal of Business Ethics* 39:3 (2002), 297–318.

57 Total, *Corporate Social Responsibility Report 2003: Sharing Our Energies* (Courbevoie: Total, 2003), 145.
58 Shell Nigeria, *Report of the Stakeholder Review of SPDC Community Development Projects Completed in the Year 2000, passim* (2000).
59 Christian Aid, Friends of the Earth, and Platform and Stakeholder Democracy Network, *Shell in Nigeria. Oil and Gas Reserves Crisis and Political Risks: Shared Concerns for Investors and Producer-Communities. A Briefing for Shell Stakeholders* (London: Stakeholder Democracy Network, 2004), 5.
60 Graduate Institute on International Studies, *Small Arms Survey 2011* (Geneva: Cambridge University Press, 2011), 148–149.
61 WAC Global Services report as quoted in Christian Aid, Friends of the Earth and Platform and Stakeholder Democracy Network, *Shell in Nigeria*, 7.
62 Aid, Friends of the Earth and Platform and Stakeholder Democracy Network.
63 Amnesty International UK, *Shell Clean Up Your Act* (pamphlet) (London: AI, 2009).
64 Frynas, 'The false developmental promise of corporate social responsibility', 596–598.
65 Table statistics compiled from data obtained from Frynas, *Oil in Nigeria*, 17; *International Petroleum Monthly*, September 2002; US Energy Information Administration, 'Nigeria', 16 October 2012. Available at: http://www.eia.gov/countries/analysisbriefs/Nigeria/nigeria.pdf [accessed 6 January 2013].

Further reading

Gao, Zhiguo (ed.). 1998. *Environmental Regulation of Oil and Gas*. London: Kluwer Law.

Gary, Ian and Karl, Terry Lynn. 2003. *Bottom of the Barrel: Africa's Oil Boom and the Poor*. Catholic Relief Services report. Baltimore, MD: CRS.

Ebenlein, Ruben. 2006. 'On the road to the state's perdition? Authority and sovereignty in the Niger Delta, Nigeria', *Journal of Modern African Studies* 44:4, 673–596.

Frynas, Jedrzej Georg. 2000. *Oil in Nigeria: Conflict and Litigation between Oil Companies and Village Communities*. Hamburg: Lit Verlag.

Joab-Peterside, Sofiri. 2007. 'On the militarization of Nigeria's Niger Delta: The genesis of ethnic militia in rivers state, Nigeria', *Niger Delta Economies of Violence Working Papers No. 21*. Berkeley: Institute of International Studies, University of California.

Ojakorotu, Victor (ed.). 2010. *Anatomy of the Niger Delta Crisis: Causes, Consequences and Opportunities for Peace*. Berlin: Lit Verlag.

Soares de Oliveira, Ricardo. 2007. *Oil and Politics in the Gulf of Guinea*. New York: Columbia University Press.

4

Protecting the Tibetan Antelope: A Historical Narrative and Missing Stories

Mao Da and Mei Xueqin

Introduction

The Tibetan antelope (*Pantholops hodgsonii*) or *chiru* is endemic to the high plains of the Tibetan Plateau. It roams an area of more than 950,000 sq. km, at an altitude of between 3,700 and 5,500 m above sea level. According to wildlife surveys, most Tibetan antelopes live in the Tibet and Xinjiang Autonomous Regions and the Qinghai and Sichuan Provinces of the People's Republic of China, while some herds may be found in parts of India (Figure 4.1).[1]

Through a long process of evolution, the Tibetan antelope has adapted perfectly to the harsh environment of the mountain-desert grassland in the Tibetan Plateau. However, it has been regarded since the 1970s as an endangered species because the balance between its population and the environment is fragile; any major turbulence, such as climate change, famine or the thriving of predators could threaten this unique species. In 1979, the Convention on International Trade in Endangered Species of Wild Fauna and Flora (CITES) added the Tibetan antelope to its Appendix I, which means that any commercial trade of the animal and its products is illegal to treaty parties. In 1981, China joined the CITES and thus committed itself to the protection of the antelope from illegal trade.

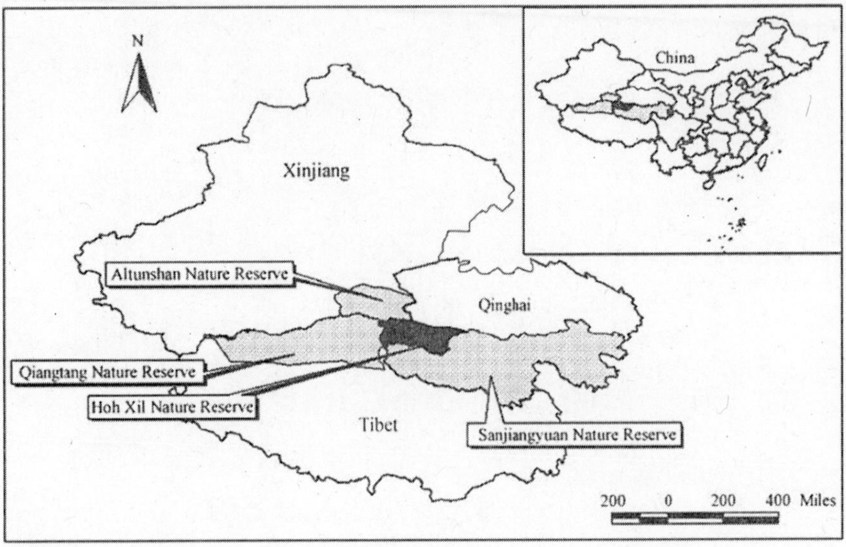

FIGURE 4.1 *Geographic distribution of Tibetan antelope in China*
Source: Zhou, H. et al. (2007), 'Genetic diversity of microsatellite DNA loci of Tibetan antelope (Chiru, *Pantholops hodgsonii*) in Hoh Xil national nature reserve, Qinghai, China', *Journal of Genetics and Genomics* 34:7, 601.

Unfortunately, the population of the Tibetan antelope dropped dramatically starting in the mid-1980s due to illegal hunting, and by the mid-1990s this endemic species of the Tibetan Plateau was on the verge of extinction. Although it is very hard to estimate the Tibetan antelope population prior to the increase of intensive illegal hunting, it is believed that there were over a million animals in the early twentieth century.[2] However, according to *The Current Status of the Tibetan Antelope Protection* (also known as 'the white paper of the Tibetan antelope protection'), issued by the National Forestry Administration of China (the primary government agency responsible for wildlife protection) in December 1998, about 20,000 Tibetan antelopes have been killed by poachers each year and the existing antelope population was between 50,000 and 75,000 in 1995.[3] Experts and wildlife protection activists then warned that if no effective measures were taken, the Tibetan antelope would vanish from the Earth within twenty years.[4]

The Tibetan antelope became a target for hunters because of its fur. It is the only source of a valuable type of wool called *shahtoosh*—a Persian word which means the 'king of wool'. Shahtoosh is often woven into precious shawls, which are known as 'ring shawls' because they are so fine that they can pass through a wedding ring.[5] For a long time, the processing, manufacture and consumption of shahtoosh was strictly limited to Kashmir or the broader region in India and Pakistan. Antelope meat was only rarely eaten or used as medicine by Tibetan herdsmen. Shahtoosh shawls were traditional clothing for the local people in Kashmir and an important part of their artwork, but the consumption of wool was too low to threaten the species' survival. However, since the mid-1980s, when gold mines were discovered in Kekexili and the Archin Mountain areas, both important habitats for the Tibetan antelope, thousands of workers armed with modern mining equipment and military weapons swarmed into the region. The Tibetan antelope soon became another 'gold mine' to miners, and the intensity of killing was compounded by continuous demand by the Western fashion market. According to a Chinese government report, the price of 1 kg of raw Tibetan antelope wool could reach 1,000 to 2,000 US dollars and a shahtoosh shawl made with 300 to 400 g of antelope wool could cost 5,000 to 30,000 US dollars on the international market.[6]

The Tibetan antelope did not disappear, however, though the species went through an extremely dangerous time in the 1980s and 1990s. Since the early stages of brutal slaughtering of the species, there have been conservation scientists, government officials, police officers, environmental activists, environmental non-governmental organizations (NGOs) and journalists who joined forces to protect the antelope. A scientific survey released in 2005 showed that the surviving Tibetan antelopes were estimated to be 149,930 in number, twice as many as in 1995. Although it is not enough to keep the species stable, these two decades of conservation efforts deserve recognition.[7]

This chapter offers first a narrative of the history of Tibetan antelope protection from 1982 to 2005. It addresses the following questions: who sought to protect the antelope? What did they do? And what changes have they brought about? The chapter also argues that there are stories missing from this mainstream narrative that deserve historians' attention—stories about environmental ethics, the politics behind wildlife conservation and Chinese prejudice towards the Western society.

The chronology of the campaign for protecting the Tibetan antelope

The twenty-year history of the Tibetan antelope protection can be divided into three phases. The first phase is from 1982 to 1994, during which a famous conservation scientist and a local Chinese government official played pioneering roles. The second phase, between 1995 and 1999, includes the institutionalization of an informal protection force, and the contribution of environmental activists and NGOs. The last phase began at the end of 1998 and ended in 2005. During this period, compared with the rather local and grassroots efforts in the two earlier stages, the central and regional governments of China took responsibility, followed by some attempts at international cooperation.

1982–1994

The influx of thousands of gold miners into Kekexili and the adjacent area of the Tibetan Plateau in the early 1980s is a prelude to the history of Tibetan antelope conservation. Before then, few people, apart from Tibetan herdsmen, geological surveyors and wildlife biologists, would encounter or interact with the antelopes.[8] After 1982, however, it was estimated that over 5,000 new miners entered into Kekexili and Archin Mountain area every year.[9]

Some gold miners soon became wild animal poachers, though there is no data on how and when it happened. Nevertheless, it is clear that once miners realized the commercial value of this animal, they greedily killed as many as they could. As witnesses described later, in the late 1980s, armed poaching was popular in Kekexili, Archin Mountain and Qiangtang (another important habitat for the Tibetan antelope, which is located in the Tibet Autonomous Region), and a group of poachers could kill hundreds, sometimes over a thousand antelopes in a single trip.[10]

Dr George Schaller was the first person who denounced the disaster of the Tibetan antelope. In 1985, Schaller came to the Tibetan Plateau to begin his research on wild hoofed animals. He was then the director of the International Conservation Program of New York Zoological Society and was already renowned for his contribution to wildlife conservation.[11] In 1988, Schaller first witnessed poachers striping the hair from Tibetan antelope fur. In 1991, he visited a poachers' tent and saw many furs for sale. Most importantly, Schaller identified that the hair of the Tibetan antelope was the only raw material for shahtoosh. He wrote that the only way to get shahtoosh wool was by killing Tibetan antelopes and that each shahtoosh shawl cost about three to four antelopes' lives.[12]

Schaller's warning in 1992 immediately caught the attention of conservationists in India, which hosted most of the manufacturers of and dealers in shahtoosh.[13] Following Schaller's work, the Wildlife Protection Society of India (WPSI) made further contributions to the protection of the Tibetan antelope.

Almost at the same time, a government authority called the Western Affair Working Council (WAWC) was established in Qinghai Province, later becoming a most important frontline body against illegal antelope hunting. Suonan Dajie, the founder of the WAWC, was from Tibet. While serving as a government leader in Suojia *xiang* (an administrative unit lower than 'county' and higher than 'village' in China), he advised the government of Yushu *zhou* to establish a special government institution to administrate the five neighbouring *xiang*, including Suojia in the western part of Yushu, in order to design specific development schemes for the region. However, when Suonan Dajie first led his colleagues to the 'human-free zone' of Kekexili, where there was supposed to be only wildlife—animals and plants—they were shocked by the environmental destruction caused by mining activities and by the number of animals killed by poachers. The dead animals they saw included Tibetan antelopes, from which the skin and fur had been brutally stripped, leaving only the complete skeleton and muscle. Sometimes, the bloody and fur-stripped antelopes were still alive when the WAWC members arrived.[14] Most of the victims were female, either pregnant or with small calves disoriented beside them. As a witness reported, in one slaughter, 'hundreds of antelopes were killed, with blood flowing like water and a field littered with corpses. In the blood lay a pregnant antelope, beside which a baby antelope was still sucking its dead mother's bloody breast... Without the mother's protection, this little orphan would soon be eaten by hawks and wolves'.[15]

The chaos they found in Kekexili soon shifted WAWC's emphasis from development to conservation. In November 1992, under the leadership of Suonan Dajie, the WAWC established two agencies, the Gold Administration Committee and the Wildlife Protection Office, to address the new challenges.[16]

Suonan Dajie and his colleagues went to Kekexili twelve more times in order to patrol the area and enforce the law, and each time they covered a territory of over 5,000 km. Compared to their opponents—thousands of gold miners and poachers, and even many gangsters—the WAWC was weak. Besides the difficulties of working in an extremely broad expanse of territory, and in a harsh natural environment, the WAWC had limited human, material and financial resources with which to fulfil their duties. According to Suonan Dajie's colleagues, the patrol team of the WAWC did not own guns themselves. In fact, the twelve patrols borrowed weapons twice from the local police office. In a few encounters with armed poachers, the patrol team had only to fire to warn off or stop the crimes. However, sometimes they would face stronger enemies, which put them into very dangerous situations.[17] On 17 January 1994, Suonan Dajie was shot dead in an armed conflict with eighteen poachers.[18] His death not only marked the end to the first phase in Tibetan antelope protection but also ignited a bigger fire for the conservation movement in China.

1994–1999

In 1995, the Qinghai provincial government established the provincial-level Kekexili Nature Reserve, following the advice of specialists. In 1997, the reserve was upgraded to a national-level reserve.[19] In spite of this high-level government action, the protection of the Tibetan antelope was still largely done by local government, environmental activists, NGOs and the media between 1994 and the early 1999. In this period, illegal antelope hunting and the shahtoosh trade reached its peak, creating a real danger of extinction for the species.[20]

Zhaba Duojie, the new leader of the WAWC, was Suonan Dajie's brother-in-law. He had served in the army and later became the executive director of the Public Security Administration of Zhiduo County. When Suonan Dajie was murdered, he 'sadly saw the frozen body of Suonan Dajie in the thick snow, which still preserved his shooting position'.[21] Zhaba Duojie then decided to give continuity to his brother-in-law's unfinished work.[22]

In September 1995, Zhaba Duojie reorganized the WAWC and gave it a fancier name, 'the Western Wild Yak Troop' (or the 'Wild Yak Troop' for short). The new conservation team was much bigger and better equipped than the previous one.[23] Nevertheless, it was considered only a semi-official armed force and most of its members were volunteers with very low wages.[24]

Despite the above progress, the WAWC received no more than 10,000 CNY (about 1,600 USD) each year from the government of Zhiduo County, which barely covered their basic living needs. For other expenses, such as additional wages, gasoline, fuel and necessary equipments, they had to raise funds by themselves. Despite all these difficulties, the Wild Yak Troop posed from its establishment an effective deterrent against the poaching of Tibetan antelopes and other crimes in Kekexili. From September 1995 to the end of 1999, they cracked down on 62 poaching cases, arrested 240 poachers and seized 56 guns and 3,180 pieces of Tibetan antelope fur. Poachers were no longer able to easily invade Kekexili from the east.[25]

Following the reorganization of the WAWC in 1995, its work attracted attention from a wider audience. Some environmentalists joined the effort—like Yang Xin. Yang was a wilderness adventurer in the 1980s, well known for his unprecedented drift along the upper stream of Yangtze River. In 1995, he decided to do something for the protection of Kekexili and the Tibetan antelope, which also inhabited the source area of Yangtze River.[26] Yang Xin's first contributions focused on building permanent protection stations in some Tibetan antelope's important habitats.[27] He funded the construction of first station in Kekexili with the revenues from his autobiography. On 19 August 1997, Yang Xin and his colleagues celebrated the completion of the first station at the site marked as the '2,952 km' of the Qinghai-Tibet Road, and named it the Suonan Dajie Nature Protection Station.[28]

Many people and groups supported Yang Xin's activities, including Friends of Nature (FON), a non-governmental organization founded in 1994. FON's membership included many social elites such as scholars, educators and journalists. Between 1995 and 1997, its members conducted some basic research on the Tibetan antelope issue. In 1997, the same year FON promoted Yang Xin's book to raise funds for the Suonan Dajie Nature Protection Station, one of its members, Xi Zhinong, a famous wildlife photographer and journalist for China Central Television (CCTV) at the time, visited Kekexili and brought back powerful images and first-hand evidence of the ecological disaster in the plateau.[29]

In 1998, FON's campaign reached its highest point. First, the group, cooperating with the World Wide Fund for Nature (WWF) office in Beijing, wrote a report and a factsheet about the Tibetan antelope crisis and circulated it to the media,[30] including foreign news agencies such as the Times, Reuters and the British Broadcasting Corporation (BBC). As a result, in June, the British newspaper *The Independent* published two related articles about this issue.[31] In September, FON, in cooperation with *China Green Times*, a newspaper supervised by the National Forestry Administration, sent a letter to the Zhiduo County government and formally invited Zhaba Duojie to Beijing to promote local conservation activities. The visit of Zhaba Duojie to Beijing proved to be a successful 'public relations' activity. It had a large impact on public opinion regarding what was happening to the animal called the Tibetan antelope, its habitat Kekexili and of the people dedicated to their conservation.[32]

Finally, in October, FON strategically used the visit of British prime minister Tony Blair to raise the profile of Tibetan antelope protection before the media. On 6 October 1998, the leader of FON and also the National Committee member of the Chinese People's Political Consultative Conference, Liang Congjie, wrote to Blair denouncing the illegal trade of Tibetan antelope products in the United Kingdom and Europe. Blair formally replied the next day, promising he would bring Liang's letter to the attention of the environmental authorities in the United Kingdom and the European Union, in the hopes of putting an end to the illegal trade.[33] Later, Blair and Liang met in Beijing. This dialogue between a Chinese environmental NGO director and a foreign country's leader, which had never happened before in China, soon made the headlines and the related articles stimulated increasing public concern over the endangered species.

This call for international cooperation by a group from China's civil society indirectly pressured the Chinese government to develop its own conservation blueprint, and particularly to support the WAWC or the Wild Yak Troop. Unfortunately, on 8 November of that year, when everything seemed to be going smoothly, WAWC's leader Zhaba Duojie was shot dead in his house. To this day, there has not been any confirmed official inquiry into the cause of his death.[34]

The death of another conservation hero inflicted heavy losses on the burgeoning campaign for the protection of the Tibetan antelope, but FON and other activists did not grieve for long. They contacted Zhiduo County and expressed their concern for the fate of the Wild Yak Troop.[35] On 19 December, the WAWC sent a letter to FON vowing to continue the conservation activities, and stating that the Wild Yak soldiers had patrolled again in Kekexili 'despite their great sorrow for the passing of their leader'.[36]

Once reassured about the commitment from local authorities, FON, WWF, the International Fund for Animal Welfare (IFAW) and other environmental groups maintained their financial support for conservation work in Kekexili. In February 1999, FON donated two brand-new jeeps to the Wild Yak Troop. In May, Liang Congjie, other FON staff, and several IFAW officers visited Kekexili to participate in a ceremony in which 374 pieces of antelope fur were destroyed at the Suonan Dajie Nature Protection Station.[37]

FON, a Chinese environmental group, was thus not the only NGO which contributed to the Tibetan antelope protection. Two international groups, WWF and IFAW, also supported FON with information, money and media resources.[38] In fact, the aforementioned report on the Tibetan antelope problem was written by Shi Lihong, who was both on the WWF staff and a member of FON. As another sign of international connectedness, Shi's writing cited extensively the report *Fashioned for Extinction: An Exposé of the Shahtoosh Trade*, which was produced by the Wildlife Protection Society of India in 1997.

1998–2005

At the end of the twentieth century, the public awareness of the Tibetan antelope protection was at its highest point—unfortunately, so was the critical situation of this species. A journalist who visited the southern part of the Yangtze River source area described how he only encountered three small herds of antelopes in a month, with no more than 24 animals in each herd.[39] More encouragingly, in a message sent to Liang Congjie by late 1999, Ge Rui from IFAW excitedly cited a reliable news source which confirmed that it was very difficult for dealers in Tibet to sell their antelope fur.[40] The implication was that the previous work of local conservation officers, environmental activists, NGOs and the media had triggered reactions from the regional and national governments in China for the protection of Tibetan antelopes.

Qinghai provincial government was the first to respond to the conservation campaign. Its deputy governor Liu Guanghe held a working meeting on 27 November 1998, just nineteen days after Zhaba Duojie's death, and instructed his colleagues and subordinates to enhance law enforcement in Kekexili.[41] Soon after, the National Forestry Administration released the official report *The Current Status of the Tibetan Antelope Protection*, declaring the Chinese government's firm commitment to protecting the endangered animal.

At the beginning of 1999, the government took more substantial action. Firstly, right after the Central Government issued the 'white paper' on Tibetan antelope protection, it launched an extensive law-enforcement campaign that took place between 10 April and 30 April in three major Tibetan antelope habitats, the nature reserves of Archin Mountain, Kekexili and Qiangtang. The campaign was led by the forest police department working under the National Forestry Administration, and was named 'Kekexili Number One Action'. The governments of the three relevant provinces and autonomous regions, namely Xinjiang, Qinghai and Tibet, all sent police officers to join the campaign.[42]

In October 1999, the Administrative Office of the Import and Export of Endangered Species of the People's Republic of China, cooperating with the

CITES Secretariat, organized the International Workshop on Conservation and Control of Trade in Tibetan Antelope in Xining. For the meeting, representatives from the governments of China, France, India, Italy, Nepal, the UK and the United States were invited, as well as members of seven well-known Chinese and international wildlife conservation NGOs.[43] At the end of the conference, the attendants endorsed the Xining Declaration on the Conservation and Control of Trade in Tibetan Antelope, which demonstrated the potential for cooperation within the international community.[44]

The Chinese government then introduced several measures to support the conservation of the Tibetan antelope. First, in 2000, it dismissed the Wild Yak Troop, which had been regarded as a semi-official armed force, and relaunched it under the Administration of Kekexili Nature Reserve, with the same nickname 'the Wild Yak Troop'. The Administration of Kekexili Nature Reserve then became the sole government power in Kekexili.[45] This institutional reform significantly strengthened the presence of the state in Kekexili. Secondly, in 2001, the Central Government included the Tibetan antelope in the list of the fifteen most endangered animals in China. It also invested more in basic research on their conservation by carrying out repeated surveys of their population and migration.[46] Thirdly, in order to mitigate the impact of the construction of the Qinghai-Tibet Railway (which had formally started in 2002) on the antelopes, the Central Government required the respective agencies to ensure that the migration route of the antelope would not be blocked.[47]

Although by the end of the twentieth century, the government had taken the leading role in Tibetan antelope conservation, the work of environmental activists and NGOs was still indispensable. Their effort to keep the WAWC or Wild Yak Troop alive, for instance, was remarkable—and crucial for the conservation efforts.

After Zhaba Duojie's sudden death, the officers of Yushu *zhou* had implied publically that the WAWC should no longer exist. By contrast, FON, as well as other environmental groups and activists, held the Wild Yak Troop in high regard because they believed that compared to many other government agencies, this local institution was the most active force for conservation.[48] Moreover, their experience in patrolling Kekexili could not be replaced easily, as many policemen from other more formal agencies, including those participating in the Kekexili Number One Action, were not familiar with the natural and social environment there.[49]

In August 1999, FON's leader Liang Congjie and seventeen journalists wrote a letter to Wen Jiabao, then the Vice-Premier of China, urging him to intervene in the WAWC issue and to save the Wild Yak Troop in any way possible. This letter resulted in a complicated process through different levels of government that reconsidered the fate of the WAWC.[50] Eventually, however, FON's support for the WAWC waned, and, due also to the strong political power of those requesting the dismissal of the Wild Yak Troop, the Wild Yak Troop was indeed dismissed within two years. Anecdotal evidence suggests Liang Congjie was very disappointed when he learned that leaders of WAWC used donations for their private expenses, and that was the factor that lead FON to withdraw its support.[51]

There were many other actions taken by NGOs in this period for the protection of the Tibetan antelope. For instance, in February 1999, FON submitted a comprehensive recommendation paper on Tibetan antelope conservation to Central Government. In this document, besides the comments on the WAWC, FON proposed a tri-provincial (regional) anti-illegal hunting campaign, which is believed to be the inspiring idea for the Kekexili Number One Action.[52] Later in the same year, WWF launched a worldwide consumer campaign against shahtoosh products. In 2000, a network of environmental websites called 'Saving Tibetan Antelope' was formed,[53] and since then FON, Green Rivers (a group founded by Yang Xin) and other NGOs have recruited and sent volunteers directly to Suonan Dajie Nature Protection Station to help conservation activities in the field.[54] Finally, from 2003 to 2004, FON conducted a new field investigation on antelope habitats and warned that gold mining was banned in Kekexili only, leaving many threats to the antelope elsewhere and to conservation in general.[55]

Following the work by government, environmental activists and NGOs, the business sector also joined in conservation activities in the early twenty-first century. In fact, some businesspeople, such as Ouyang Rongzong, had already been deeply involved in WAWC's work and had donated over one million CNY to the Wild Yak Troop since 1995.[56] The new contributors included companies famous in China and worldwide, such as Ericsson, UT Star, H. Brothers, Hengyuanxiang Textile and Taikang Life. The form of their contribution varied, as some companies like Ericsson and UT Star donated money while others offered special services like insurance or sponsored movies.[57]

By the mid-2000s, the government, civil society, media and business corporations were all actively participating in Tibetan antelope protection. Thus fight to protect antelopes became a war that touched different sectors from the entire nation. In consequence, hunting and trade activities decreased dramatically and, as mentioned earlier, the antelope population had almost doubled in the ten years from its low in 1995 to the upturn in 2005.[58] It could be said that the struggle to avoid the extinction of an endemic wildlife animal in the Tibetan Plateau had been reasonably successful.

The missing stories

The historical narrative above is not much different from the story told in mainstream Chinese literature, which is rather hero-centric, ecology-centric and nationality-centric. However, further examination of archives and recent scholarship offers deeper insights to the movement for the protection of the Tibetan antelope. Basically, there are three stories behind the main narrative that have been largely ignored. Firstly, local authorities, while celebrated for fighting poachers, also harboured a strong desire to exploit the natural resources of the large area inhabited by the Tibetan antelope. Such plans may challenge the belief that their fundamental goal was the protection of wildlife. Secondly, the Chinese government, the media and the environmental NGOs avoided linking the Tibetan antelope issues to the protection of the tiger in India. This omission reflects the complicated politics behind conservation activities. Thirdly, Western consumers have showed more behaviour change than the villain role ascribed to them by the mainstream Chinese literature would allow, and the impact of their self-education should not be underestimated.

The ambition of developing Kekexili

It is well known that the original motivation of Suonan Dajie for coming to Kekexili was to develop the natural resources there, which had little to do with Tibetan antelope. When Suonan Dajie volunteered to work in Suojia *xiang* in 1987, his heartfelt goal was to improve the local economy and the living standards of its local people. At the beginning, his only strategy was tax exemptions, as the Suojia herdsmen were too poor to submit surplus produce to the government. Even without paying taxes, however, life was still difficult in Suojia *xiang* because the local economy depended mostly on low-productivity stock farming. Suonan Dajie clearly knew that 'if Suojia relies only on the hips of cattle and sheep, it will never prosper'.[59]

While Suonan Dajie desperately looked for an alternative means of developing Suojia, a group of geological surveyors brought him new hope. As the famous journalist Liu Jianqiang described in his book, Suonan Dajie joined the surveyors to assess the water resources in Suojia. One day, after returning from a potential dam construction site, they celebrated their progress by drinking heavily. On that night, the surveyors suggested to him, 'why don't you go to Kekexili? There is gold there'. Hearing this, Suonan Dajie got very excited and wondered whether 'perhaps Kekexili could save Suojia'.[60]

That was the origin of Suonan Dajie's interest in Kekexili, a remote and vast place almost forgotten by local people, and also of the establishment of the WAWC in 1992. However, when he first arrived in Kekexili with a handbook of industrial minerals, illegal gold miners had preceded him, and the untold damage to the natural environment, including the slaughtering of the Tibetan antelope, astonished him. The ambition of developing Kekexili temporarily gave place to conservation concerns.

The developing goal did not disappear with the death of Suonan Dajie in 1994, though. His successor Zhaba Duojie had an even more systematic project to exploit the natural resources and did not see any contradiction between development and wildlife conservation. On 20 July 1995,

Zhaba Duojie submitted a report to the government of Zhiduo County, summarizing his investigation on the Kekexili region. This report gained him further support from his superiors to reorganize the WAWC and to continue Suonan Dajie's work.

Zhaba Duojie's report was mostly about the utilization of the natural resources in Kekexili rather than their preservation. In fact, Tibetan antelope conservation was only a small part of it. It was divided into two parts. In the first part, it listed six categories of resource in Kekexili and described their situation at the time. These resources include gold, other minerals, wildlife, coal, salt and grasslands. According to the report, apart from the wild animals, all resources were abundant and available for development. For example, on silver deposits, Zhaba Duojie stated that the WAWC had signed a five-year contract with two companies for their development. Such business deal brought seven million CNY in benefits for the local government.[61]

In the second part of the report, Zhaba Doujie suggested five measures. The first one was stricter control of gold mines. The report said that the WAWC should expel the illegal gold miners from Kekexili and support state-owned or collectively owned companies to obtain mining concessions. In addition, while making sure the grassland was not damaged, the WAWC should encourage these companies to employ mechanical technology and conduct structured, well-planned mining activities. Only the second measure was about fighting wildlife poachers. The third measure was more comprehensive, covering the development of salt lakes, silver and coal. Its basic plan for exploiting mineral resources was to establish agencies dealing with different minerals and sell mining rights to interested companies. It also mentioned the promotion of tourism in Kekexili, which might increase the income for local government and the local population. The fourth measure emphasized the development of stock farming by establishing state-owned farms and introducing commercial stocks to increase profits. The final measure was about setting up an office building as an information and trade hub in Geermu, a major city in the central area of Qinghai Province.[62]

At the end of the report, Zhaba Duojie expressed his ideal more explicitly:

> Over the past several years, due to various reasons, the WAWC's pace has not yet been fast enough, but its political influence has been deep and far-reaching… our goal must be achieved, and the long-sleeping western lion will feed the sons and daughters of Zhiduo for their growth and sustenance, as a mother's milk.[63]

To the general public, the work of the Wild Yak Troop was to patrol the wide range of terrains in Kekexili and fight the illegal hunting of protected wild animals. In fact, the other important task of the WAWC was to survey the natural resources and to seek opportunities to convert them into economic value. Bearing the above report by Zhaba Duojie in mind, this is not surprising at all. According to WAWC's official newsletter, between 1996 and 1998, its staff continuously explored new mineral, fisheries and brine shrimp (*Artemia salina*) resources in the heartland of Kekexili. It also affirmed that WAWC signed a cooperation agreement with a gold mining company and started fishing in the Cuorendejia Lake.[64]

In short, when the media and environmental NGOs praised the heroic feats of Suonan Dajie, Zhaba Duojie, the WAWC and the Wild Yak Troop for wildlife conservation, they seldom mentioned their long-held desire of exploiting the natural resources in Kekexili and improving local economy. From an ecological point of view, development in Kekexili, whether mineral mining or tourism, rather undermines the mission of protecting the Tibetan antelope, because the survival of the species depends fundamentally on a healthy natural habitat.

This is the first gap in the Tibetan antelope story, given that wildlife protection must often deal with both the health of a larger ecological system and the livelihood of local people. Although it is not easy to pass judgement on whether the WAWC's development scheme was right or not, the Qinghai provincial government ruled in 2000 that all mining, fishing and hunting activities in the Kekexili Nature Reserve ought to be banned.[65] This decision put an end to the old development dream of local authorities in Zhiduo County, and it might also have hindered the solution of other serious problems such as human poverty, which Suonan Dajie sought to address at the beginning of his time there.

Tiger bones for shahtoosh

The Tibetan antelope and shahtoosh problem exposes conflicts among the countries involved, particular in the complicated bilateral relationship between China and India.

A Chinese newspaper article in February 2000, for instance, cited the hostile reaction of an Indian businessman with regard to Chinese actions against the illegal hunting and trading of the Tibetan antelope or its products:

> Although the Tibetan antelope comes from China, China does not own the technique to process them into shahtoosh. Therefore their action is a business scheme against India and its purpose is to destroy the shahtoosh industry in Kashmir.[66]

On the other hand, Chinese officials often criticized India indirectly for its inadequate control of the manufacture and trade of shahtoosh.[67] In fact, most antelope fur would be processed into shahtoosh in Jammu and Kashmir, a state exempted from the ban on hunting antelope for its shahtoosh-related industries within India. That was why the Indian government and civil society groups had little to respond to China's criticism.

However, China was not innocent in terms of the responsibility for not protecting the Tibetan antelope effectively. Besides the lack of government control of the gold rush in Kekexili during the 1980s, which led to the illegal hunting in the first place, and the insufficient investment in conservation and support for local authorities, the Chinese demand for tiger-derived products was also a significant factor in increasing the trade in Tibetan antelope fur.

The Wildlife Protection Society of India, a non-governmental organization focused on wildlife conservation in India, has dedicated much of its efforts to the conservation of the Indian tiger. In fact, their logo is the face of a tiger. In its 1997 report *Fashioned for Extinction*, WPSI disclosed that there had been a barter trade between antelope fur and tiger-derived products such as bones and fur, as well as some other wild animal products including leopard bones, leopard fur, beaver fur and musk. Such trade was not discovered until 1993. When the WPSI staff first detected it, they were surprised to find out that Indian dealers could make 600 per cent profit by selling tiger bones in Tibet and shahtoosh wool in India.[68]

WPSI further asserted that though both the Indian and Chinese governments took measures to control this crime, the demand for tiger and Tibetan antelope products were intertwined and offered a great incentive to hunters and dealers. As Belinda Wright, one of the authors of *Fashioned for Extinction*, claimed during the Xining Workshop in October 1999, 'if the illegal trade in shahtoosh is not curbed, it might well prove the last straw for both the Tibetan antelope in China and the tiger in India'.[69]

The Indian environmentalists' discovery, however, was not welcomed by its counterparts and other social groups in China. As mentioned earlier, the WPSI's report became an important information source for Chinese campaign for the conservation of the Tibetan antelope. However, compared to other topics in the report, the connection between the illegal trade of tiger bones and fur and the poaching of antelopes was rarely mentioned in Chinese literature. In other words, both Chinese civil society and the government used information selectively in their communication with the public, excluding facts that could be seen as negative to the country's image.[70] Furthermore, there is anecdotal evidence indicating that in the international arena on wildlife traffic, both the Chinese government and civil society had agreed on an implicit strategy to avoid linking the barter trade issue to the general discussion of Tibetan antelope protection or, at the worst, to the allocation of responsibility among countries.

Nevertheless, China's main aim of distancing itself from the tiger-bone-for-shahtoosh trouble did not pose a serious threat to the potential cooperation between China and other countries, given that both the Chinese and Indian governments could not afford to fail in saving the Tibetan antelope and tiger. For example, in the Xining Workshop, the Indian delegates did not blame China for the tiger issue, but sought the possibility of multilateral cooperation between India, Nepal and China.[71] This proposal came to fruition after the meeting, and in fact the Chinese government had been willing to cooperate even when it was uncertain about the Indians' attitude.[72]

The evil fashion?

In the narrative of mainstream Chinese literature on the endangered Tibetan antelope, 'Western' countries at large were often criticized for their consumption of shahtoosh products. These countries or regions include the United States, the United Kingdom, Japan, France, Italy, as well as Hong Kong. Due to their share in the shahtoosh trade, all of these countries or regions sent delegates to the Xining Workshop in October 1999.

Chinese authors or reporters often used the word 'greedy' to describe the wealthy people of the Western societies who loved and looked for shahtoosh, and drew the conclusion that their 'bloody' or 'barbarous' fashion was the 'essential' cause of the extinction crisis of the Tibetan antelope.[73] As Ge Rui from IFAW once said, 'it is the fashion market and the endless vanity of the rich that drive the Tibetan antelope up a wall'.[74] Such story framing is, however, somehow simplistic and fails to analyse the motivations of consumption behaviour. A more detailed examination of the historical data offers a more balanced understanding of the issue, or at least the revelation that morality alone could not fully explain why shahtoosh became so desired in Western society.

First, it must be admitted that shahtoosh shawl is a fascinating garment, mostly worn by women. As mentioned before, this 'king of wool' or 'ring shawl' has been a highly valuable product for centuries in the central Asian region. Traditionally, it was one of the most treasured dowry items for Kashmiri brides. In modern times, it still attracts consumers by its softness, lightness, beauty and warmth. 'Once you own one shahtoosh, you want more and more and more,' one wealthy New Yorker confessed, 'they're so light that you don't feel them hanging around your neck, and they drape in this special way that is extremely luxe'.[75]

Irresponsible consumption indeed is an important cause of environmental degradation, but the pursuit of high-quality commodities might not be such a serious moral issue unless the negative impacts were deliberately ignored. In fact, many Western consumers of shahtoosh did not know the exact material source of this wool and hence bore little moral burden when buying the product. In fact, shahtoosh dealers usually tell their customers that 'they (shahtoosh products) are made from the chin hairs of wild goats or ibex which have been shed onto bushes, trees, and rocks and then painstakingly collected, tuft by tuft, by Tibetan nomads'.[76]

The mystery of the source of shahtoosh wool supplied a good rationale for the rich to pay high prices for it. One observer suggests that the high value of shahtoosh shawl comes not only from its high quality but also from the supposed hard work by Tibetan nomads to collect the hair of some wild animals. From such a perspective, buying shahtoosh was seen as morally innocent or even good—a high price for 'fair trade' and a benevolent substitute for animal fur, which has been regarded as a less than honourable material for garments since the 1980s. Thus, it is not surprising that in November 1994 there was a charity sale of shahtoosh shawls in New York City to benefit a philanthropic programme for terminally ill patients at the city's hospital. Besides the participation of some local celebrities, the event brought in Michael Jackson, who sang and talked to a dying child. The highly well-to-do public ordered shahtoosh shawls during the event and the seller agreed to make a donation of 10,000 USD to the hospital. But neither the buyers nor the seller expected that such open and public transaction would become a clue for the US Fish and Wildlife Service to investigate the shahtoosh trade.[77]

Although some may wonder to what extent shahtoosh consumers, like the New York socialites, knew the actual process of the production of shahtoosh, in fact even scientists and some dealers were puzzled for a long time. A 1999 article of *Vanity Fair* illustrates how difficult it was for Dr Schaller and his friends to find the truth in the late 1980s and 1990s:

> The wool dealer, Michael Sautman, the president of the California Cashmere Company, Inc., told me (Bob Colacello, the author of the article of *Vanity Fair*) how he and Schaller came to make the connection between antelope hides and shahtoosh shawls. After receiving an inquiry from a famous Italian cashmere company about raw shahtoosh wool, and based upon my doubt as to how the wool was obtained, I decided to contact George Schaller, who I knew was the foremost expert on Tibetan wildlife. When I talked to George, and we put together his knowledge of the animal and my knowledge of the fiber, all of a sudden we were able to come to a simultaneous conclusion about the trafficking and production of the wool in India and its final application. Before that, George didn't know what the wool was being used for, and I didn't know—had no confirmation—that the wool was obtained by killing animals. We filled in the missing parts of the story for each other.[78]

After finding the truth, Schaller not only sent his warning to India and China but also sought to influence the fashion industry and consumers domestically. In 1995, he and his Wildlife Conservation Society colleagues wrote letters to one hundred American fashion designers and retailers informing them about how shahtoosh was made and encouraging them to promote alternatives like pashmina. He also gave lectures on the theme at high-income social events, reaching out for the main consumers of shastoosh.[79] With the same recognition and concern, the Wildlife Trade Monitoring Network (TRAFFIC) admitted in 1997 that some wealthy consumers 'may not know that they are buying into the extinction of a species' and then conducted a trade monitoring programme in cooperation with WWF and IUCN.[80]

The efforts by Schaller and wildlife conservation organizations to publicize the truth were soon followed by law enforcement actions in several countries or regions. In the United States, as mentioned earlier, some wealthy consumers, mostly women, received subpoenas ordering them to give up their shahtoosh shawls and provide all information about the suppliers in October 1999. In Hong Kong, the former Agriculture and Fisheries Department (now the Agriculture, Fisheries and Conservation Department) conducted several searches against the sale of shahtoosh shawl between 1997 and 1999, and made great efforts to upgrade their technology on identifying shahtoosh wool from other materials, which was critical for subsequent litigation against dealers.[81] In India, *Hindustan Times* reported on 29 November 1999 that two gentlemen were arrested for illegally holding shahtoosh shawls. One of them was the president of a foundation for education and art, and the other one was a collector of antiquities. As the report said, they were suspected of breaking the Wildlife Protection Act of India and might be sentenced to a minimum of one year imprisonment and Rs 5,000 fine, up to a maximum of six years imprisonment and Rs 25,000 fine.[82]

There were wealthy consumers and fashion designers who indeed did not care about animal rights. In the Middle East, a princess declared that 'this shahtoosh thing is all a fiction of the animal-rights fanatics'. In the United Kingdom, the London Metropolitan Police admitted that despite a clear message sent to the traders and the public, customers still ask dealers for shahtoosh. In that case, the police officers would leave brochures for traders and guide them to warn their customers of the legal implications.[83] Also, as revealed by Chinese environmentalists, some Western fashion magazines continued to market shahtoosh products even after the true story about its extraction had been well disclosed to the public. For example, *Harper's Bazaar* advertised a shahtoosh shawl at the cost of 2,850 USD in its June 1998 issue. Likewise, *Vogue*, in its 1999 June issue, supposedly touted shahtoosh as a necessity for attending a luxurious event or banquet.[84]

By and large, approaching the problem of a shahtoosh market in Western society from a common sense perspective, there will be always good and bad behaviour. However, the fact that a significant share of Western consumers came to realize their mistakes and correct them was seldom mentioned by Chinese environmental activists, NGOs, journalists or the government. Such an omission deepens the existing misunderstanding of the Western society by Chinese people.

On 7 December 1999, Siobhan Peters, an officer from the Economic Section of the British Embassy in Beijing, wrote a letter to Liang Congjie, the leader of FON, arguing that Mr Liang was mistaken in his complaints about the Western fashion industry regarding their attitude towards the Tibetan antelope issue. She pointed out that the suspected shahtoosh advertisement on the June issue of *Vogue* was actually about pashmina. She further clarified that after receiving complaints from readers, a fashion designer who had previously expressed that she 'couldn't live without shahtoosh' had publicly renounced her beloved treasures.[85] So, was it not time for Chinese environmentalists to get rid of prejudices based on the Western–Eastern dichotomy?

Conclusion

The twenty-year history of Tibetan antelope protection, including both the mainstream narrative and the hidden stories, reveals much about the development of wildlife species conservation in China.

Firstly, the salvation of the Tibetan antelope from extinction should be seen as a result of the cooperation between grassroots organizations and government officers, as well as many mediating actors, such as environmental NGOs and journalists. It also resulted from the combination of domestic efforts, foreign aid and international cooperation. Notwithstanding, the protection of the Tibetan antelope, unlike the panda, a national symbol of China, has experienced a typical bottom-up trajectory in which the central and regional governments were almost absent in its first decade (mid-1980s to 1995). As far as internal–external driving forces are concerned, it could be said that both the domestic conservation power and foreign contribution were equally important. Also, as determined by the international nature of the issue, the cooperation between China and other relevant countries or regions, which were either supplying or demanding Tibetan antelope fur and products, provided an integrated solution to the problem.

The complexity of this protection history should also be highlighted. For example, protecting the Tibetan antelope is not only a legal responsibility but fundamentally reflects ethical motivations. As illustrated in this chapter, the original motivation of local officials to enter the habitat of the Tibetan antelope shows that wildlife conservation is frequently related to the livelihood of people, directly or indirectly. And, the development-oriented concerns of the local authorities, in particular the WAWC, demonstrate that there may be conflicts between the goals to preserve nature and to improve economy. Furthermore, conservation activities are not isolated from political and cultural influences. As seen in the 'shahtoosh for tiger bone' connection, it is not only the non-Chinese culture that values shahtoosh but also the Chinese culture addicted to tiger products have affected the hunting of and trade in the Tibetan antelope products.

Lastly, the content and way of telling this protection story also deserves attention, because the mainstream Tibetan antelope conservation history has been socially constructed by specific social groups in China in the past fifteen years. Despite their different focuses, Chinese environmentalists and government framed a common story to legitimize the conservation movement in China, which included the environmentally heroic image of the local conservationists and the legal and moral wrongs of the governments or rich consumers from the other countries or regions involved. As examined in this chapter, the story told by Chinese environmentalists and the Chinese government is incomplete, ignoring the complicated motivations for conservation, deliberately avoiding some important issues that were regarded as negative to the national image, and giving an unbalanced picture of Western society. It must also be admitted that such selective story somehow 'benefited' the conservation movement in China at the time, by creating environmental role models and villains for the general public. However, in the long run, if Chinese environmentalists and the government aim to gain more from the wildlife conservation movement, including the continuous protection of the Tibetan antelope, some important questions, such as the relationship between conservation and the alleviation of poverty, the need for a better understanding of national interests and the perils of intercultural misunderstandings, can be neglected no longer.

Notes

1 Qisen Yang, Lin Xia and Xiaomin Wu, 'Qingzang tieluxian shang de yesheng dongwu tongdao yu Zanglingyang baohu', *Bulletin of Biology* 5 (2005), 16; National Forestry Administration of China, 'Zhongguo Zanglingyang baohu xianzhuang' (FON Archives, 1998); Belinda Wright, and Ashok Kumar, *Fashioned for Extinction: An Exposé of the Shahtoosh Trade* (New Delhi, India: Wildlife Protection Society of India, 1997).

2 Ya'na Cai, 'Zanglingyang weishenme hui binwei (shang): baohu shengwu duoyangxing', *City and Disaster Reduction* 1 (2010), 38; Author unknown, 'Zanglingyang·Kekexili', *China's Ethnic Groups* 11 (2008), 81.

3 National Forestry Administration of China, 'Zhongguo Zanglingyang baohu xianzhuang', 1998.

4 Congjie Liang, 'A letter to Tony Blair dated 6 October 1998', (FON Archives, 1998).

5 Cai, 'Zanglingyang weishenme hui binwei (shang): baohu shengwu duoyangxing', 41.

6 National Forestry Administration of China, 'Zhongguo Zanglingyang baohu xianzhuang', 1998.

7 Yuan Shi, 'Xizang Zanglingyang zongshu jizeng, binwei yijiu', *Green Leaf* 7 (2006), 24–25.

8 Yulian Gao, 'Zanglingyang daolie fanzui ji baohu duice', *Journal of Yili Normal University (Natural Science)* 3 (2009), 35; Zhaba Duojie, 'Baowei Kekexili' (FON Archives, 1998).

9 Yue Gu, 'Guanzhu Zanglingyang', *West China Development* 1 (2001), 24–25.

10 Danping Sun, ' "Shatushi": Canhai Zanglingyang de yuanxiong', *Man and the Biosphere* 2 (2000), 48.

11 Ya'na Cai, 'Zanglingyang weishenme hui binwei (xia): baohu shengwu duoyangxing', *City and Disaster Reduction* 2 (2010), 36.

12 Cai, 'Zanglingyang weishenme hui binwei (xia): baohu shengwu duoyangxing', 34; Sun, ' "Shatushi": Canhai Zanglingyang de yuanxiong', 47.
13 Belinda Wright, 'Shahtoosh Trade and India', (Presented at the International Workshop on Conservation and Control of Trade in Tibetan Antelope, 13 October 1999, FON Archives).
14 Jianqiang Liu, *Tianzhu: Zangren Chuanqi* (Lasa: Tibetan People's Press, 2009), 93, 95.
15 Liu, *Tianzhu: Zangren Chuanqi*, 97.
16 Liu, *Tianzhu: Zangren Chuanqi*, 94.
17 The literature on violent conflicts between poachers and rangers is rather large; among others, see Louis Warren, *The Hunter's Game: Poachers and Conservationists in Twentieth-Century America* (New Haven, CT: Yale University Press, 1997); Roderick P. Neumann, 'Disciplining peasants in Tanzania: From state violence to self-surveillance in wildlife conservation', in Nancy Lee Peluso and Michael Watts (eds), *Violent Environments* (Ithaca, NY: Cornell University press, 2001).
18 Jun Yan, 'Zhaba Duojie diexue Yushu', in Congjie Liang and Xiaoyan Liang (eds), *Wei Wugao de Daziran* (Tianjin: Baihua Literature and Art Publishing House, 2000), 154.
19 Deqian Wangmu, 'Chumo Zanglingyang', *Tibetan Literature* 4 (2003), 66.
20 Gaowen Zhang, 'Daolie Zanglingyang fanzui yanjiu', *Forestry of China* 1A (2007), 47.
21 Yan, 'Zhaba Duojie diexue Yushu', 154.
22 Yan, 'Zhaba Duojie diexue Yushu', 154.
23 Wen Jing, 'Zanglingyang he ta de baohuzhe', *Business World* 12 (1999), 76.
24 Yan, 'Zhaba Duojie diexue Yushu', 55.
25 Yan, 'Zhaba Duojie diexue Yushu', 155.
26 Weiqun Wang, 'Xue're Changjiang yuan', in Congjie Liang and Xiaoyan Liang (eds), *Wei Wugao de Daziran*, 46–57.
27 ingguo Wei, 'Zanglingyang xueran Kekexili', *Western Forum* 3 (2002), 34.
28 China Central Television, 'Baowei Kekexili', *China Report* (television programme script, FON Archives), (year unknown).
29 Fanxu Zeng, 'Huanbao NGO de yiti jian'gou yu gonggong biaoda', *Journal of International Communication* 10 (2007), 15.
30 Friends of Nature and World Wide Fund for Nature, 'Zanglingyang Baogao' (FON Archives, 1998); Friends of Nature, 'Zanglingyang zhenxiang' (FON Archives, 1998).
31 Anne Hanley et al., 'Rare antelope sacrificed for European rich and fashionable', *The Independent*, 20 June 1998, 1 (FON Archives); Peter Popham, 'These animals are dying out and all because ladies love shahtoosh', *The Independent*, 20 June 1998, 3 (FON Archives).
32 Fanxu Zeng, 'Huanbao NGO de yiti jiangou yu gonggong biaoda', 15–16.
33 Liang, 'A letter to Tony Blair dated 6 October 1998', 1998; Tony Blair, 'A letter to Liang Congjie dated 7 October 1998', (FON Archives, 1998).
34 Yan, 'Zhaba Duojie diexue Yushu', 152–153.
35 Friends of Nature, 'Minjian huanbao zuzhi "Ziran zhiyou" guanyu baohu Zanglingyang wenti de baogao he jianyi' (FON Archives, 1999).
36 Western Affair Working Council, 'A letter to Friends of Nature dated 19 December 1998' (FON Archives, 1998b).

37 Author unknown, 'Zhongguo Kekexili Zanglingyang baoweizhan', *Photo Story* 1 (2000), 5.
38 Cai, 'Zanglingyang weishenme hui binwei (xia): baohu shengwu duoyangxing', 37; International Fund for Animal Welfare, 'Guoji aihu dongwu jijinhui juankuan baohu Zanglingyang', *China Nature* 2 (1999), 3.
39 Gu, 'Guanzhu Zanglingyang', 25.
40 Rui Ge, 'A letter to Liang Congjie dated 3 December 1999' (FON Archives, 1999).
41 The People's Government of Qinghai Province, 'Guanyu Kekexili Zanglingyang deng yesheng dongwu baohu gongzuo zhuanti xietiao huiyi de jiyao' (FON Archives, 1998).
42 Author unknown, 'Xiang wei baohu yesheng dongwu kejinzhishou de zhongguo senlin gong'an ganjin men zhijing! Yuan senlin gong'an shouhu zhu Zanglingyang ningjing de tiantang!', *Forest & Humankind* 2 (2003), 24–25.
43 Chinese civil society environmental groups like FON were, however, not formally invited.
44 The attendants to the 1999 International Workshop on Conservation and Control of Trade in Tibetan Antelope in Xining, China, 'Xining declaration on the conservation and control of trade in Tibetan antelope' (FON Archives, 1999).
45 Wei, 'Zanglingyang xueran Kekexili', 34.
46 Qinghua Liang, 'Zanglingyang jiudi baohu de jianyi', *Environmental Protection* 11B (2008), 25.
47 Cai, 'Zanglingyang weishenme hui binwei (xia): baohu shengwu duoyangxing', 37.
48 Friends of Nature, 'Minjian huanbao zuzhi "Ziran zhiyou" guanyu baohu Zanglingyang wenti de baogao he jianyi' (FON Archives, 1999); Congjie Liang et al., 'A letter to Wen Jiabao dated 18 August 1999' (FON Archives, 1999).
49 National Forestry Administration of China, 'Guanyu yinfa "Qinghai, Xinjiang, Xizang sanshengqu jizhong kaizhan daji feifa liesha Zanglingyang xingdong de zongjie" de tongzhi' (FON Archives, 1999).
50 Liang et al., 'A letter to Wen Jiabao dated 18 August 1999', 1999; Bureau for Letters and Calls, the Central Committee of the Communist Party of China, '(Wen) 99–36' (FON Archives, 1999); The General Office of the State Council, 'Guanyu zhuansong Wen Jiabao tongzhi pishijian de han, Zhongban Guoban xinpizi (1999) 213 hao' (FON Archives, 1999); D. S. Mu, 'A letter to the Agriculture and Forestry Department of Qinghai Province' (FON Archives, 1999).
51 Zhu Wu, *Niudu Xingdong* (Hong Kong: China Cultural and Art Publishing House, 2008), 52.
52 Friends of Nature, 'Minjian huanbao zuzhi "Ziran zhiyou" guanyu baohu Zanglingyang wenti de baogao he jianyi', 1999.
53 Cai, 'Zanglingyang weishenme hui binwei (xia): baohu shengwu duoyangxing', 37.
54 Liang, 'Zanglingyang jiudi baohu de jianyi', 27; Yan Zhou, 'Zanglingyang cong zheli zouguo: huanbao zhiyuangzhe zai Kekexili', *Tibet Tour* 5 (2004), page unknown.

55 Qinghua Liang, 'Zanglingyang jiudi baohu de xianzhuang diaocha', *Environmental Protection* 10B (2008), 53.
56 Qiuping Wang, 'Ouyang Rongzong he ta de Zanglingyang shiye', *People's Political Scene* 7 (2000), 38.
57 Cai, 'Zanglingyang weishenme hui binwei (xia): baohu shengwu duoyangxing', 37; Author unknown, 'Zanglingyang·Kekexili', 81.
58 Another research on the Archin Mountain Nature Reserve shows that the estimated antelope population there had increased from 12,000 in 1995 to 40,000 in 2004. See Zhiheng Cao and Dalin Wang, 'Xinjiang Zanglingyang shuliang zengduo', *West Leather* 12 (2004), 46.
59 Liu, *Tianzhu: Zangren Chuanqi*, 89.
60 Liu, *Tianzhu: Zangren Chuanqi*, 90.
61 Zhaba Duojie, 'Guanyu Kekexili diqu xianzhuang de zonghexing diaocha baogao', in Rongzong Ouyang (ed.), *Mengduan Kekexili* (1995; Beijing: Intellectual Property Publishing House, 2011), 34–36.
62 Zhaba Duojie, 'Guanyu Kekexili diqu xianzhuang de zonghexing diaocha baogao', in Rongzong Ouyang (ed.), *Mengduan Kekexili*, 36–38.
63 Zhaba Duojie, 'Guanyu Kekexili diqu xianzhuang de zonghexing diaocha baogao', in Rongzong Ouyang (ed.), *Mengduan Kekexili*, 38–39.
64 Western Affair Working Council, *Newsletter* 9:12 (1996) (FON Archives); Western Affair Working Council, *Newsletter* 1, 5, 6, 7 (1997) (FON Archives); Western Affair Working Council, *Newsletter* 10 (1998a) (FON Archives).
65 Deqiang Hou, 'Kekexili, Zanglingyang de shengcunqu haiyou duoda?' *Reporters' Note* 8 (2005), 14.
66 Sun, ' "Shatushi": Canhai Zanglingyang de yuanxiong', 49.
67 For example, Administrative Office of the Import and Export of Endangered Species of the People's Republic of China, 'Weile Zanglingyang de mingyun' (FON Archives, 1999).
68 Wright, 'Shahtoosh Trade and India', 1999.
69 Wright, 'Shahtoosh Trade and India', 1999.
70 Metropolitan Police (London), *The Illegal Trade in Shahtoosh* (brochure, FON Archives, 1999).
71 Author unknown, 'Chiru and Shahtoosh' (Presented by an Indian government representative at the International Workshop on Conservation and Control of Trade in Tibetan Antelope, FON Archives, 1999b).
72 Lynne O'Donell, 'Shawl Casts Pall over Antelope', *The Australian* 23 October1999 (FON Archives); Author unknown, 'The strategy for participating to the 1999 International Workshop on Conservation and Control of Trade in Tibetan Antelope in Xining, China' (FON Archives, 1999a).
73 Bo Zhang, 'Zanglingyang he "yeman" shishang', *Civilization* 6 (2003), page unknown; World Wide Fund for Nature, 'Shishang: Zanglingyang de siwang zhi zhou', *China Nature* 1 (2000), 16–17.
74 Jiang Qing and Qian Sun, 'Hujiu! Zhongguo Zanglingyang mianlin miedingzhizai', *Journal of Green Great World* 3 (1999), 47.
75 Bob Colacello, 'O. K., Lady, Drop the Shawl', *Vanity Fair* November 1999, page unknown (FON Archives).

76 Xiang Lu, and Lei Wu, 'Qiangkou xia de shengling: Zanglingyang', *Environmental Education* 5 (2003), 58–59; Wright and Kumar, *Fashioned for Extinction*.
77 Colacello, 'O. K., Lady, Drop the Shawl'.
78 Colacello, 'O. K., Lady, Drop the Shawl'.
79 Colacello, 'O. K., Lady, Drop the Shawl'.
80 Wildlife Trade Monitoring Network, 'High Fashion Shawls Threaten Species with Extinction', 19 December 1998 (FON Archives).
81 Zhixin Zhang, 'Xianggang Tebie Xingzhengqu dui Zangliangyang rong feifa maoyi de kongzhi' (Main points of the presentation at the 1999 International Workshop on Conservation and Control of Trade in Tibetan Antelope in Xining, China, FON Archives).
82 Author unknown, 'Shahtoosh Shawl Pallu Seized, Two Arrested', *Hindustan Times*, 29 November 1999 (FON Archive).
83 Andy Fisher, 'Operation charm: Tackling the Shahtoosh trade in the United Kingdom' (Presented in the 1999 International Workshop on Conservation and Control of Trade in Tibetan Antelope, Xining China, FON Archives).
84 Cited from: Bo Zhang, 'Zanglingyang he "yeman" shishang', page unknown.
85 S. Peters, 'A letter to Liang Congjie dated 7 December 1999' (FON Archives).

Further reading

Feng, Yongfeng. 2010. *Langwu tuteng*. Beijing: Intellectual Property Publishing House.

Liang, Congjie and Xiaoyan Liang (eds). 2000. *Wei Wugao de Daziran*. Tianjin: Baihua Literature and Art Publishing House.

Murray, Geoffrey and Ian G. Cook. 2004. *The Greening of China*. Beijing: China International Press.

Schaller, George B. 1997. *Tibet's Hidden Wilderness: Wildlife and Nomads of the Chang Tang Reserve*. New York: Harry N Abrams.

Wang, Ming (ed.). 2008. *Emerging Civil Society in China, 1978–2008*. Beijing: Social Sciences Academic Press.

Wang, Zongren. 2010. *Zanglingyang de naxie shier*. Shanghai: Xuelin Publishing House.

5

Blood on the Ice: The Greenpeace Campaign Against the Harp Seal Slaughter

Frank Zelko

In the early 1970s, a group of peace and environmental activists in British Columbia pioneered a new form of environmental activism. They decided to call themselves 'Greenpeace', a term they felt best expressed their efforts to unite the peace movement with environmentalism. Greenpeace's founders were the first environmentalists to adopt the Gandhian non-violent protest strategies employed by the peace and civil rights movements. They combined this with the Quaker notion of 'bearing witness'—the idea that a crime or atrocity can be challenged by observing it and reporting it to others—and hitched it to a media strategy heavily influenced by Marshall McLuhan, the Canadian communications scholar who developed such enduring concepts and aphorisms as 'the global village' and 'the medium is the message'. In 1976, after several years of protesting against nuclear testing and whaling in the Pacific, Greenpeace turned its attention to the annual harp seal slaughter that took place on the ice floes of eastern Canada at the end of winter. This would prove to be the young organization's most difficult and problematic campaign. This chapter examines Greenpeace's

---

This chapter draws on material from *Make It a Green Peace!: The Rise of Countercultural Environmentalism*, by Frank Zelko (2013). Reproduced with permission of Oxford University Press, USA.

attempt to end the seal slaughter (the goal of which was the production of luxury fur coats) and the fierce resistance it encountered from the mostly impoverished Newfoundlanders who were the chief labour force of the fur industry. The anti-sealing campaign, more than Greenpeace's anti-nuclear or anti-whaling protests, exemplifies a conflict that has been played out over and over again during the past several decades between environmentalists intent on preserving a part of the natural world they value and the working people whose livelihoods depend on exploiting it. From the forests of the Amazon to the North Atlantic fisheries, environmentalists have often found themselves in the unenviable position of being pitted against rural working class or indigenous people struggling to make a living, a conflict that is usually complicated by the actions of corporations and governments.[1]

Greenpeace's 1975 anti-whale campaign could be plausibly framed as an attempt to preserve an endangered species rather than as an animal rights issue; after all, there was no doubt that certain species of great whales were threatened with extinction. However, the fate of the harp seal, from an ecological standpoint, was less clear-cut. Although Canadian and Norwegian hunters continued to slaughter hundreds of thousands of seal pups every year, the harp seal population, though considerably smaller than it had been during previous centuries, was nonetheless relatively stable.[2] Furthermore, unlike whales, seals did not seem to be possessed of an extraordinary intelligence, which was one of the major arguments against whaling. What was undeniable, however, was that baby harp seals were utterly adorable, a fact that made their slaughter—usually achieved by a skull-crushing blow from a home-made club—seem all the more brutal. Herein lay a dilemma: in a world in which millions of cute animals are butchered or subjected to cruel experiments on a daily basis, would it be possible to adopt the harp seal as a symbol of humankind's wanton ecological destruction without running a gratuitously emotional campaign that demonized the mostly impoverished Newfoundlanders who slaughtered them?

Every year in February and March, hundreds of thousands (in earlier times, millions) of female harp seals haul themselves onto the ice floes of eastern Canada in order to whelp. The fishermen of Newfoundland, many of whom were forced to remain idle throughout the winter, supplemented their generally meagre incomes by 'hunting' the doe-eyed, fluffy white harp seal pups. To many middle-class city dwellers who had become insulated and disconnected from the harsh vicissitudes of rural life, the annual slaughter of the harp seal pups seemed to be a vestige of a brutal and barbaric past. The 'swilers',[3] as they are known in Newfoundland, simply walk up to a defenceless pup and smash it on the head with a spiked club known as a *hakapik*, a Norwegian word that amply evokes the club's function in numerous languages. The pup is quickly skinned and the swiler moves on to the next one, often leaving behind a mother seal pathetically nudging the pup's bloody corpse. Various animal welfare groups had been protesting against the hunt since the mid-1960s, and although they had forced some improvement in the management of the hunt, hundreds of thousands of seal pups are still being slaughtered each winter.

In 1975, Paul Watson, a young Greenpeace activist who subsequently became one of the world's most prominent and radical environmentalists, convinced Greenpeace's leaders to employ the organization's patented confrontational protest style on the ice floes off the coast of Newfoundland, Labrador and Quebec. The harp seal, Watson insisted, was on the road to extinction as a result of the hunt. From the start, however, Watson made it abundantly clear that from his perspective, the seal campaign was not going to be about population biology and maximum sustainable yield. It would, instead, be about brutality, blood and death. The sealers, he emoted, 'greet the mothers and their babies with club and knife', turning the ice from a 'peaceful nursery to [a] bloody carnage', bringing 'a horrible death to the seals and international shame to Canadians'. Swilers, he insisted, were 'colder than the ice upon which they trod'. They dispatched 'baby after baby, clubbing them, kicking them and in some cases removing the skin while the baby still lives and struggles'. Watson also made it clear that as with Greenpeace's stand on whaling, mere conservation would not be good enough: 'The seal hunt', he insisted, 'must end completely'.[4]

The seal hunt took up only a small portion of the swilers' working lives—a mere three or four weeks towards the end of the winter. Most spent the warmer months on fishing boats or in processing plants and the winter working in the forest industry. Despite the short amount of time swilers devoted to it, the income earned from sealing could be quite substantial in certain communities, frequently constituting the difference between extreme hardship and getting by. In earlier times, as one scholar noted, the hunt was essential for many communities. However, since the mid-twentieth century its economic value can best be described as supplemental.[5]

Sealing constituted something of a rite of passage for many of the province's workingmen, and the region's folklore is filled with stories of the hardships and triumphs of the swilers.[6] Since the act of killing a seal is not particularly skillful or dangerous, the swilers' stories emphasized their battles with the elements and with unscrupulous capitalists. They tended to view themselves as poor, humble and hardy folk living on the margins of civilization, battling the awesome forces of nature, and exploited by ruthless shipowners and fur traders who cared little for their safety or economic well-being. Newfoundland history is replete with tragic stories of swilers succumbing to sudden snowstorms and plunging through thin ice into the frigid waters of the Gulf of St. Lawrence. One of the more notable examples is the Newfoundland Disaster of 1914, which was vividly retold by Cassie Brown in her book, *Death on the Ice*.[7] For two days, a group of one hundred and twenty sealers were trapped in a blinding snowstorm on the shifting ice floes, unable to find their ship. Eighty froze to death on the ice, a tragedy that was compounded by the fact that the ship's captain, eager to make up his quota, had forced the sealers off the boat despite the horrendous conditions. Shipowners typically took two-thirds of a voyage's proceeds. The remainder was divided up among the crew, with the captain receiving the lion's share. Adding salt to the wounds was the fact that the swiler, as one indignant Newfoundlander put it, 'is obliged to pay hospital dues and is taxed by the merchant to pay not only for the tools and materials used in the fishery, but a further sum of three pounds, ten shillings for the privilege of being allowed to hazard his life to secure a fortune for the merchant'.[8]

Historically, therefore, the life of a swiler bore a similar degree of hardship and indignity to that of a coal miner in an early twentieth-century Appalachian company town. And rather than constituting a 'hunt', in any reasonable sense of the term, the work patterns and labour practices of the seal industry were akin to those of the industrial slaughterhouse. Nevertheless, the fact that the activity took place in 'the great outdoors' rather than inside a factory meant that the swilers could develop a sense of autonomy and expertise, as well as the feeling that they were testing themselves against the harsh vicissitudes of nature. Perhaps this helps explain their tenacious defence of an industry in which, from an outsider's perspective, they appear to occupy the role of an exploited labouring class performing difficult and dangerous work for relatively little remuneration.[9]

As with whaling, the Norwegians were the major technological innovators in the sealing industry. By the late 1960s, most of the swilers were working for Norwegian firms, some of which were registered in Canada, while the few independent Newfoundland sealing operations could only sell their furs to Europeans through Norwegian middlemen. Swilers received an average of \$2–3 for a single pelt, which increased in value to \$100–125 by the time it was part of a luxury fur coat. Only a very small percentage of this money ever found its way back to Canada. According to historian Briton Cooper Busch, by 1971, the sealing industry in Newfoundland 'may safely be said to have come into Norwegian hands'.[10]

Between 1949 and 1961, swilers killed an average of 300,000 harp seal pups per year. According to David Sergeant, a biologist working for the Canadian Fisheries Research Board, this was far too many to sustain the hunt in the long term, and had already more than halved the birth rate from 750,000 in 1950 to a mere 350,000 in 1961. The entire harp seal population was estimated to be less than one and a half million.[11] Until the early 1960s, neither the sealers nor the Canadian government had taken an active interest in conservation, the sole measure being a vague gentleman's agreement between Canadian and Norwegian sealers that seals should only be taken from the beginning of March through early May.[12] This hands-off policy was in stark contrast to the more statist approach that generally characterized Canadian wildlife management practices throughout the twentieth century. In fact, historian Tina Loo argues that Canadian wildlife managers have long engaged in a 'normative project of social, economic, and political change', one that was often at odds with the needs of local people and particularly indigenous Canadians.[13] The situation in Newfoundland was different, no doubt in part due to the fact that Newfoundland did not become part of Canada until 1949. Furthermore, since much of the hunt took place more than twelve miles offshore it was outside the government's jurisdiction. However, from the 1960s onward, the federal government became a staunch advocate and facilitator of the hunt. The swilers did not always appreciate the efforts of professional wildlife biologists. Nevertheless, no matter how much swiling tarnished Canada's image abroad, the Canadian government has remained steadfast in its support of the industry.

By the mid-1960s, conservation-minded scientists were calling on the Canadian government to regulate the slaughter. In addition, animal welfare activists, incensed by what they saw as the unmitigated cruelty of the hunt, began to publicize the annual slaughter in an effort to alert the metropolitan populations of North America and Europe to what they perceived as the barbaric practices of Newfoundlanders. Ecological and conservation issues were only of passing interest to these activists, many of whom belonged to the various Canadian branches of the Society for the Protection of Cruelty to Animals (SPCA). Rather, it was the cruelty of the hunt that raised their ire. In addition to causing great pain and suffering to the pups—and to the mothers who lost them—the hunt, it was felt by many, brutalized the swilers, turning them into cold-hearted savages. For middle-class SPCA members in the suburbs of Toronto or Vancouver, it was difficult to imagine the mindset that enabled a man to pitilessly club to death one of nature's most beautiful creatures, and then proceed to skin its warm and potentially still living body.[14]

Swilers did not fit easily into any recognizable social category. Indigenous communities, after all, also hunted seals, and few non-aboriginal Canadians would begrudge them this right. However, where native hunting practices were ennobled by thousand year traditions and deep cultural and mythological connections to their prey, the swilers were just poor white folk who clubbed seals for the international fur trade. In reality, indigenous sealing and swiling were much more similar than many would care to admit. The methods of killing the seals were virtually identical, and by the mid-twentieth century, both groups were intimately bound to the international market economy. Perhaps the only significant difference was that the indigenous hunters included a substantial amount of seal meat in their diets, while Newfoundlanders would only dine on the occasional flipper. Nevertheless, the indigenous hunters were sheltered under the protective blanket of sacred tradition, leaving the profane Newfoundlanders to bear the brunt of middle-class opprobrium.

In 1964, the harp seal issue came to the attention of a wider audience when a Montreal production company, Artek Films Limited, signed a contract with the CBC (Canadian Broadcasting Corporation) to produce a series of thirty-minute features on fishing and hunting in Quebec. After filming several episodes on topics such as duck shooting and moose hunting, the film crew, with little foreknowledge of the harp seal hunt, flew to the

Magdalen Islands off the coast of Quebec, where they hoped to film the harps in their natural habitat and perhaps witness one or two being hunted. Instead, they arrived in the middle of swiling season and were shocked by scenes of swilers clubbing and skinning seals with apparently gay abandon. This was not like skilled hunters picking off the odd caribou with a telescopic rifle; the swilers raced from seal to seal, bashing and skinning as quickly as they could in order to maximize their productivity. The documentary, titled *Les Phoques de la Banquise*, provoked outrage throughout Canada and beyond. In a film not short on gruesome scenes, one in particular stood out and, for anti-sealing protestors, came to symbolize all that was brutal and degrading about the hunt. The infamous scene shows a swiler taking his knife to a bucking and kicking harp seal, one that was clearly very much alive, and beginning to skin it. It ends with the flayed creature racing madly across the ice, screaming deliriously and leaving a trail of blood behind it.[15]

Both the swilers and the Canadian government, which by now strongly supported the annual hunt, contested the film's authenticity, claiming that the film crew had staged the skinning and paid one of the swilers to do what he would not have done in the normal course of his job.[16] But such charges did little to diminish the film's visceral impact, which led *Canadian Audubon* magazine to declare that, whether exaggerated or not, the film 'served to focus general attention on a practice which, whether limited or general, had to be outlawed'.[17]

Prior to Greenpeace's involvement in the seal hunt, the most high-profile protestor was the indefatigable Brian Davies. In 1964, while Davies was the executive secretary of the New Brunswick SPCA, he attended a gathering of government officials and seal industry representatives who were drafting the regulations for the 1965 hunt. The meeting led Davies to conclude that 'an over-capitalized sealing industry was intent on killing the last seal pup in order to get a return on its equipment, [while] those who profited from the seals gave not one thought to their suffering'. Under pressure from various humane societies, the Canadian fisheries minister offered to take three representatives to the 1965 hunt in order to prove that it was as humane as possible. One of the three was Davies. It was a decision that the minister and his successors would come to regret, as Davies became virtually a permanent presence on the March ice floes for the next three decades.[18]

While the SPCA was ostensibly concerned with making the hunt more humane, rather than ending it altogether, it soon became clear that Davies and various like-minded members wanted to go further. By 1966, Davies' New Brunswick chapter of the SPCA decided to pursue a policy of abolition. This put them out of step with the organization's national office, which issued an official statement supporting the hunt and the methods employed by swilers. Although they felt that the use of clubs and gaffs was still cruel, it represented, they argued, the best available method for the time being. For Davies, merely putting a halt to the cruelty was not enough: 'For my part', he wrote in his book, *Savage Luxury*,

> I believe my efforts have reduced the cruelty of the hunt, but that was not my primary goal. The question I pose for the moral discrimination of Canada does not concern itself so much with how these animals are killed, but rather whether they should be killed at all. I see the seal issue as representing a showdown for wildlife. These animals are symbolic, and if they can't be saved it is probably not ever going to be possible to save any substantial population of wild creatures. The world will gradually fill with filth and one day, empty of all but man, this planet will become the loneliest place in the universe. *Perhaps in saving the seals, man may save himself.*[19]

For Davies, the SPCA's grudging stamp of approval for the hunt was simply unconscionable. If even those who were supposedly defending the seals were supporting the hunt, it was clear that change could only occur if the international community pressured the Canadian government. With this in mind, Davies embarked on a decade-long media campaign designed to shame the Canadian government into ending the hunt. Although he never employed Greenpeace-style direct-action tactics in his protests, Davies nonetheless proved to be a skilled media manipulator. In 1966, he convinced *Weekend* magazine, a weekly supplement that appeared in dozens of major Canadian newspapers, to publish an article that clinically but dispassionately described the swilers going about their business. In response, Davies received almost 5,000 letters, the vast majority supporting his position, as well as donations to his 'Save the Seals' fund.[20] He then trekked off to England where he set himself the goal of convincing London's *Daily Mirror*—Britain's largest circulation newspaper with a readership of over fifteen million—to publish a lurid exposé of the seal hunt. The *Mirror* duly sent a reporter and a photographer to accompany Davies onto the ice in 1968. Davies' reward came in the form of a front-page article accompanied by a picture of a bloodstained sealer, his club raised and poised to strike another doe-eyed pup. This, the *Mirror*'s headline blared, was 'The Price of a Sealskin Coat'. Davies continued his campaign in Europe and the United States for the next decade with similar success.[21] Canadian embassies were soon inundated with letters calling for an end to the hunt. The Brussels embassy, for example, received a petition signed by over four hundred thousand school children. In the United States, popular publications such as *Life* magazine also criticized the hunt, and protestors picketed the Canadian embassies in Washington and New York.[22] In fact, such protests, plus the evidence Davies presented at Congressional Hearings, were significant factors in helping to pass the US Marine Mammal Protection Act of 1972.[23]

In the early 1970s, the media interest in the hunt began to wane. Protestors such as Davies had little to offer other than more images of pups being slaughtered. Greenpeace, on the other hand, offered the prospect of direct confrontation with the swilers. Their initial plan was to arrive on the floes ahead of the swilers and spray the white-coated baby seals with a harmless permanent dye that would ruin the commercial value of their pelts. In addition, they stated in their press release, 'Greenpeace people will place themselves bodily between the sealer's club and its intended victim', as well as 'harassing the sealers constantly in an effort to slow the progress of the hunt'. Such actions, they hoped, would directly save the lives of many seals and 'focus world attention on the fact that harp seals are being slaughtered to the brink of commercial and biological extinction'.[24] From the beginning, the campaign was based on an uneasy blend of ecology and moral outrage. Bob Hunter, Greenpeace's president, was certainly aware of the pitfalls and contradictions inherent in such an approach: The hunt, he recognized,

> was an issue that brought out the worst forms of anthropomorphism and yet at the same time the highest forms of compassion. We knew we would have to walk a tightrope between a balanced 'scientific' analysis that the hunt itself was simply bad for the ecology of the ocean ... and the depths of emotion that the killing of 'babies' generated in the breasts of millions of urban people, who, otherwise, with their cars and swimming pools and electric gadgets, were the worst environmental destroyers of all.[25]

Drawing on the work of various university scientists, Greenpeace insisted that the hunt was not only 'demonstrably hideous and savage', but that there was incontrovertible scientific evidence that if it continued for much longer, 'the whole harp seal species [would] vanish forever, leaving nothing more than blood stains on the ice floes'. Like Brian Davies, Greenpeace saw the harp seals as a gateway species: 'Any heightened public sense of responsibility toward one species—such as the whale or the seal—inevitably has the same effect on people's thinking about lynx, beaver, polar bears or birds'. Greenpeace, therefore, was working 'toward an overall change in attitude toward all living creatures'. The alternative was 'the slow death of human moral consciousness, the ultimate and inevitable death of an ecological system which can in time reach out to damage mankind itself'.[26] This rhetorical blend of wildlife conservation and moral outrage, combined with photos of the whitecoats before, during and after their slaughter, had worked successfully in the past for groups such as Davies' International Fund for Animal Welfare (IFAW). When combined with the possibility of direct confrontation between swilers and protestors on the stark ice floes, it proved to be an irresistible formula for grabbing media attention. Within a day of announcing their plans, Newfoundland's newspapers printed headlines such as 'War with Greenpeace—we must win', while Newfoundland politicians were quoted as saying that the first Greenpeace protestors to step onto the ice would be 'mobbed' by irate locals.[27]

By 1976, the Canadian government had succeeded in convincing many of the more traditional conservation organizations that the harp seal was not an endangered species and that the swilers' hunting methods were humane. Measures such as start and stop dates, catch limits, strictly defined quotas for the various hunters, licensing procedures and the presence of government supervisors on the ice led organizations such as the World Wildlife Fund, Canada Audubon and the Ontario Humane Society to withdraw their opposition to the hunt.[28] In many ways, the environmental philosophy of such groups was closer to the scientific conservation of government wildlife biologists than to that of Greenpeace or the IFAW. By this time, Brian Davies was unashamedly running an animal rights campaign. Greenpeace, however, was hedging its bets. Most of its public rhetoric was grounded in the discourse of holistic ecology: seals were a vital part of the marine ecosystem and the hunters were killing them in unsustainable numbers, threatening them with extinction. But it soon became clear that many of the key activists—and many of Greenpeace's supporters—had come to take an abolitionist stance against sealing. While this was consistent with their attitude towards whales, the rationale for taking such a position on seals was neither as clear nor as compelling.

On 2 March 1976, the majority of the Greenpeace anti-sealing crew left Vancouver for the long train, ferry and car ride to the remote fishing village of St. Anthony on the north-western coast of Newfoundland. Awaiting them were two chartered Bell Jet Ranger II helicopters that would fly them out to the pack ice. Watson, according to Hunter, had a 'militaristic streak' and delighted in giving crew members specific titles, such as 'squad leader', 'flight assistant' and 'squad quartermaster'. For himself, he reserved the title 'expedition leader'. During the whale campaign the previous summer, Greenpeace's arrival at various ports on the west coast had been greeted with great cheer and goodwill. None, of course, were expecting similar scenes in Newfoundland, but few were prepared for the genuine anger and sheer hatred that the locals directed towards the meddlesome mainlanders.

As Greenpeace's vans pulled into St. Anthony, the small squadron of Greenpeace activists was greeted by a mob of enraged placard-waving, fist-shaking locals. Hunter saw about a dozen menacing young toughs in the front who were swinging ropes with nooses. The mob quickly surrounded the vans and began to rock them as though intent on pushing them over. Hunter tried to remember 'the best method of protecting my head while being stomped'. Watson and some of the other Greenpeacers were wearing orange-coloured arctic survival suits, apparel that further distinguished them from the locals, whose attire was considerably more modest. Furious locals continued to scream obscenities at Watson, threatening him with the blunt end of their pickets.[29] At this point, Walrus Oakenbough, a long-haired hippie with a large drooping moustache who was one of the more deeply countercultural members of Greenpeace, strode up to a belligerent swiler, jabbed his finger in the man's chest and screamed:

> *Listen, I haven't heard one of you guys say one word about Mother Earth! And that's what this is all about! We're here to protect the seals, the whales, the birds, everything! It's all part of Mother Earth! And you're*

not gonna stop us, because it's Mother Earth's will. Those seals are my seals too! So just get out of our way, get out of our way, that's all![30]

Such language further emphasized the cultural gulf between the Vancouver eco-hippies and the swilers. To locals such as Calvin Coish, 'Greenpeace came through as a bunch of freaky know-it-alls from way over on the west coast'. Many of the swilers vowed that they 'wouldn't think twice about giving [Greenpeacers] a bash on the side of the head'. To the swilers, the idea of 'saving' a seal pup made no more sense than 'saving' a fish. Certainly, it was appropriate to try to prevent a species that they viewed as a resource from being unduly depleted. But the idea that an entity called Mother Earth believed that it was wrong to kill seals seemed patently absurd. In their minds, God had placed the seals there for their use.[31] Those who justified the hunt frequently referred to Genesis, Chapter one, Verse 26, with its famous declaration that man should 'have dominion over the fish of the sea, and over the birds of the air, and over the cattle, and over all the earth, and every creeping thing that creeps upon this earth'. It was a theme that was also stressed by the priests who frequently blessed the sealing ships before their departure for the ice floes.[32]

Both the provincial government in Newfoundland and the federal government in Ottawa strongly supported the sealing industry and the swilers, a situation that long predated the 1970s protests and continues to this day. In response to Greenpeace's appearance on the scene, the Canadian government had just passed an order-in-council making it illegal to spray seals. An order-in-council is a statute or law that is passed by the federal cabinet and does not need to be approved by the parliament. Somewhat melodramatically, Hunter despaired that Greenpeace had 'underestimated the totalitarian streak that existed in Ottawa'.[33] This development compounded the problems that Greenpeace faced as a result of amendments to the Seal Protection Act. These included banning everyone, apart from those associated with the seal hunt, from flying lower than two thousand feet over a seal herd or landing a helicopter within half a mile of a seal. These regulations were transparently designed to prevent groups such as IFAW and Greenpeace from protesting. The government argued that the amendments were necessary to prevent people from 'disturbing' the seals during their breeding and nursing phase. However, as Hunter caustically observed, the law effectively stated, 'you may not disturb a seal unless you are definitely going to kill it'. George Orwell himself, he continued, 'could not have invented a nicer title for a piece of legislation aimed at the destruction of an animal'.[34]

With the odds stacked firmly against Greenpeace, Hunter felt it was time for a quick change of tactics. Clearly, the federal government was not going to alter its position any time soon, but the local landsmen might be persuaded to drop their opposition to Greenpeace, and, if Hunter played his cards right, to support them on some issues. While the others were settling into their boardinghouse, Hunter arranged a quick private meeting with Roy Pilgrim, the leader of the anti-Greenpeace protesters. During his time among the crowd of angry locals, Hunter had surmised that the landsmen—the small-time swilers who were not crewmembers on the large sealing ships—were particularly incensed by Greenpeace's plan to spray the seals with dye. Furthermore, it quickly became evident that they did not think particularly well of the Norwegian companies that dominated much of the sealing industry. Hunter was well aware that the landsmen took a relatively small number of seals compared to the predominantly Norwegian-owned ships. Here was an opportunity, he felt, to build a coalition with the landsmen against the wealthy and mostly foreign-owned sealing corporations.

With this in mind, he proposed the following deal to Pilgrim: Greenpeace would give up the spraying plan in exchange for a promise by Pilgrim that nobody would interfere with their helicopters. In addition, if Pilgrim would allow Hunter to try to recruit landsmen to Greenpeace's cause, he would leave the local swilers in peace and restrict the protest to the factory ships. From Hunter's perspective, this was a very favourable compromise. After all, spraying the seals with dye was now illegal and would only result in the protestors being arrested on the first day of the hunt. Furthermore, Greenpeace's intention had always been to focus their activities on the factory ships rather than the landsmen. Such a deal, Hunter hoped, would enable Greenpeace 'to outflank Ottawa and pull off a worker-conservationist alliance that would dumbfound everybody'. By this time, the little fishing village was swarming with reporters from influential media outlets such as America's NBC and the *Washington Post*, Germany's *Stern* and France's *Gamma News Agency*, as well as all the major Canadian newspapers and TV stations. Pilgrim, for his part, did not want to see his people once again depicted as angry Arctic rednecks intent upon beating up the noble seal savers. He and Hunter shook hands and agreed to abide by the terms Hunter had laid out.[35]

The local media was not impressed with Hunter's apparent compromise. Wick Collins, a columnist for the St. John's *Evening Telegram* argued that it was 'no more than a tactical withdrawal in the face of determined opposition from the strong minded people of St. Anthony'. As soon as these 'publicity hounds' were 'back on safe ground in mainland Canada, they will resume their verbal assault on the Newfoundland sealers'.[36] Paul Watson and his supporters within Greenpeace were also less-than-happy. Watson strongly objected to the idea of giving up the dye, but Hunter insisted that it was the only way they could mount a successful campaign. At the meeting that evening, Watson attempted to explain, in ecological and economic terms, why Greenpeace was against the hunt, eliciting heckles and boos from the rowdy audience. Hunter then strode to the microphone and played his ace:

> Out of respect for the serious economic hardships experienced by the people of Newfoundland, the Greenpeace Foundation will drop its plans

> to spray the seal pups with green dye … instead, Greenpeacers will go out to the Front, to the icebreakers operating in international waters, focusing primarily on the Norwegians, and we will throw our bodies between those seal hunters and the seals.

Hunter's speech was greeted with wild cheers and jubilation, with most of the locals interpreting it as a capitulation.[37]

As a result of Hunter's compromise, Greenpeace would no longer have to worry about local swilers preventing their helicopters from taking off for the distant ice floes. But they would have to pay a price for it. The next day, newspapers across Canada were reporting Greenpeace's plan to abandon their spraying tactic and to form an alliance with local swilers.[38] The Vancouver Greenpeace office was bombarded with angry phone calls from people demanding their money back and accusing Greenpeace of selling out. The newly formed Toronto Greenpeace crushed all their Greenpeace buttons under their heels and mailed them personally to Hunter in St. Anthony. Nevertheless, Hunter remained optimistic:

> with a little 'luck', so long as we could get the choppers out to the ice, we would recover, and, if everything went perfectly, we might yet emerge with a formula for bringing the environmentalists together with the grass-roots people in Newfoundland against the government and the handful of fur barons who had so successfully exploited both seals and the sealers for centuries.[39]

Greenpeace's strategy, never too clear to begin with, was shifting constantly as the campaign progressed. From the start, Watson, Walrus and similarly minded Greenpeacers wanted to pursue an animal rights-based agenda of saving as many individual seals as possible and advocating the abolition of the hunt. Hunter, while sympathetic to this view, was pragmatic enough to realize that such an approach would create too many enemies. It was difficult enough to cope with the restrictions of the Seal Protection Act: if angry landsmen had tried to prevent Greenpeace's helicopters from taking off, then the campaign would be almost entirely ineffective. Although nobody within Greenpeace wanted to admit it, the landsmen of St. Anthony had forced the organization to make a significant compromise. Instead of crying for the hunt's abolition, Greenpeace was now officially endorsing the landsmen's right to hunt while condemning the mostly Norwegian factory ships operating on the front. Animal rights and deep ecology had, temporarily at least, taken a back seat to a more pragmatic and traditional form of wildlife conservation.[40]

On March 12, the first contingent of protestors flew to Belle Island off the north-east coast of Newfoundland, where they spent two miserably cold days setting up their camp. The temperature fell to minus thirty-five degrees Celsius and a howling gale blew across the island. With only their tissue-thin tents for protection, the crew spent much of the time cocooned in their sleeping bags. Moustaches froze and any exposed skin was soon burned by the freezing wind. On the morning of March 15, Watson, Walrus and several others climbed into a helicopter and headed for the ice floes. Within twenty minutes, they spotted two Norwegian ships breaking their way through the ice. From twenty-five hundred feet, the Greenpeace 'action squad' could see streaks of seal blood painted across the blindingly white surface. As they descended, they could see the swilers dragging bundles of pelts towards the ships, where cranes hauled them aboard. Jumping out of the helicopter, the Greenpeacers had their first sight of the baby harp seals. To Watson, they were 'beautiful beyond expectation. Chubby little bundles of soft white fur, their round, jet-black eyes glistening with tears, they cried, sounding exactly like human infants in distress'.[41] The Greenpeacers immediately began to charge across the ice, heading for the nearest sealers. Jet Johnson, a commercial airline pilot from Vancouver, was the first to put Greenpeace's nonviolent, direct-action strategy into action on the ice. As a swiler was readying to club another whitecoat, Johnson bumped him aside and threw himself on top of the seal pup, pinning it to the ice by its flippers and shielding it from the sealer's raised hakapik. It was, according to Hunter, 'the first seal in history to be so protected by the loving flesh of a human being'. Walrus attached himself to a swiler, following him around the ice and blocking him every time he came across a pup. The furious and clearly confused swiler soon retreated to the ship.[42]

Watson, too, was throwing himself on top of seals. He soon found himself being chased by two inspectors from the Fisheries Ministry, who demanded that he stop interfering with the hunt. The swiler, Watson and the officials formed a bizarre conga line as they shuffled across the ice from seal to seal. As Watson came closer to one of the ships, he noticed that the blocks of ice churned up by the icebreaker's steel-reinforced bow were crushing many whitecoats. Spotting a pup that was in the path of the ship, Watson raced across the ice, bent down and, with some difficulty, picked up the surprisingly heavy animal. The ungrateful seal bit Watson on the cheek, before resigning itself to its fate and allowing him to carry it away from immediate danger. For Watson, this was a critical moment:

> I looked down into its ebony eyes which looked back quizzically with such innocence that I burst into tears.... Now I was personally involved, not simply making a protest of principle. I had saved that particular pup's life, held it in my arms, felt its warm body against mine.[43]

It was at such moments in the life of a Greenpeacer that any abstract thoughts of animal rights, ecology and conservation were expunged and completely overwhelmed by a wave of pure emotion and instinct. Such a visceral experience, and the passion it summoned forth, was something new to the environmental movement. It certainly was not one that the average Sierra Club member or Friends of the Earth activist was ever likely to experience.

The apogee of the protest, and one of its most enduring images, occurred later that day when Hunter and Watson decided to blockade a sealing ship. While Greenpeace cameramen gathered around them to film and photograph the action, Hunter and Watson stood in the path of the icebreaker, their backs to its bow, forcing it to either halt its progress or run them down. It was an event marked by an odd verisimilitude: on the one hand, the danger was very real; much like driving a Zodiac in front of a whaler, it was a game of chicken in which a slight miscalculation could be fatal. On the other hand, the presence of the three cameramen shouting out questions and directions gave it the air of a film set. In a sense, it was the perfect metaphor for Greenpeace's style of protest: it was simultaneously artificial and real, spontaneous, yet scripted. The photographs show Hunter standing, legs apart, staring determinedly ahead, his right arm extended to a slightly more nervous-looking Watson, who clasps it in a revolutionary handshake. Hunter admitted that he was trembling vigorously, but was able to allay his fear by keeping his mind 'centered as much as possible on the Clear Light, a Tibetan Buddhist meditation technique'. As the ship, called the *Arctic Endeavour*, made its initial run towards Hunter and Watson, a crewman warned them: 'Ya better move, b'yes, the ole man ain't one ta tink twice about runnin' ya into the ice'. Hunter yelled back: 'Tell the old bastard to do what he wants, we're not moving'. The captain took up Hunter's challenge and began to thrust the giant icebreaker forward. However, Hunter and Watson refused to move, thus forcing the ship to come to a halt.[44]

It was a classic media moment, one that was seen on televisions and in the print media throughout much of the world. It was also, as Hunter recounts, an episode that reinforced his belief that Greenpeace were involved in what he liked to refer to, in an era of pre-9/11 innocence, as a jihad:

> In the final few seconds before the ship had stopped, and the sound of the ice had been like a mountain-sized molar breaking apart in the middle of my head, I had felt a blaze of anger like a blowtorch. It was righteous wrath. It brought with it absolute conviction and an ecstatic, exultant feeling of strength.[45]

As the protest continued, the CBC aired a television documentary on its popular *Fifth Estate* programme detailing Greenpeace's anti-nuclear and anti-whaling campaigns and generally lionizing Hunter and his crew. The film elicited a grudging respect for Greenpeace from a small number of locals. In the village of Raleigh, for example, Hunter claimed that seventy people signed a petition saying they were willing to accompany Greenpeace to the front to oppose the factory ships. Roy Pilgrim's younger brother, Doug, perhaps as part of some long simmering sibling rivalry, went so far as to start the local St. Anthony branch of Greenpeace, although it was not fated to last long. Once Greenpeace and the media departed, according to Hunter, the younger Pilgrim was disowned by his brother, left by his wife and beaten up by some of the local men. Doug Pilgrim and the sympathetic villagers were clearly in the minority, and a miniscule one at that, as anyone scanning the Newfoundland newspapers in March 1976 would have quickly realized. The St. John's *Evening Telegram*, for example, called the CBC documentary 'as neat a bit of propaganda as we have ever seen'. The host of the programme, the well-known television personality and future Governor General of Canada, Adrienne Clarkson, deserved 'a medal of honor for doing such a neat job of corrupting the truth'. Greenpeace and Davies, the *Telegram* thundered, were engaged in a 'propaganda war over the seal hunt', one that involved 'lies, deceit, misrepresentation, suppression of the truth and skillful use of the half-truth'.[46] This kind of invective was pervasive in the editorial and letters pages of the major Newfoundland newspapers; even the reportage was larded with sarcasm towards the protestors.[47]

Despite his efforts, Hunter's vision of a worker-conservationist coalition was not to be realized. The international media had come to see a confrontation on the ice: they were not particularly interested in a story about a grassroots campaign to form an alliance between Greenpeace and the landsmen. The successful formation of such an alliance would have required Hunter, or somebody with similar negotiating skills, to remain in the region for much longer than a few weeks. The opposition of key figures such as Watson, who continued to insist that all sealers were Greenpeace's enemies, also doomed the alliance. Furthermore, Hunter had not fully realized just how deep the cultural roots of sealing ran.[48] However distasteful the practice might appear to the outside world, for most Newfoundlanders, swiling was a way of life—a valued part of their culture that they were not prepared to give up without a fierce struggle. To the outside observer, it appeared that the swilers were naively engaged in maintaining their status as an exploited underclass—a cheap, brutalized labour force that could be easily manipulated by European fur barons. In academic jargon, they were victims of 'false consciousness' or a 'culture of poverty'. Such explanations, however, are themselves predicated on certain cultural assumptions about people's motivations. They provide little genuine insight into why Newfoundlanders tenaciously defended a brutal, bloody and heavily subsidized industry that only provided them with a moderate, short-term income—one that could easily be replaced by other forms of employment.[49] The swilers still await their Clifford Geertz—an anthropologist who can offer a 'thick description' of their culture to the outside world. Whatever the deeper reasons for their attachment to seal hunting, however, it was not a trait that was going to be overturned by a mere fortnight of protest.[50]

From the perspective of most Newfoundlanders, the anti-sealing movement appeared to be nothing more than a 'protest business', one that was too lucrative to abandon despite the obvious absurdity and hypocrisy of IFAW and Greenpeace. Newspaper reports frequently portrayed Brian Davies as a jetsetter who had deviously converted public ignorance and sympathy into a steady stream of cash for his own self-enrichment. According to Jeremiah Allen, a political scientist at the University of Lethbridge in Alberta, groups such as Greenpeace were more like traditional businesses or bureaucracies whose primary motive was 'the perpetuation of the firm, rather than ending the Atlantic seal hunt'. In such a scenario, the 'firm' is best served, not by the elimination of the hunt, which would remove the group's *raison d'être*, but by its continuation.[51] While organizational health was certainly a factor in Greenpeace's decision-making calculus, Allen was guilty of considerable exaggeration. By extension, one could argue that nineteenth-century abolitionists would have been best served by the perpetuation of slavery and that their actions were carried out with this in mind. Such an analysis completely discounts the evangelical fervour that marks many radical protest groups, as well as reducing human passion and commitment—with all their flaws and inconsistencies—to mere variables in economic equations. It also ignores the myriad cultural and ideological influences—from holistic thought to Quakerism, to animal rights—that shaped Greenpeace's actions.

Despite Hunter's efforts, Greenpeace was not able to defuse Newfoundlanders' enmity. The influence of Greenpeace's animal rights contingent, with its insistence that sealing be abolished, combined with the intransigence of the sealers and the Canadian government, meant that there was little common ground between the two sides. The animal rights advocates within Greenpeace and elsewhere would not be content until the hunt was eliminated, while the swilers and their supporters were simply not prepared to consider such a drastic step. The lack of space for a compromise meant that victory for one side could only be achieved at the expense of utter defeat for the other.

Greenpeace continued its anti-sealing protests for several more years. By the early 1980s, however, the direct-action approach to the seal slaughter began to lose impact. Thus anti-sealing advocates began to concentrate instead on closing the European market that largely sustained the industry, a campaign that had considerable success. The 1983 European Community ban on the importation of harp seal products seemed like a great victory for animal rights activists and for the seals themselves, but it proved to be a Pyrrhic one. While the major market for seal products may have been suddenly eliminated, the slaughtering of seals was never outlawed. Therefore, the sealing industry, with the help of substantial government subsidies and the strong support of the swilers, was able to gradually establish new markets for its products. It has been successful to the point where the slaughter has reached an even higher level than when Greenpeace first entered the fray. Perhaps a campaign that had focused more on ecology and less on the rights of individual animals may have yielded a better long-term outcome. Through international and domestic pressure, anti-sealing groups may have forced sealers and the Canadian government to establish stricter and sharply reduced quotas, while enabling the industry to continue to operate at a reduced, though still viable, level. While the industry would doubtless have been angered by efforts to reduce their kill, such a strategy may have minimized the outrage among many Newfoundlanders and their representatives in Ottawa, making it easier to set up supplementary employment schemes that would gradually have reduced the swilers' dependence on sealing as an important source of winter income.

Somewhat ironically, Greenpeace can legitimately claim that by keeping the issue in the media spotlight, they contributed to the creation of one of the world's more sustainable wildlife harvests.[52] While this is scant consolation for animal rights activists, for those who take a more pragmatic and ecological approach to environmental issues, it can be seen as at least a partial victory. Certainly, hundreds of thousands of newborn harp seals are still hakapiked to death every year. The species as a whole, however, does not appear to be in any imminent danger, and earlier claims that harp seals were on the road to extinction appear, in hindsight, to have been somewhat exaggerated. Nonetheless, for activists such as Bob Hunter and Paul Watson, who devoted (and in Watson's case, continue to devote) a good deal of their lives to protecting a charismatic and beautiful creature, this was hardly a cause for celebration. For them, the depressing reality was that after more than three decades of campaigning by IFAW, Greenpeace and others, there was still a substantial portion of the population for whom a harp seal remained a mere 'natural resource'.

Notes

1 For an intelligent and sensitive discussion of this subject, see Richard White, ' "Are you an environmentalist or do you work for a living?": Work and nature', in William Cronon (ed.), *Uncommon Ground: Rethinking the Human Place in Nature* (New York: W. W. Norton, 1996).

2 Briton Cooper Busch, *The War Against the Seals: A History of the North American Seal Fishery* (Kingston & Montreal: McGill-Queen's University Press, 1985), 248–252; Janice Scott Henke, *Seal Wars!: An American Viewpoint* (St. John's, Newfoundland: Breakwater Books, 1985), chapter 3.

3 N.B.: 'Swiling' rhymes with 'smiling'.

4 *Greenpeace Chronicles*, Fall (1975), 3.

5 Author's interview with Chesley Sanger, St. John's, June 2007. Sanger, a native Newfoundlander, is an emeritus professor of geography at Memorial University and has a deep knowledge of the history of sealing and whaling in the region.

6 In 1913, the Newfoundland House of Assembly reported: 'There are few young men in the colony who have not been on the "ice" and an expedition is looked on as a test of manhood.' Quoted in Busch, *War Against the Seals*, 57.

7 Cassie Brown, *Death on the Ice: The Great Newfoundland Sealing Disaster of 1914* (Toronto, ON: Doubleday Canada, 1972).

8 Quoted in Farley Mowat and David Blackwood, *Wake of the Great Sealers* (Toronto, ON: McClelland & Stewart, 1973), 91.

9 For more on the class dimensions of the seal hunt, see John-Henry Harter, 'Environmental justice for whom? Class, new social movements and the environment: A case study of Greenpeace Canada, 1971–2000', *Labour/Le Travail* 54:Fall (2004), 83–119. For a good general discussion of work and environment, see Chad Montrie, *Making a Living: Work and Environment in the United States* (Chapel Hill: University of North Carolina Press, 2008).

10 Busch, *War Against the Seals*, 246–247. For some fascinating historical photographs of Newfoundland sealers, see Shannon Ryan, *Seals and Sealers: A Pictorial History of the Newfoundland Seal Fishery* (St. John's, Newfoundland: Breakwater Books, 1987).

11 D. E. Sergeant, 'Harp seals and the sealing industry', *Canadian Audubon* 25:2 (1963), 34; Calvin E. Coish, *Season of the Seal: The International Storm over Canada's Seal Hunt* (St. John's, Newfoundland: Breakwater Books, 1979), 72.

12 At this time, Canadian control was restricted to a distance of twelve miles from the Canadian shore. The 200-mile limit that applies today was established in 1977. See Busch, *War Against the Seals*, 248.

13 Tina Loo, *States of Nature: Conserving Canada's Wildlife in the Twentieth Century* (Vancouver: University of British Columbia Press, 2006), 6. Loo's study is the best critical scholarly history on the subject. Studies that celebrate Canadian wildlife management include: J. Alexander Burnett, *A Passion for Wildlife: The History of the Canadian Wildlife Service* (Vancouver: University of British Columbia Press, 2003) and Janet Foster, *Working for Wildlife: The Beginning of Preservation in Canada* (Toronto, ON: University of Toronto Press, 1978).

14 Despite appearing brutal and bloody, most biologists seem to agree that the clubbing and bleeding method is the most humane, as well as the most efficient method of dispatching the pups. The first blow usually renders the seal unconscious, the second kills it. Its movement thereafter is simply the result of reflexive twitches that occur once it is unconscious or brain dead. For a useful overview (albeit from a pro-sealing perspective), see Henke, *Seal Wars*, chapter 4.

15 Coish, *Season of the Seal*, 74; Henke, *Seal Wars*, 68–72.

16 Coish, *Season of the Seal*, 74. Two years later, a sealer from the Magdalen Islands signed an affidavit declaring that the film crew had paid him to 'torment the said seal and not to use a stick, but just to use a knife to carry out this operation where in normal practice a stick is used to first kill the seals before skinning them'. Quoted in Coish, *Season of the Seal*, 95. Despite such apparent evidence, one is left wondering why Artek, which appeared to have no intention of making a propaganda film, would need to embellish a documentary that was already studded with images of cruelty and gore.

17 *Canadian Audubon*, November–December, 1964, 75.

18 Brian Davies, *Savage Luxury: The Slaughter of Baby Seals* (New York: Taplinger, 1971), 17–21.

19 Davies, *Savage Luxury*, 207–208. Italics in original.

20 Davies, *Savage Luxury*, 68–69.

21 Davies, *Savage Luxury*, 150; The 1968 hunt was marked by the appearance of several veterinarians on the ice who were burdened with the gruesome task of examining the smashed skulls of the harp seal carcasses in order to determine if they had been killed 'humanely'. In a twelve-hour period, they examined 361 carcasses for fractures, heamorrhages and lesions. They concluded that 97 per cent of the pups had in all likelihood been rendered unconscious by the blows from the club before they were skinned. Coish, *Season of the Seal*, 106–107.

22 Davies, *Savage Luxury*, 111–112.

23 Janice Henke, 'Canada and the WTO in the 21st Century', *Sustainable eNews*, January 2008. Available at: http://www.maninnature.com/MMammals/Seals/Seals1o.html [accessed 10 March 2011]; Richard Ellis, *The Empty Ocean: Plundering the World's Marine Life* (Washington, DC: Shearwater Books, 2003), 203.

24 Greenpeace press release, 1976 (no exact date). Rex Weyler's personal papers.

25 Robert Hunter, *Warriors of the Rainbow: A Chronicle of the Greenpeace Movement* (New York: Holt, Rinehart and Winston, 1979), 250.

26 Greenpeace, 'Save the Seals Expedition'. Direct mail fund-raising letter from early 1976. From Patrick Moore's personal papers.

27 St. John's *Evening Telegram*, 12 March 1976; Hunter, *Warriors*, 251.

28 George Wenzel, *Animal Rights, Human Rights: Ecology, Economy and Ideology in the Canadian Arctic* (Toronto, ON: University of Toronto Press, 1991), 47.

29 Hunter, *Warriors*, 257–259; Paul Watson and Bob Hunter interviews. Had Greenpeace had access to the Newfoundland newspapers, they might not have been as surprised by the locals' viciousness. The editorial and letters pages of the St. John's *Evening Telegram* and the Corner Brook *Western Star* were filled with furious denunciations well before their arrival.

30 Quoted in Hunter, *Warriors*, 260. Italics in original.

31 Interestingly, though perhaps not surprisingly, local religious leaders were strong backers of the hunt. The Roman Catholic archdiocese of St. John's, for example, circulated a letter of support, suggesting 'it would be far more appropriate if the emotional rhetoric given to the humane harvesting of the seals were applied to the plight of the unborn and suffering children of the world'. Quoted in the St. John's *Daily Mail*, 15 March 1977. Many letters in the Newfoundland newspapers voiced similar sentiments, bemoaning a society that seemed to care more for seals than human foetuses.

32 Coish, *Season of the Seal*, 179–180. In the 1981 film *Bitter Harvest* (Northern Lights Films), a priest is shown speaking exactly these words as a sealing ship departs for the floes. Busch also makes the telling point that it is *sealing*, rather than the seals, that occupies the most important role in Newfoundland's folklore. Newfoundlanders have none of the traditions respecting the spirit and power of the seals that are common in old northern European or Native American folk traditions. Perhaps because the Newfoundland seal hunt was, almost from its inception, a commercial venture, seals have always been seen as a mere resource. See *War Against the Seals*, 41–42.

33 Hunter, *Warriors*, 260–261. The following year, all the parties in the Canadian House of Commons passed a unanimous resolution supporting

the continuation of the seal hunt. It is unlikely, therefore, that the Trudeau government's actions represented a 'totalitarian streak'. See *International Herald Tribune*, 26 March 1977.

34 Hunter, *Warriors*, 286–287.
35 Hunter, *Warriors*, 261–263.
36 *Evening Telegram*, 13 March 1976, 13.
37 Watson interview; Hunter, *Warriors*, 264.
38 For example, see the *Montreal Star*, 10 March 1976. To Newfoundlanders such as the schoolteacher and writer Calvin Coish, 'The sudden swing to the side of the landsmen seemed like a desperate attempt by Greenpeace to counter the unexpected hostility of the Newfoundland sealers'. See *Season of the Seal*, 126.
39 Hunter, *Warriors*, 263.
40 Watson and Hunter interviews.
41 Paul Watson, *Sea Shepherd: My Fight for Whales and Seals* (New York: W. W. Norton, 1982), 92. Harp seals' eyes are constantly lubricated by tears to protect them from salt water. Unlike terrestrial mammals, they lack ducts to drain away the tears. Thus, they look like they are constantly crying. See David M. Lavigne, 'Harp Seal: *Pagophilus groenlandicus*', in William F. Perrin, Bernd G. Würsig, and J. G. M. Thewissen (eds), *Encyclopedia of Marine Mammals* (New York: Academic Press, 2008), 543–544.
42 Hunter, *Warriors*, 279–280; Interviews with Jet Johnson and Paul Watson.
43 Watson, *Sea Shepherd*, 93–94.
44 Hunter, *Warriors*, 290–291.
45 Hunter, *Warriors*, 291–293. Italics in original.
46 Hunter interview. 'Cruel Propaganda', *Evening Standard*, 19 March 1976.
47 This was my unmistakable impression after reading through all of the March 1976 issues of the St. John's *Evening Telegram* and the *Western Star*, which is based in the west Newfoundland town of Corner Brook.
48 Hunter and Watson interviews. Fred Bruemmer, a Canadian nature photographer who wrote widely on the hunt, described it as an exhilarating release from the boredom and grinding poverty of winter, as well as representing a traditional rite of the early spring. See Fred Bruemmer, *Life of the Harp Seal* (Montreal: Optimum, 1977).
49 On subsidies, see the report written by the Canadian Institute for Business and the Environment, 'The Economics of the Canadian Sealing Industry', 11 June 2001. Available at: http://www.ifaw.org/sites/default/files/2001_The%20economics%20of%20the%20Canadian%20sealing%20industry.pdf.
50 George Wenzel has done this for indigenous sealers in the Canadian Arctic. See *Animal Rights, Human Rights*.
51 Jeremiah Allen, 'Anti sealing as an industry', *Journal of Political Economy* 87:2 (1979), 427. From another angle, John-Henry Harter argues that Greenpeace has always had an inherently anti-working class bias. In fact, he goes so far as accusing them of 'devastat[ing] two entire economies and communities: those of the Inuit and the Newfoundland sealers'. Clearly, the story is far more complex. For one thing, Newfoundland provincial politics have been dominated by the Conservative, and to a lesser extent, the Liberal Party. The socialist NDP has barely gained a toehold. Harter appears reluctant to acknowledge that sometimes the interests of the working class are best served

by allying themselves with capitalists in order to defeat environmentalists. See Harter, 'Environmental justice for whom?'

52 Sanger interview. For an analysis of the effectiveness of both the anti-whaling and anti-sealing campaigns, particularly since the 1980s, see Gloria Yolanda Guevara, 'Assessing the effectiveness of transnational activism: an analysis of the anti-whaling and anti-sealing campaigns', Doctoral diss., University of Southern California, 2008.

Further reading

Busch, Briton Cooper. 1985. *The War Against the Seals: A History of the North American Seal Fishery*. Kingston & Montreal: McGill-Queen's University Press.

Dale, Stephen. 1996. *McLuhan's Children: The Greenpeace Message and the Media*. Toronto: Between the Lines.

Daston, Lorraine and Mitman, Gregg. (eds). 2006. *Thinking with Animals: New Perspectives on Anthropomorphism*. New York: Columbia University Press.

DeLuca, Kevin Michael. 2005. *Image Politics: The New Rhetoric of Environmental Activism*. New York: Routledge.

Hunter, Robert. 1979. *Warriors of the Rainbow: A Chronicle of the Greenpeace Movement*. New York: Holt, Rinehart and Winston.

Jordan, Grant and Maloney, William. 1997. *The Protest Business? Mobilizing Campaign Groups*. Manchester: Manchester University Press.

Loo, Tina. 2006. *States of Nature: Conserving Canada's Wildlife in the Twentieth Century*. Vancouver: University of British Columbia Press.

Ryan, Shannon. 1994. *The Ice Hunters: A History of Newfoundland Sealing to 1914*. St. John's, Newfoundland: Breakwater Books.

Wapner, Paul. 1996. *Environmental Activism and World Civic Politics*. Albany: State University of New York Press.

Watson, Paul. 1982. *Sea Shepherd: My Fight for Whales and Seals*. New York: W. W. Norton.

Wenzel, George. 1991. *Animal Rights, Human Rights: Ecology, Economy and Ideology in the Canadian Arctic*. Toronto: University of Toronto Press.

Weyler, Rex. 2004. *Greenpeace: How a Group of Ecologists, Journalists and Visionaries Changed the World*. Vancouver: Raincoast Books.

Zelko, Frank. 2013. *Make It a Green Peace! The Rise of Countercultural Environmentalism*. New York: Oxford University Press.

6

The Struggle for Justice in Bhopal: A New/Old Breed of Transnational Social Movement

Stephen Zavestoski

Introduction

In the early morning of 3 December 1984, a toxic cloud rose over the city of Bhopal, India. The gas escaped from a runaway chemical reaction in a pesticide manufacturing plant operated by the subsidiary of an American multinational corporation named Union Carbide. Conservative government estimates put the number of immediate deaths at 3,800 while other estimates range as high as 15,000. Thousands more have died since the disaster, not to mention chronic illness among survivors and contamination-related disease within the generation born after the disaster. Mobilization of disaffected survivors of the disaster occurred overnight and soon became a social movement that over the next three decades would evolve new modes of challenging the injustices triggered by the disaster. The movement is old, but an examination of its history can reveal what is new about transnational social movement organizing in the context of a globalizing world.

This chapter's main intent is to examine the history of the Bhopal struggle to illustrate that when the forces of globalization introduce new and complex forms of risk and hazard, mobilization against these threats and harms faces its own set of unique challenges. A slogan painted on the wall outside the former Union Carbide factory hints at the nature of these challenges—'Bhopal: The Real Face of Globalization'. On one hand, the slogan refers to 'Bhopal the historical site of the world's worst industrial disaster' and warns that disasters will happen when transnational corporations seek to benefit from the processes of globalization that make it easier to move their operations to different parts of the world where there may be cheaper labour or new markets to tap. On the other hand, the slogan can refer to 'Bhopal the global social movement' which is the civil society response necessitated by globalization's tendency to expose vulnerable populations to environmental hazards.

The Bhopal disaster illustrates that when absentee multinational corporations contaminate communities, and support of state political or judicial elites is not forthcoming, social movements are compelled to work transnationally to find ways to have their grievances addressed. This explanation of global social movement emergence differs somewhat from those put forward in the increasingly broad and deep body of research that focuses on the history, evolution, prevalence, processes and impacts of transnational social movement organizations.[1] An analysis of the Bhopal movement, especially its transnational manifestations that are the focus of this chapter, reveals how a movement arising to counter globalization's tendency to expose the powerless to environmental hazards builds bridges and balances local–global relationships.

A new/old breed of transnational social movement

The scale of the Bhopal disaster—from the deaths due to chemical exposure to the fundamental transformation of the material conditions of people's existence—was unprecedented. Additionally, the disaster occurred at a time when virtually no international agreements regulating industrial hazards existed and when the global anti-toxics movement was in its infancy. These factors—the scale of the disaster and the political and institutional context in which it occurred—forced the emergence of a new breed of transnational social movement that was ahead of its time. Working on an unregulated frontier with no precedent for how to respond to a corporate-caused disaster at the scale of Bhopal created a number of challenges specific to the movement in Bhopal. As a result, the strength of the movement's international ties and its effectiveness at using its global network have waxed and waned over the course of its history. The remainder of the chapter examines the types of relationships the Bhopal movement has developed and utilized throughout its history.

The Bhopal movement and the global anti-toxics movement

While the movement has always had as its primary goals the provision of health care and the securing of fair compensation for survivors and their descendants, it has also tried to garner international support by experimenting with framing its struggle in a variety of ways that might resonate with audiences outside of Bhopal. The movement's slogan 'No More Bhopals' has been employed to call for corporate accountability and human rights and to make sweeping criticisms of globalization. But as a slogan, 'No More Bhopals' appeals primarily to people for whom 'Bhopal' represents the potential for future disasters. The slogan was used to great effect by those advocating for new post-Bhopal policies and regulations that would prevent future Bhopals, or at least guarantee certain rights for those living in potential disaster zones. But policy responses triggered by the 'No More Bhopals' framing—such as community right-to-know legislation in the United States—were largely meaningless to survivors dealing with chronic health problems and a government that constantly put up obstacles to the collection of what little compensation survivors had been promised. Just as some of the research discussed earlier would predict, focusing on the Bhopal disaster as a tool to leverage new international regulations on the chemical industry—a strategy the movement could have pursued—would have detracted from the movement's ability to meet the immediate needs of Bhopal survivors. The development of a symbiotic relationship with the global anti-toxics movement became a key tactic for managing this dilemma.

On one hand, the global anti-toxics movement was able to use the *idea* of Bhopal to push for regulation of industrial hazards and the rights of the victims of industrial disasters. Bhopal became the de facto cause for the global anti-toxics movement, a movement itself rooted in lessons learned by the consumers movement of the mid-twentieth century and labour movements dating even earlier. Based on this lineage, the global anti-toxics movement developed tactics for pressuring otherwise unaccountable transnational corporations to clean up their acts. In some cases, even the fear of such pressure prompted corporations, for better or worse, to act voluntarily to establish codes of conduct.[2] While the global anti-toxics movement was using the Bhopal disaster to lobby for international standards, the Bhopal movement used the network of the global anti-toxics movement to ensure that the rest of the world would not forget the Bhopal disaster, as well as to organize some of its legal and corporate campaigns against Union Carbide and later Dow Chemical. But this relationship developed unevenly, only really benefitting the Bhopal struggle in the last 15 years. To understand the ebb and flow of the relationship, we need to go back prior to the Bhopal disaster to what might be considered the founding of the global anti-toxics movement.

When the Bhopal tragedy occurred in 1984, the global anti-toxics movement was officially two years old. But its roots can be traced back to at least around 1971 when people like David Weir, who later published *The Circle of Poison* with Mark Schapiro,[3] began discovering in the developing world pesticides and other toxic products that had been banned in the United States and Europe. Weir's book was followed in 1982 by *A Growing*

Problem: Pesticides and the Third World Poor, by David Bull.[4] That same year, Anwar Fazal, a Malaysian activist who at the time was the first person from a developing country to head the International Organisation of Consumers Unions (IOCU; later known as Consumers International), organized a meeting in Penang, Malaysia, to explore the possibility of an international network of activists aimed at halting 'the indiscriminate sale and misuse of chemical pesticides throughout the world'.[5] Fazal, who had led IOCU's campaign for a code of conduct to regulate the marketing of infant formula, drew on his extensive network ties to organize the May 1982 meeting where the Pesticide Action Network (PAN) was born. At its inaugural meeting, which included the authors Weir and Bull, participants proposed a model based on a communication network with three main components: regional centres that would serve as action hotline centres; data hotline centres; and a newsletter. The idea was to link the communication network to Consumer Interpol, a global citizen alert system on hazardous products and processes created by IOCU. Linked to IOCU, Consumer Interpol was designed to draw on IOCU's ability to launch global campaigns against products or companies. According to Fazal,

> If a specific company is involved, we will make sure that as much effort is made at the source of the problem as is made at chasing the particular products in different parts of the world. We will go to the factories where these hazardous goods are made, and to the company that manufactures them. With this kind of a Consumer Interpol, we can give a multinational response to the multinationals.[6]

PAN's formation was rooted in Fazal's understanding that problems created by multinational actors needed multinational reactions. IOCU had learned a great deal about how to challenge the power of multinationals, how to create global communication networks, how to negotiate treaties and agreements at the international level and how to split off 'subsidiaries', like PAN, that could take on new issues while IOCU remained focused on its core objectives. PAN quickly developed its own identity and new alliances and areas of focus that would not have been possible for IOCU. In particular, PAN aimed to build regional networks of grassroots farmworker, women's, environmental and other organizations, while advocating for codes of conduct and other international agreements on behalf of the network.

Within two years of its founding, PAN had already held several regional meetings in Latin America, Africa and Europe and engaged in negotiations with the UN's Food and Agriculture Organization on the development of the International Code of Conduct on the Distribution and Use of Pesticides that was approved in 1985. In fact, Fazal and Monica Moore, the founder of Pesticide Action Network North America, were in Bangkok in December 1984 for a meeting on the UN Food and Agriculture Organization's proposed Code of Conduct. Upon hearing the news of the Bhopal disaster, the two spontaneously organized a silent protest on the steps of the conference centre where the FAO meeting was taking place.

Also in 1984, PAN organized and launched its international 'Dirty Dozen' campaign. PAN's dirty dozen included aldicarb, toxaphene, chlordane and heptachlor, chlordimeform, chlorobenzilate, DBCP, DDT, the 'drins' (aldrin, dieldrin and endrin), EDB, HCH and lindane, paraquat, parathion and methyl parathion, pentachlorophenol and 2,4,5-T. At the worldwide launch of its campaign on 5 June 1985, actions included protests at plants manufacturing chemicals on the list such as the Dow plant in New Zealand that produced the herbicide 2,4,5-T. In the development of the Dirty Dozen campaign, PAN's leaders debated whether the target of the campaign should be specific corporations or specific chemicals. In the end, the chemical-based approach won out for strategic reasons.

This is the context of the global anti-toxics movement, into which the Bhopal movement was born. PAN, which emerged as a direct response to the globalization of the chemical industry and in particular the pesticide hazards it was spreading around the world, had already established itself as a network for sharing information about toxic hazards and as a key NGO voice in nascent negotiations for international chemicals management treaties and corporate codes of conduct.

PAN operated over the same uneven global terrain on which the Bhopal movement found itself in 1984. To address this unevenness, the organization developed a decentralized model for its international network. Establishing regional offices in Africa, Asia, Latin America, Europe and North America allowed each regional office to provide regionally specific support to the grassroots organizations in its region working on pesticide and related environmental issues. But regional offices also collected data on pesticide use and patterns of health effects that could be aggregated with other regional offices to paint a global picture. In this manner, PAN was able to serve the needs of local farmers and others with concerns about pesticide and chemical exposures, while also building capacity to negotiate at the international level for new chemicals management treaties. With its roots in the consumers movement, which had gained experience at the international negotiating table, PAN was able to insert itself into the UN dialogue on how to protect people from chemical hazards. How the Bhopal movement fit into the framework for the global anti-toxics movement that PAN had constructed is the focus of the next section.

Early Bhopal organizing

Immediately following the disaster, PAN was unsure how best to support the as yet unorganized movement in Bhopal. Similarly, activists in Bhopal barely had time to think about how to connect with existing global networks as they struggled to figure out how to respond locally. Inside the Bhopal movement, survivor organizations jockeyed for position and often came into conflict with one another over how best to organize.

Most activism fell into the category of protest and was aimed at demanding that Carbide and the government begin providing care and compensation. Within months, the main groups involved in these protests—a combination of Bhopal-specific organizations and larger national organizations—formed a loose-knit movement. Conflicts among the various movement organizations emerged almost immediately. Sarangi, for example, writes that the Zahreeli Gas Kand Sangharsh Morcha (known as the Morcha) and Nagarik Rahat Aur Punarvas Committee (NRPC), which formed within the first week after the disaster, had immediate disagreements: 'The NRPC viewed Morcha as doing politics instead of providing help, and the Morcha thought of NRPC as a bunch of reformists with dubious motives'.[7] As one example of its strong political orientation, the Morcha patently refused to accept support from organizations in the United States or elsewhere outside India, for fear that the government would portray Bhopal activists as disloyal and unpatriotic and that organizations from the United States could be linked to US intelligence.

Initially, disagreements tended to focus on whether to direct efforts on demanding action from the government and Union Carbide, or on the more mundane task of trying to care for sick people and provide livelihood to those who had lost the sole earners in their families. Those favouring the provision of health care understood the need for epidemiological research into the extent of the effects of the disaster in the population. Yet activists had few resources to undertake the extensive collection of public health data needed to understand the range and seriousness of the impacts.[8] What little epidemiological data activists were able to gather in the first few months following the disaster were destroyed in 1985 when Bhopal police raided the offices of a makeshift clinic activists were using.

PAN continued to provide moral support through the early years of the Bhopal struggle, as did many other national and international organizations. But the unprecedented nature of the Bhopal disaster created challenges for the movement formed in its aftermath. The disaster immediately took on great symbolic meaning that attracted activists from near and far, and brought them together in a political, economic, legal and cultural context that initially prevented any of them from achieving their goals of securing adequate relief and rehabilitation for survivors.

These conflicts mostly ended within a year when the only groups remaining active were survivor-led organizations. But even into the early 1990s, the movement's energy by necessity was focused on pressuring the government and Union Carbide to provide adequate health care and compensation to the survivors. This inward focus reached a peak in 1989 and the several years afterward when the movement spent most of its time and energy challenging the amount and terms of the 1989 settlement decision. The $470 million settlement, negotiated between Union Carbide and the Government of India,[9] was a mere fraction of the $3 billion figure that had been raised, by some accounts, by the Union Carbide CEO himself. In addition, the terms of the settlement absolved Union Carbide of any future liability for damages related to the disaster. Responding to what the movement believed was an insultingly unjust settlement became the focus of attention for at least the next three years and required the movement to develop new strategies for bringing the world's attention to Bhopal and for overturning the 1989 settlement.

Building a global social movement network

Even during periods of great inward focus, the movement understood the importance of maintaining global awareness of the plight of Bhopal survivors. The Bhopal Group for Information and Action (BGIA), which was formed in early 1986 by a core group of activists that had weathered the chaos and conflicts of the first post-disaster year, played a central role in balancing the demands of local organizing with the need to build a network of supporters beyond Bhopal. In its inaugural newsletter, BGIA wrote,

> For the victims of the Bhopal Gas Disaster, the trauma is far from over.... In the absence of an adequate and effective programme of healthcare and rehabilitation, the disaster continues.... Many NGO's and individuals are involved in vital work aiming to lessen the impact of the continuing tragedy.... Given the magnitude of the problem, it is clear that only such multi-pronged efforts can keep the issue alive and provide directions for finding short and long term solutions.... A need has been greatly felt... for a stable, well organised and accessible centre at Bhopal, which could be a clearing house for information, and which in addition, could provide basic support to all the other groups working in/on Bhopal and issues raised by it.[10]

The group goes on to explain that among its aims and objectives is to collect and document information, generate information by commissioning and conducting research, disseminate information, lobby for action and collaborate with other groups engaged in work on the Bhopal issue. The group had already benefited from the global connections of its members. A Bhopal native who was studying at the California Institute of Technology at the time of the disaster became a key source of information about Union Carbide, providing to Bhopal activists the names of Carbide's executives and information about the chemicals it had been processing in Bhopal. Paul Shrivastava, another Bhopal native who was working as an academic in the United States, also became an important ally and published widely on the management failures and other aspects of the tragedy.[11] Global connections occurred in the other direction as well. Ravi Rajan, an early member of

BGIA, later pursued an advanced degree at Oxford and currently teaches at the University of California, Santa Cruz, where he has served as President of the Board of Directors of PAN North America and published on the Bhopal tragedy.[12]

In another example of the movement's early global reach, members of what would become the BGIA attended a meeting of activists in the Netherlands in May 1985 to discuss the broader issue of air pollution, especially in the context of Bhopal. According to BGIA, 'Out of this meeting grew a new global network linking environmental groups concerned about these issues. AIRPLAN, as the network is called, coordinates international campaigns and is a forum for exchange of information and action plans.'

BGIA understood from its inception the importance of helping the rest of the world remember Bhopal while activists on the ground in Bhopal worked year after year to secure healthcare and compensation. Printing its monthly newsletter in English was a strategic move to maintain communication with the audience of English-speaking Indians throughout the rest of India, and more importantly, the rest of the English-speaking world. This is evident in the newsletter's second issue, when in a plea for support from readers the authors write: '... we see our small group here as a mere extension of a shared desire of a vast community to sustain work on Bhopal and related issues'.[13]

Newsletter readers would have included members of the network Ward Morehouse of the Council on International and Public Affairs was building in the United States. Having spent time in India during the 1960s and 1970s while researching science and technology policy, Morehouse became almost instantly committed to the fight against Union Carbide and devoted much of the rest of his career to the Bhopal struggle. Morehouse organized nearly 50 organizations, ranging from trade and labour unions to environmental, church and consumer groups, into the Citizens Commission on Bhopal. Morehouse also created the Bhopal Action Resource Center, BGIA's counterpart in the United States. Among the members of the Citizens Commission on Bhopal was the Highlander Research and Education Center, an organization dedicated to grassroots organizing in the Appalachian region of the United States, which encompasses Institute, West Virginia, where Union Carbide operated a methyl isocyanate plant. Highlander had begun earlier in the 1980s a successful community environmental health programme to support activists organizing around toxics. Following the Bhopal tragedy, Highlander worked with Bhopal activists to build solidarity with people in the United States who had been affected by Union Carbide. Among the efforts of the Citizens Commission on Bhopal were an early book-length account of the Bhopal tragedy by Morehouse and Subramaniam, and the report 'No Place to Run: Local Realities and Global Issue of the Bhopal disaster',[14] a joint effort of the Highlander Research and Education Center, the Society for Participatory Research in Asia and the Centre for Science and Environment in Delhi.[15]

By late 1986, Morehouse's Bhopal Action Resource Center had joined with Asian Regional Exchange for New Alternatives, the Bhopal Disaster Monitoring Group of Japan, Bhopal Never Again Action Group of the Netherlands, Bhopal Trade Union Solidarity Group and Bhopal Victims Support Committee both of the United Kingdom and the International Organisation of Consumers Unions, which was based in Malaysia at the time, to form the International Coalition for Justice in Bhopal. Morehouse brought a small group of Bhopal survivors to the United States in 1989 where they gave talks to member organizations of the Citizens Commission on Bhopal, held press conferences and protested at the Union Carbide shareholders meeting. These examples of its global reach illustrate how the Bhopal movement was ahead of its time. At least ten years before the widely praised 'blue-green' alliances formed at the Seattle World Trade Organization protests, Bhopal activists were building relationships with labour activists and environmentalists, among others. But at the same time, these relationships proved difficult to maintain.

When the International Coalition for Justice in Bhopal lost momentum in the 1990s, BGIA and Bhopal Action Resource Center worked hard to build new international networks. These included the short-lived International Network of Victims of Corporate and Government Abuse (which included the White Lung Association, Dalkon Shield Information Network and a survivor group from Minamata, Japan, among others) and the Asian Victims for a Hazard Free Environment. Each of these networks more or less disappeared by 1994. The International Coalition for Justice in Bhopal had slightly more staying power, but by 2000 was revamped as the International Alliance for Justice in Bhopal, and later became the International Campaign for Justice in Bhopal. The failure to sustain any of the transnational coalitions over an extended period of time had to do with the costs of maintaining such relationships, which are discussed in more detail below.

Balancing the local and the global

Bhopal activists learned some key lessons in their first ten years of organizing. Balancing efforts to keep the memory of Bhopal alive through its international organizing with the political and legal battles in India had taken a toll. According to one of Bhopal's long-time activists, it took ten years for the movement to realize that it needed to separate the health care needs of the community from the larger political struggle in which the movement was engaged.

This realization, prompted in part by the report of the 1994 International Medical Commission on Bhopal, helped the movement understand that it would need to find its own ways to begin the healing in the absence of government support. The idea of community healing became embodied in the Sambhavna Trust, which was formed in 1996 to operate a health clinic that would provide care to the affected communities. Sambhavna was designed to collect community health data while administering treatment. In the absence of government policies to conduct health research and provide adequate health services, activists had built their own research health care facility.

With the emergence of the Sambhavna Trust, and the need to raise money to fund the clinic the Trust had set up, the Bhopal movement finally hit upon a significant opportunity for the support of Pesticide Action Network. Although PAN had been supportive of the Bhopal effort right from the beginning, its support mostly took the form of statements of solidarity with the victims and an open offer to provide whatever sort of support the local Bhopal movement asked of it.

PAN's support became more substantial when in 1994 a Bhopal activist visited the United Kingdom to spread awareness about the lack of government response to the disaster and the need for community-based health care delivery. As a result of this visit, the Bhopal Medical Appeal was created and the UK branch of PAN (previously known as Pesticides Trust), headed by an activist named Barbara Dinham who had been involved with PAN almost from its inception in 1982, used its non-profit status to oversee the money raised through the Bhopal Medical Appeal. The Bhopal Medical Appeal raises money for Sambhavna, the community health clinic, by placing ads in major British newspapers on each anniversary of the disaster. Although the Bhopal Medical Appeal launched a similar advertising campaign in the United States, it failed to generate sufficient contributions to warrant its continuation. By 1999, the PAN North America regional office began overseeing an account through which North American funders and individual donors could contribute to the movement.

The clinic offices also provide space for the International Campaign for Justice in Bhopal (ICJB), which was formed in 2002 out of the ashes of the failed networks and coalitions of the 1990s. The Bhopal Medical Appeal and PAN-UK are members of the ICJB, but the ICJB itself receives no money from the Bhopal Medical Appeal. Instead, the ICJB is a network of international partners responsive to the agenda-setting of four Bhopal-based survivor groups.

The other significant event of the mid- to late 1990s was the involvement of Greenpeace and the eventual creation of a Greenpeace India office. Beginning with a tour of India by Greenpeace activist Annie Leonard in 1993 to identify sources of environmental activism in the country, Greenpeace slowly developed a relationship with the Bhopal movement. Bhopal became the centrepiece of Greenpeace International's 'Global Toxic Hotspots' campaign. In 1999, Greenpeace produced and circulated globally a report titled 'The Bhopal Legacy'.[16] The report documented the levels of dioxins, PCBs and other chemicals still contaminating the site 15 years after the gas leak. Greenpeace also provided funding for survivor tours to Europe and the United States to raise awareness of the ongoing Bhopal struggle.

Rejuvenated, the movement used its momentum, and the infusion of energy from the 2001 merger of Union Carbide with the much more publicly recognizable chemical giant Dow, to strike out in new directions. In 2003, Bhopal activists convinced Amnesty International that the suffering of Bhopal victims represented a corporate human rights violation. In response, Amnesty published a report documenting the injustices experienced by Bhopal victims over the previous two decades, and made Bhopal a centrepiece of its corporate accountability campaign.[17] The significance of Amnesty's involvement lies in the fact that the organization had previously focused almost entirely on state violations of human rights.

Why weren't the earlier international networks as successful as the one that emerged in the late 1990s? Interviews with movement activists and analysis of movement communications suggest the benefits of maintaining transnational relationships were simply not outweighing the costs. Up until the mid-1990s, long-distance travel was still quite expensive and most organizations in the coalitions formed by the Bhopal movement still communicated by typed or even handwritten letters. Bhopal activists attribute their more recent success at building and sustaining transnational relationships to a number of factors that only began converging in the late 1990s. These factors include the maturation of the Internet as a communication and organizing tool, allowing more rapid communication that could be broadcast to a much wider audience. Perhaps as important, according to one interviewee, the world's social justice activists became more sensitive to the implications of the type of economic globalization being driven by the developed countries of the world and their free trade agreements. In other words, the emergence of an organized resistance to top-down globalization, in particular, and the growth and maturation of civil society more broadly, made it possible for the costs of transnational organizing to be outweighed by the benefits.

Lastly, in an ironic twist chemical industry corporations surely did not foresee, their global spread resulted in a global class of chemically exposed citizens. By the late 1990s, these citizens had begun to use information and communication technologies to share information and experiences in ways that could build solidarity networks and create a global presence that had previously not been possible. PAN had effectively set up the infrastructure for the sharing of information on pesticide risks. But it was the heightened global awareness of the questionable behaviours of multinational corporations that made possible company-specific campaigns. For example, when Dow Chemical purchased Union Carbide in 2001, Bhopal activists suddenly became linked to a global chain of communities fighting for their health in the face of chemical contamination originating from Dow plants, its subsidiaries or its products. Bhopal activists and PAN members, among others, formed the Dow Accountability Network and housed it in the PAN North America office.

The Dow Accountability Network also illustrates how the Bhopal movement has avoided compromising its core values at the expense of participating in transnational networks. As the Dow Accountability Network began to take shape, it was apparent to activists in the ICJB that the network was framing itself as a supporter of corporate reform. In an email between two ICJB activists obtained during archival research on the movement, concerns about the 'corporate reform' position of the network are made explicit: 'I repeat my earlier concern about the corporate reform [greener products, yoga for workers, meditation for executives...] line of thinking that appears to dominate in the dow accountability network'. The email goes on to add that 'a demand for greener products legitimises corporate rule/power... in the process we dont want to end up as supporters of corporate reform'.[18] This exchange offers yet another example of the Bhopal movement's strategic balancing of transnational relationships with a commitment to its core constituency and its unchanging goals of health care, fair compensation and to bring Union Carbide executives to India to stand trial.

Meanwhile, other transnational efforts offered mixed results. Events like the 2002 World Summit on Sustainable Development in Johannesburg and 2004 World Social Forum in Mumbai, both of which Bhopal activists attended, provided the opportunity for solidarity building through face-to-face contact among activists, but no concrete gains on the ground for Bhopal survivors. Attendance at such international events was largely made possible by the support of Greenpeace. Similarly, Greenpeace funded Bhopal survivors to go on tours around the world and to attend the Dow shareholders annual meeting in Midland, Michigan, United States. Through these meetings and travels, a snowball effect developed whereby the movement's international network began growing stronger and stronger. One outcome, for example, was the development of an organization of university students in the United States known as Students for Bhopal, built initially on the strength of several chapters of Association for India's Development, an organization that depends heavily on Indians residing in the United States to support its work for just and sustainable development in India.

The constant struggle to balance an international campaign with attention to the core demands of the Bhopal organizations—which parallels the struggle between advocating for international agreements to protect people from future 'Bhopals' and advocating for the rights of survivors to fair compensation and care—has been especially evident in the last five years. The run-up to the twentieth anniversary celebration, for example, represented a high point in terms of international awareness and the extent and strength of the international network of Bhopal supporters.

In addition to the above-mentioned appearances at international meetings, in 2003 international partners in the global anti-toxics movement used their connections to put a Bhopal activist on the programme of a meeting of the Intergovernmental Forum on Chemical Safety (IFCS), a World

Health Organization-administered body with the charge of facilitating and advocating international efforts to bring order to global policies aimed at global chemical safety. One aim of raising the issue of Bhopal before the delegates of 126 countries was to push for the adoption of the precautionary principle and a 'polluter pays' mandate in future chemicals management treaties. Delegates, many of whom were participants in the subsequent preparatory meeting for the UN Environment Programme's 'Strategic Approach to International Chemicals Management', advocated for precautionary principle and polluter pays language to be included in the final agreement. But at the final negotiating stages, the US delegation blocked consensus until both principles were struck from the agreement. Keenly aware of the potential to exhaust valuable resources in the pursuit of such goals, the Bhopal movement has had little direct involvement with the chemicals treaties of which PAN has been such a central participant.

By allowing its partners in the global anti-toxics movement to take on such goals, the Bhopal movement has been able to control the shifts in where its work focuses—from local, state and national levels to regional and international levels. For example, activity in the United States, organized now almost exclusively by Students for Bhopal, has declined in the last three years. Furthermore, the movement's relationship with Greenpeace was terminated after a number of incidences in which Greenpeace activists failed to respect the ICJB's request for Greenpeace's actions to be promoted under the banner of the ICJB. Though not officially terminating its relationship with Amnesty International, Bhopal has received less attention from Amnesty International.[19]

The Bhopal movement's transnational relationships have waxed and waned over its entire history. Most recently, the movement has shifted its energy from international organizing to some very important developments within India. Due to Dow Chemical's desire to invest heavily in India's chemical infrastructure, Bhopal activists have found new leverage points at which to apply pressure. In a well-orchestrated use of Indian 'right to knowledge' and US 'right to information' laws, the movement has revealed efforts by Dow Chemical to persuade the Government of India to take 'key actions to achieve [Bhopal] legacy issue resolution for Dow' so that Dow could go forward with plans to invest upwards of $1 billion in India.[20] Along with its efforts to block Dow's attempts to invest in India, the movement has been increasingly focused on forcing the Government of India and state government of Madhya Pradesh to fulfil their promises to deliver clean drinking water to residents of neighbourhoods with well water contaminated by chemicals left behind by Union Carbide at the factory site. Meanwhile, the movement has been successful at organizing students and alumni at the prestigious Indian Institutes of Technology across India to protest the presence of Dow recruiters on their campuses. In another domestic development, villagers of Shinde and Vasuli in Pune recently succeeded in their year-long struggle when the state's chief minister announced that a planned Dow Research and Development Centre would not be located near the villages. In their protest, which included arrests and police beatings, villagers explicitly linked Dow and the risks of its proposed facility to Bhopal. The ICJB featured the struggle prominently on its website as part of its 'Dow, Quit India' campaign.

Balancing the local and global is just one dimension of the complex social movement strategy that arose in response to an unprecedented tragedy with rather clear-cut corporate culpability. Not only did the movement need to figure out how to operate at a range of levels, it also had to juggle a range of different issues. Although not discussed at great length in this chapter, the movement has at various times shifted its focus from the immediate medical care of affected individuals, to compensation demands, to monitoring of the allocation of settlement funds, to economic rehabilitation for survivors, to legal challenges of the settlement and criminal trials against corporate executives, to broader efforts at corporate reform. The variety of issues, and the range of levels on which the issues were taken up, also meant that the campaign has fought its battles in an array of venues: courtrooms on two continents, the streets of Bhopal, in front of the Prime Minister's residence in Delhi, at Permanent People's Tribunals and International Medical Commissions, at shareholder meetings of Union Carbide and Dow, and at international meetings like the World Summit on Sustainable Development, the Intergovernmental Forum on Chemical Safety and the World Social Forum. In short, the Bhopal struggle evolved a strategy for balancing all of these demands as it adapted to address the unprecedented nature of the disaster and its aftermath.

Conclusion

The motto 'Bhopal: The Real Face of Globalization' reminds us that globalization introduces new hazards to vulnerable populations. The main objective in detailing the evolution of the Bhopal movement has been to illustrate that the forces of globalization that facilitated the global expansion of the petrochemical industry are accompanied by counterforces in the form of social movement challenges to environmental hazards introduced by the industry. Threats to people's existence introduced by multinational corporations necessitate civil society responses that include, among other strategies, transnational organizing. But transnational organizing, as the Bhopal movement illustrates, must be balanced with local organizing aimed at meeting constituents' immediate needs.

What have been the outcomes of the Bhopal movement's efforts to balance local and global organizing? On one hand, immediately following the disaster the chemical industry developed a 'Responsible Care' programme that called for members of the industry to take voluntary steps towards meeting safety standards. Superfund and 'Right to Know' legislation was passed in the United States to protect the public from toxic hazards. India, though less responsive, saw the formation of a Ministry of Environment and a number of new environmental laws. And although less directly an outgrowth of Bhopal, a series of international agreements on the disposal, trade and manufacture of chemicals have come out of the UN in the last 15 years.

The institutional responses described earlier have more or less resulted in the prevention of a Bhopal repeat. The trade-off has been chronic low-level releases of toxic chemicals, the effects of which are often far removed in time and place from the physical assault. Yet these 'slow Bhopals' are altering the physical means of existence just as the 1984 disaster did for its thousands of survivors. The Bhopal movement must be examined more closely before we can understand the potential for movements to respond to these 'slow Bhopals'. Perhaps more significantly yet, as humans continue to change the Earth's climate, future Bhopal-like events are bound to interact with droughts, floods and other human-induced 'natural' disasters in ways that will magnify and complicate responses to chemical or industrial disasters.

In its twenty-ninth year, the Bhopal movement is relatively old for a social movement. But one thing is certain: new strategies will evolve from this old movement as it continues to counter the forces of globalization that resulted in suffering for so many thousands of people in Bhopal. Whether future movements learn lessons from Bhopal—like how domestic movements can balance local needs with the demands of building and sustaining global network ties—will likely shape how effectively civil society responds to the next generation of Bhopal-like disasters.

Acknowledgements

This research was funded in part by a University of San Francisco Jesuit Foundation Grant and by a grant from the American Sociological Association's Fund for the Advancement of the Discipline. The author wishes to thank both funding sources, without which this research would not have been possible, and the many people in and outside of Bhopal who have been involved with the movement for justice and who shared their experiences.

Notes

1 See Donatella della Porta and Sidney Tarrow, 'Transnational processes and social activism: An introduction', in Donatella della Porta and Sidney Tarrow (eds), *Transnational Protest & Global Activism* (Boulder, CO:

Rowman & Littlefield, 2004), 1–17; Donatella della Porta, Massimiliano Andretta, Lorenzo Mosca and Herbert Reiter, *Globalization From Below: Transnational Activists and Protest Networks* (Minneapolis: University of Minnesota Press, 2006); John A. Guidry, Michael D. Kennedy and Mayer N. Zald (eds), *Globalizations and Social Movements: Culture, Power, and the Transnational Public Sphere* (Ann Arbor: University of Michigan Press, 2000); Sanjeev Khagram, James V. Riker and Kathryn Sikkink (eds), *Restructuring World Politics: Transnational Social Movements, Networks, and Norms* (Minneapolis: University of Minnesota Press, 2002); and Valentine Moghadam, *Globalization and Social Movements: Islamism, Feminism, and the Global Justice Movement* (Boulder, CO: Rowman & Littlefield, 2008).

2 Lisa Whitehouse, 'Corporate social responsibility, corporate citizenship and the global compact: A new approach to regulating corporate social power?' *Global Social Policy* 3:3 (2003), 299–318.

3 David Weir and Mark Schapiro, *Circle of Poison: Pesticides and People in a Hungry World* (Oakland, CA: Institute for Food and Development Policy, 1981).

4 David Bull, *A Growing Problem: Pesticides and the Third World Poor* (London: Oxfam, 1982).

5 PAN International, 'Pan International calls for halt to global pesticide proliferation', Press Release (Penang, Malaysia: International Organisation of Consumers Unions, undated).

6 Mattew Rothschild, 'Consumers take the offensive against multinationals: An interview with Anwar Fazal, President, International Organization of Consumers Unions', *The Multinational Monitor* 3:7 (1982).

7 Satinath Sarangi, 'The movement in Bhopal and its lessons', *Social Justice* 23:4 (1996), 100–108.

8 Pushpa S. Mehta, Anant S. Mehta, Sunder J. Mehta and Arjun B. Makhijani, 'Bhopal tragedy's health effects: A review of methyl isocyanate toxicity', *Journal of the American Medical Association* 264 (1990), 2781–2787.

9 A 1985 piece of legislation, the Bhopal Gas Leak Disaster Processing of Claims Act, appointed the government as the representative of all plaintiffs and took away the rights of individuals to file cases on their own behalf. The legislation had the potential to guarantee even the poorest survivors representation in legal proceedings and it also took away the power of the ambulance-chasing American attorneys who had flocked to Bhopal aiming to sign up people for class-action suits. Instead, it was used by the Government of India to negotiate a settlement with Union Carbide without involving the survivors.

10 Bhopal Group for Information and Action, 'Information & Action', *Newsletter of the Bhopal Group for Information and Action*, Issue 1 (June 1986).

11 Paul Shrivastava, *Bhopal: Anatomy of a Crisis* (Cambridge, MA: Ballinger, 1987); Paul Shrivastava, 'Technological and organizational roots of industrial crises: Lessons from Exxon Valdez and Bhopal', *Technological Forecasting & Social Change* 45:3 (1987), 237–253.

12 S. Ravi Rajan, 'Bhopal: Vulnerability, routinization, and the chronic disaster', in Anthony Oliver Smith and Susanna M. Hoffman (eds), *The Angry Earth: Disaster in Anthropological Perspective* (New York: Routledge, 1999), 257–277; S. Ravi Rajan, 'Toward a metaphysic of environmental violence: The case of the Bhopal gas disaster', in Nancy L. Peluso and Michael Watts (eds),

Violent Environments (Ithaca, NY: Cornell University Press, 2001), 380–398; S. Ravi Rajan, 'Missing expertise, categorical politics and chronic disasters—the case of Bhopal', in Anthony Oliver Smith and Susanna M. Hoffman (eds), *Culture and Catastrophe: The Anthropology of Disaster* (Santa Fe, NM: School of American Research (SAR) Press, 2002), 237–260.

13 These examples are drawn from the Bhopal Group for Information and Action's 1986 newsletter: AIRPLAN, Newsletter of the Bhopal Group for Information and Action, Issue 2, (July 1986).

14 Anil Agarwal, Juliet Merrifield and Rajesh Tandon, *No Place to Run: Local Realities and Global Issue of the Bhopal Disaster* (Tennessee: Highlander Research and Education Center, 1985).

15 Ward Morehouse and M. Arun Subramaniam, *The Bhopal Tragedy: What Really Happened and What it Means for American Workers and Communities at Risk* (New York: Council on International and Public Affairs, 1986).

16 I. Labunska, A. Stephenson, K. Brigden, R. Stringer, D. Santillo and P. A. Johnston, 'The Bhopal legacy: Toxic contaminants at the former Union Carbide factory site, Bhopal, India: 15 Years After the Bhopal Accident (Technical Note 04/99)', (Exeter, UK: Greenpeace Research Laboratories, Department of Biological Sciences, University of Exeter, 1999).

17 Amnesty International, *Clouds of Injustice: Bhopal Disaster 20 Years On* (London: Amnesty International Publications, 2004).

18 The author was given access to an email database by activists within the movement.

19 The exceptions are a 2009 report, 'Dodging responsibility: Corporations, governments and the Bhopal disaster'. Available at http://www.amnesty.org/en/library/info/NWS21/004/2012/en [accessed 1 March 2013], support for a 2012 campaign against the London Organising Committee of the Olympic and Paralympic Games' relationship with Olympics sponsor Dow Chemical and occasional coverage in the Amnesty International magazine *Wire* (see July/August 2012 issue, 'Carrying the Torch', 4–5).

20 A. Liveris, 'Transcription of letter from Andrew Liveris, Dow Chemical CEO, to Ronen Sen, Ambassador of India to US'. Available at: http://legacy.bhopal.net/assets/3617/Letter_SEC_Bhopal_May_08.pdf [accessed 1 March 2013].

Further reading

Edelstein, Michael. 2004. *Contaminated Communities: Coping with Residential Toxic Exposure*. Boulder, CO: Westview.

Erikson, Kai. 1994. *A New Species of Trouble: Explorations in Disasters, Trauma, and Community*. New York: Norton.

Everest, Larry. 1986. *Behind the Poison Cloud: Union Carbide's Bhopal Massacre*. Chicago: Banner Press.

Fortun, Kim. 2001. *Advocacy After Bhopal: Environmentalism, Disaster, New Global Orders*. Chicago: University of Chicago Press.

Jones, Tara. 1988. *Corporate Killing: Bhopals Will Happen*. London: Free Association Books.

Keck, Margaret and Sikkink, Kathryn. 1998. *Activists Beyond Borders: Advocacy Networks in International Politics*. Ithaca, NY: Cornell University Press.

Lapierre, Dominique and Moro, Javier. 2002. *Five Past Midnight in Bhopal: The Epic Story of the World's Deadliest Industrial Disaster*. New York: Warner Books.

Sinha, Indra. 2008. *Animal's People: A Novel*. New York: Simon & Schuster.

Smith, Jackie, Chatfield, Charles, and Pagnucco, Ron (eds). 1997. *Transnational Social Movements and Global Politics*. Syracuse: Syracuse University Press.

Smith, Jackie and Johnston, Hank (eds). 2002. *Globalization and Resistance: Transnational Dimensions of Social Movements*. Boulder, CO: Rowman & Littlefield.

Tarrow, Sidney. 2005. *The New Transnational Activism*. New York: Cambridge University Press.

7

Rubber, Trees and Communities: Rubber Tappers in the Brazilian Amazon in the Twentieth Century

Lise Fernanda Sedrez

On 22 December 1988, the leader of the rubber tappers' union in the heart of the Brazilian Amazon Francisco Alves Mendes Filho, or simply Chico Mendes, was killed in an ambush. Acre, the state where the crime took place, is a remote area in the north-west of Brazil and no stranger to violence. Mendes' predecessor had also been murdered in a similar fashion, eight years earlier. It is fair to say that few Brazilians, besides those in environmentalist circles, took notice of the significance of the Mendes' killing at the time. In fact, two days later, a character of a very popular soap opera, Odette Roitman, was also murdered—on screen. Between the Christmas and New Year's Eve of 1988, it would have been more likely to find people on the streets discussing the killing of Roitman than the death of Chico Mendes. Yet a quarter century later, Chico Mendes is a household name, and the rubber tappers' struggle is part of the Brazilian political agenda in many ways. Schools have been named after him and his image is present in most environmentalist events. There is a large extractive reserve of about one million hectares with his name, besides several parks and preservation areas. An important division within the Ministry of Environment goes by the name *Instituto Chico Mendes de Conservação de Biodiversidade* (Chico Mendes Institute for Conservation of Biodiversity).

The death of Mendes and the international impact of his murder have definitively changed much of the environmental movement in Brazil. Yet, although much has been written about Mendes' death, I argue that it was in his life and in the trajectory of the community to which he belonged that we must seek the seeds of this coming of age of Brazilian environmentalism.

Rubber tappers, the forest and their common history

In 1996, environmental historian Richard White wrote an influential article on labour and nature, which included a sharp criticism of mainstream environmentalism in the United States. According to White, many environmentalists insisted on viewing nature and labour as incompatible realities, and that protection of nature implied protection from human labour. This was a factual and strategic mistake. Instead, White states, 'work itself offers both a fundamental way of knowing nature and perhaps our deepest connection to the natural world'.[1] Indeed, the relation between labour and nature constitutes a key aspect of the history of the rubber tappers' movement. It was through labour that they learned to know the forest, created their communities and developed their own understanding about strategies of survival and organization. Their narrative, therefore, relates directly to the way they laboured and to the natural environment they lived in—the Amazon rainforest.

Defining the Amazon region is not easy. It is a large, intricate set of ecosystems that range from dry savannah to high-altitude rainforest. Even the most visible part of it, the Amazon River basin, combines very different ecosystems with blue, yellow and black rivers adding to its complexity. By any standards, the Amazon represents the largest chunk of tropical rainforest on the planet—almost two-thirds.[2] *Hevea brasiliensis*, the most important rubber tree, grows naturally in a large extension of the forest although not in close clusters. Extraction of its sap, the raw material for natural rubber, is work-intensive and requires long and often solitary trips deep into the forest. Attempts to establish rubber tree plantations have failed, most spectacularly in the 1940s in Fordlandia.[3] The rubber tapper economy in the Amazon is part of a long narrative of boom and bust cycles of extractions of natural resources—spices, gold, rubber and Brazil nuts.[4]

Although the rubber tree occurs throughout the Amazon, it is in the extreme west of Brazil that rubber extraction played a significant historical and economic role, changing the national political borders. The occupation of Acre as a Brazilian territory actually owes much of its history to the international rubber market. Until the mid-nineteenth century, the lands of Acre belonged 'without a doubt' to Bolivia, as the Brazilian authorities admitted. However, Latin America's increased integration into the international part of what is called 'the Second Conquest of America' and the global demand for rubber by the 1880s changed this viewpoint. Rivers helped thousands of poor immigrants from the arid Brazilian Northeast to get to this remote region and return with tonnes of rubber to the traders in Manaus. This first wave of Brazilian rubber tappers led to conflicts with the Bolivian authorities, bloody confrontations with indigenous communities and the fortunes of a few rubber barons in Manaus. Eventually, it also led to the creation of the short-lived Independent Territory of Acre and later to the Brazilian territory of Acre in 1903.[5] Bolivia had lost a rubber-rich region, and the rubber barons of the Amazon had flexed their muscles and forced the federal government into a dangerous diplomatic negotiation. At the end of the day, Acre, the new territory, was certainly a gain for the young Brazilian republic, which eventually paid Bolivia for the territory with money and the promise of an easier path to export Bolivia's rubber through the construction of a large railroad, the Madeira-Marmoré. Brazil's Minister of Foreign Affairs, Barão do Rio Branco, considered the acquisition of Acre a geopolitical priority. But as much as a diplomatic victory, the acquisition of Acre was a clear sign of the power of the local elites and their private armies in the Amazon.

The conflict with Bolivia was just one chapter of a history of the violence that surrounded the formation of the rubber fields in Acre. Indeed, the modern alliance of Indians and rubber tappers, a rightly celebrated aspect of the modern rubber tappers' movement, was slow to come to fruition and had to overcome an ugly past. Conflicts between Indians and rubber tappers go back to the first wave of rubber tappers in the late nineteenth century. They then were employed by the owners of the *seringais* (rubber tree estates) to exterminate or tame, whichever was less troublesome, the Indian population. Hunting episodes called *correrias*, which were armed forays into Indian villages, took place until at least the 1940s, wiping out tribes and communities in order to open large areas for economic exploitation.

At the same time, the crash of the rubber economy in the early twentieth century changed many aspects of the rubber tappers' communities. Rubber estates became more complex productive units with the addition of basic agriculture and trade in furs, feathers and bones. Without the continuous influx of north-east immigrants, labour was scarce. The local communities established more peaceful contact with indigenous villages and became culturally, as much as ethnically, *caboclos*.[6]

The second wave of immigrants to the rubber production areas arrived during the Second World War. To supply much-needed rubber to the Allies, the Brazilian government recruited over 30,000 people, mostly men from the drought-stricken areas of the Northeast, to become rubber tappers. They were the 'rubber soldiers' in the 'battle for rubber'. With little experience of life in tropical forests and very poor sanitary conditions, thousands died of malnutrition or disease in the Amazon, and very few returned to their hometowns. Some, however, married local women and established themselves in the region.[7] Such was the case of Chico Mendes' father.

The third wave of immigrants reached Acre in the late 1960s and early 1970 under the auspices of the military dictatorship. Cattle ranchers and loggers counted on the largesse of the federal union to bring modernity to Acre. With the perspective of fast and massive returns, they had little patience with or interest in local communities, Indians or rubber tappers and their traditional uses of the land.

Viscerally different conceptions of the Amazon were in play. While for the new arrivals, the main resource was land, for the rubber tappers it was the forest which was their breadbasket— the land itself, deprived of the forest, meant very little to them.[8] Governmental support also helped cattle ranchers obtain legal titles for the land, which had eluded or had not been a priority for rubber tappers up until then. Once they became the legal owners of larger tracts of land— which might or might not include *seringais* or rubber estates—the ranchers would burn down or clear-cut the forest. Many turned wide tracts of forest into huge grazing or logging properties called *latifúndios*. Others divided their property into small plots and sold them to landless workers in the south of Brazil, thus alleviating the pressure for land reform in these very productive areas.

For the military government, it was a win-win situation. They could suppress social unrest in the South, where land-reform initiatives were seen as a sign of communist infiltration, and could assure the economic occupation of the Amazon in areas they saw as vulnerable borders. Moreover, there was a clearly racist perception that Southern agrarian workers, who were the descendants of Italian and German immigrants, were 'better workers', less lazy and more productive than the *caboclos* and Indians who, they believed, wasted the economic potential of Amazon. In Acre, however, the government would find that their plan was not so easily executed.

The rubber tapper communities and the union

Extracting the milky sap from rubber trees involves more than simply drawing V-shaped cuts in the trunk. It requires a careful and complex social organization with several important component parts. The most important of these is the rubber estate, the *seringal*, which usually includes several families and workers. Each *seringal* has a *colocação*, or homestead composed of the productive unit, the area for the individual houses and some land set aside for yucca and other plants where the rubber tapper family raises small animals (such as chicken, pigs, and some cows), gathers fruit and hunts or fishes. *Colocações* are not private property, but part of the *seringal*. They are criss-crossed by lines or *linhas*, which are little more than rough trails in the middle of the forest, each with a name, where the rubber trees are located.

The main paths between *colocações* and *seringais* are called 'landings' or *varadouros*, and the shortcuts are the 'beaches', or *varações*.[9] Supplies arrive in ox-carts to the *seringais* through the landings, so these are supposedly better roads. Often, however, landings are no wider than a couple of feet so only mules, not carts, could reach the *seringais*. Most often rubber tappers walk from one homestead to another and from one rubber state to another. Braving the forest, crossing the *igarapés*, which are the shallow rivers of the Amazon, rubber tappers measure distances according to hours of walking which they estimate to be about three miles per hour. Gomercindo Rodrigues, an agronomist and officer in the rubber tappers' union, recalled long journeys in which he had to walk at a fast pace over for over fourteen hours carrying his backpack just to attend a union meeting in a *seringal*. The next day after the meeting was over, he would walk another ten to fourteen hours until he reached the next *seringal*.[10]

Rubber tappers thus experienced the forests with their bodies. On their long walks they fought mosquitos, hung their hammocks in safe places and learned how to distinguish landings, fords and doglegs. Rodrigues describes his introduction to this unique way of life in the forest as a slow, often painful, and sometimes embarrassing learning process, but as important as his previous academic training at the university in Mato Grosso for his activities in the rubber tappers' union.

Rubber tapping is a solitary occupation during which rubber tappers can go many days without seeing another human being. Rodrigues observed that rubber lords (*seringalistas*) and foremen traditionally encouraged this isolation in order to foster individualism and mistrust among rubber tappers—which makes the success of the rubber tappers' organization in the 1970s even more remarkable.[11] But they did organize from the bottom–up, re-creating their own identity as a community of forest people.

Their organization was, in part, a reaction to the increasing encroachment of cattle ranchers onto rubber-producing areas. In the Acre River valley in the early 1970s, thousands of hectares of forests were razed. Numerous rubber tapper families who were evicted migrated to urban slums in Rio Branco or Bolívia.[12] The threat of complete obliteration of the rubber tapper way of life forced them to realize that they shared a common fate. Even in the areas where deforestation was not yet present, communities discussed the expansion of the cattle activities and the precariousness of their own claim to the forest were they to remain isolated. They needed to unite.

The organization of rural workers lagged behind the formation of urban unions in most of Brazil. Although Brazilian history has many examples of peasant resistance to expropriation, it was only in 1963 that rural workers constituted CONTAG—the National Confederation of Agricultural Workers. The military coup in 1964 was a hard blow to the organization. However, by the early 1970s, CONTAG had reached out to rubber tappers and by 1976 several communities in Acre, supported by a progressive Catholic Church, had organized local chapters of unions associated to CONTAG.

CONTAG offered support and expertise for the rubber tappers, helped them to organize and encouraged them to challenge the cattle ranchers. However, it was the rubber tappers themselves who developed the confrontation strategy which would define a new trajectory for their communities: the *empate*.

Resistance and direct action

Empate, in the Amazon vocabulary, means to prevent, to hinder or to stop an action. During the first *empate* after the creation of the rubber tappers' union in March 1976 at the *seringal* Carmen, workers did exactly that: they prevented, hindered and stopped deforestation. Learning that the new owners planned to raze the forest and sell the land in small plots, rubber tappers in the area alerted CONTAG which, in turn, spread the word throughout the region to its associates. Rubber tappers and other rural workers from the region gathered their families, a total of sixty people, armed themselves and walked to the area that was to be clear-cut. They had to face gunslingers and *peões* (farmhands). It was not a peaceful confrontation but one that combined some guerrilla strategies, some cunning and some virtual trench warfare, but it worked well enough to attract the attention of the federal government and the media. Eventually some agreement was reached and compensation offered to the workers, but the real gains of the Carmen *empate* were not plots of land. This was the first time rural workers via their own organization had been able to stop deforestation in the Amazon. After much deliberation and evaluation, the model of the Carmen *empate* was repeated in several other places although from then on workers in the *empates* had to be as peaceful as possible without ever retreating.[13]

Wilson Pinheiro took over the leadership of the rubber tappers' union soon after the Carmen *empate*. Pinheiro had a trajectory common to many other rubber tappers, of high mobility within the region. Born in a small community in the Amazon, Pinheiro had worked humble jobs in the city and tried his luck in the gold fields in Rondônia with little success and high costs to his health. In the 1950s, he finally entered the Acre forest and began to work on a rubber homestead. A hardworking and experienced rubber tapper, forty-seven years old and highly respected by the community, he was a natural choice for leadership. Pinheiro, also known as Wilsão, organized several *empates* after 1976 and announced that the rubber tappers' union would not allow deforestation actions in Acre. He was murdered on 21 July 1980.[14]

Empates became a defining strategy in the rubber tapper movements and involved relatively large numbers of workers and their families considering the low densities in the region. These loose networks of local unions acquired a necessary institution framework in 1985, when Chico Mendes organized the first national meeting of rubber tapper leaders in Brasilia and created the

Conselho Nacional de Seringueiros (National Rubber Tappers' Council). From then on, the Council would organize *empates* and be the official voice of the multiple voices of rubber tappers throughout Brazil.

The Nazaré *empate*, against the Bourdon Group, which took place ten years after the Carmen *empate*, epitomized the evolution of this tactic. In June 1986, Bourdon threatened to clear-cut 700 ha of forest, which included a rubber tapper's homestead. To prevent it, the National Rubber Tappers' Council brought together rubber tappers from the entire Acre River valley, over ninety men and women, a photographer who was connected to the group, some sympathetic agronomists and one anthropologist all to protect a single rubber tapper's homestead against a powerful ranching group. Some walked four hours to get to the area; others travelled from even farther. When they arrived, they discussed the case, planned their actions and played soccer. It was a Soccer World Cup year, and rubber tappers were no different from most Brazilians in their fierce love for the sport. The next day, a committee led by Big Raimundo (Chico Mendes' cousin and a local resident) and Maria Canção went to meet with the workers in the logging operation. They carried a Brazilian flag casually picked up from the World Cup decorations in the union hall. Often workers in the deforestation operation were recruited from the rubber tapper community. The presence of rubber tapper families and the negotiations of the committee convinced several employees to interrupt their work. It was a temporary victory. The Bourdon Group took the case to the courts and obtained permission to deforest all the planned area except for the rubber homestead. But more than spectacular events, the *empates* were part of a well-thought out campaign of attrition and consistent victories. As a result of the Nazaré *empate*, the Bourdon Group sold its land in the Xapuri region and abandoned the area.[15]

Although definitively important, *empates* were not sufficient to preserve the homesteads. Thus they were only one of the tactics used by rubber tappers. The workers appealed to the courts. They organized national and international networks. They invited the media and like-minded journalists to witness their daily work. They connected to other rural workers and leftist parties. They also built schools, and made literacy a priority in their agenda. Following the success of the first *empate* in 1976, the rubber tappers' union decided they needed to diversify their actions to strengthen their communities. They created the Rubber Tapper Project (*Projeto Seringueiro*), which aimed to establish schools and cooperatives in the rubber estates. The schools were initially for adults as the almost total illiteracy of the rubber tappers prevented them from carrying on even those basic accounting tasks necessary for the success of the cooperatives. Soon after, however, entire families attended the classes, which were planned around the working schedule of the rubber estates. The community commitment to the schools was complete. Inspired by the Brazilian educator Paulo Freire's pedagogic methods, schoolteachers wrote their own teaching material for their students, using experiences and the real-life questions from the rubber tapper lives.

The first text produced for the schools was entitled '*Poronga*', which is the name of the kerosene lamp worn by rubber tappers on their heads when they go to work before dawn. Like the lamp, the schools were supposed to light the way for the rubber tapper community.[16]

The Rubber Tapper Project also proposed a cooperative as a natural complement to the schools and the worker union. The first experience failed, however, because according to Gomercindo Rodrigues it was not perceived as an initiative of the rubber tappers, but as an 'idea from the outside'. This first cooperative was therefore dismantled, and Mendes, his cousin Big Raimundo and Rodrigues walked over 1,000 km in the Xapuri estates during the following two years to discuss the idea of cooperativism with rubber tappers, patiently visiting hundreds of homesteads. Eventually they obtained funding from Canada's Development and Peace Agency to establish a new cooperative, this time with larger support from the community. Through trial and error, this cooperative would become the basis for the future concept of extractive reserves.

It was the combination of all these institutional and legal tools and the sheer force of direct action which was able to halt or at least to reduce the speed of deforestation in Acre. At the same time, it became clear that successful resistance needed to be proactive and had to propose alternatives to the model of development once advanced by rubber barons and now by cattle ranchers.

The nature and inspiration of the rubber tappers' movement

The rubber tappers' movement in the 1970s was shaped by a number of different influences. In the first place, the late twentieth-century-rubber tapper culture owns much to the millenary indigenous Amazon experience. As Timmons and Roberts point out, 'Indians and later the rubber tappers have combined the cultivation of a variety of crops in small clearings with the gathering of forest products for food, medicine, and building materials'.[17] Another crucial influence was the Catholic Church. At that point, Liberation Theology was widespread within the Church's rank and file particularly in the Amazon. The institution offered a protective umbrella for several social movements including the incipient rubber tappers' unions.[18]

Besides the Catholic Church, the movement also derived part of its organizational structure from socialist literature and socialist activists. Actually, Mendes owed his primary education to an old communist, Euclides Fernando Távora. Távora was a veteran from the Prestes Column, a communist movement which had shaken the Brazilian hinterlands in the 1920s. He had been imprisoned in the Fernando de Noronha Island during the Vargas Era, taken part in a number of other popular movements during the mid-1900 and moved to Acre in the early 1960s where he lived as a rubber tapper for several years. Távora befriended Mendes' father and received permission to teach the young Chico to read and write as long it did not interfere with the boy's work on the homestead. Years later, Mendes related to Gomercindo Rodrigues how Távora created his very personalized method of teaching using newspaper clippings and 'news broadcast in Portuguese from three international radio stations: the BBC in London, Radio Moscow, and the Voice of America in the United States'. More significantly, Távora 'taught him important lessons about union organizations and discipline'.[19] Often Mendes attributed to this very unorthodox education his skills in dialogue with the US Senate Budget committee or World Bank executive directors.

Mendes was not the only socialist leader in the movement, though. Although the military dictatorship violently pursued socialist activists in Brazil from 1964 to 1979, Marxist and socialist literature found its way to Acre via the Catholic Church's *comunidades eclesiais de base* (ecclesial base communities) and CONTAG's community organizers. After 1979, Brazil had adopted a slow and limited political liberalization, and these ideas could circulate more openly. When the *Partido dos Trabalhadores*, the Workers' Party, was finally created, many of its founders openly declared themselves socialists—including several from Acre.

In the 1980s, however, the movement was also strongly influenced by its contact and alliances with environmentalists. It was not only a question of strategy—it is possible to identify in the transformation of the discourse of rubber tapper leaders how they reframed their own experiences and became more aware of their connection with the forest. In a conversation with José Augusto Pádua, a Brazilian historian and environmentalist, Mendes declared he was 'grateful to his environmentalist friends, because he had learned from them several concepts and words which helped him better understand and explain some problems and alternatives which he had somehow began to elaborate'.[20] Padua notes that the incorporation of concepts and language from more traditional environmentalists was only possible because they resonated with the concerns and problems the rubber tappers faced in their daily lives. He also points out that this learning process went in both directions: 'in this process, many extractive workers recognized themselves as environmentalists and many environmentalists got to know better the violence in land conflicts and learned to be solidary with those who had suffered the burden of hundred years of injustice.'[21]

The rubber tappers' movement was not merely the sum of multiple influences. It was an organization of workers, concerned with their own physical survival and immediate material needs. These workers shared similar work-related challenges and they organized under structures such as CONTAG, an agrarian workers' institution, calling it a *sindicato*, or a workers' union. The union challenged the idea of the forest as private property not only because of environmental concerns but also because of the explicit socialist background of union members. Mendes and other leaders of the movement helped to found the Workers' Party in Acre. Some of them latter pursued political careers in the Party, as in the cases of Jorge Vianna, who would become the governor of Acre, and Marina Silva, who would become the Ministry of Environment in Brazil. Two months before his death, Mendes wrote a political testament, in which he dreamed of a 'world socialist revolution that unified all peoples of the planet in one ideal and one conception of socialist unity, and put an end to all the enemies of the new society'.[22]

It is important to acknowledge this dual origin to avoid the trap of oppose environmentalist and working-class agendas. In fact, Stefania Barca correctly defines the rubber tappers' movement as a form of 'working-class environmentalism', a category within the broader definition of 'environmentalism of the poor'.[23] As does White, Barca emphasizes how the people who live out of their physical labour—performed in industries, agriculture or in extractive activities—typically acquire a socially constructed knowledge of nature and the costs of nature degradation through their work and often through their bodies. According to Barca, the struggle of the rubber tappers against deforestation in the Amazon was one of the most striking examples of 'the relevant role played by rural workers in the formation of a popular environmental consciousness'.[24]

Nevertheless, as much as it was an environmental movement and a workers' movement, the rubber tapper narrative also related to the struggle of ordinary people for survival as a community. Rubber tappers, although defined by the work they do, are not only workers, but also members of a community. Nor is the movement only defined by union leaders. The community, the families and the way they are organized among themselves are at the centre of their struggle. This centrality of the concept of the community is better understood when we analyse the role of women in the construction of the movement.

The rubber tapper community was patriarchal and quite male-oriented. As the community resulted from mostly male migratory waves, as described earlier, women were objects of dispute and conflict—or simply pawns in demonstrations of power. Gomercindo Rodrigues mentioned cases in which rubber lords and hired guns would abduct and rape wives and daughters of rubber tappers if they were particularly beautiful.[25] And yet, women were fundamental in the formation of the rubber tapper environmental movement. First, they also had the legal right to homestead, and their land could not be sold by the men of the family without their express authorization. In more than one situation, lack of consent by a female homesteader gave the union legal standing to challenge fraudulent land titles. Although women are largely neglected by most historians of the region, Christina Sheibe Wolff documented the presence of women in the first disputes for land rights since the late nineteenth century in Alto Juruá, Acre.[26]

Second, in a community with high male mobility, women were often responsible for the organization of communities particularly in areas where the Catholic Church was stronger. Third, the productive unit is often a family unit in which women and children carry on tasks as fundamental for the survival of the rubber tapper activities as the tasks of the men who actually tapped the trees. For instance, women are traditionally responsible for the processing of Brazil nuts or the preparation of medicinal plants. When the extractives cooperatives were created, women fought to include these activities as part of their chapters. Finally, women took active part in the *empates*, sometimes carrying their children. In a moving passage, Gomercindo Rodrigues described how in the last *empate* before Chico Mendes' murder, women's actions convinced the federal police to hold its fire:

> There were 159 people, including men, women, and children at the site [Equador, near Cachoeira]. We walked quickly. Less than an hour later we were already near the clearing site. We saw the police move in, in formation, and with their guns they took the characteristic 'ready to fire' stance. The women, led by the schoolteachers of Cachoeira, and the children started to sing the national anthem. It was an indescribable scene. Since the national anthem is one of the principal patriotic symbols, the soldiers must stand at attention and, if armed, present arms during the singing. That was how about fifty police stood—we singing the national anthem and the armed police standing at attention, presenting arms, with the lieutenant saluting.[27]

The image of the wives of rubber tappers facing *peões* and gunslingers is a powerful one, and one that has been observed in other Amazonian conflicts in which forest peoples have been involved.

As a result, even in this very patriarchal society women held important roles from the very beginning. Mary Allegretti is only one of these examples. Allegretti, a young anthropologist from Paraná who was writing her doctoral thesis on the rubber tapper communities, was probably as fundamental for the creation of the extractive reserves as Chico Mendes. She partnered with Mendes to draft the structure and the project for the reserves and worked tirelessly for forging the connections with international environmental NGOs such as Friends of the Earth. Marina Silva, who would eventually become the Ministry of Environment during the Lula administration in the early twenty-first century, is another. Waldiza Alencar was not only one of the founders of the rubber tappers' union, but it was in her homestead that the first meeting for the creation of the union took place.

The active presence of women, even when their role as workers was not fully recognized, highlights the community aspects of the rubber tappers' movement which goes beyond the mere realization of economic activities or the constitution of a labour force. It is a struggle that is fought not only in the working place but also in the houses, in the homesteads, in the family life and in the multiple social and personal connections that rubber tapper communities established with allies and neighbours. Perhaps this 'community aspect' is part of the 'environmentalism of the poor', as conceived by Martínez Alier and Guha,[28] but it is an aspect that must be acknowledged more forcefully, as it shapes the way these movements relate to nature and conceive their strategies.

Building networks in dangerous times

Violence over natural resources in the Amazon hardly ended with the killing of Chico Mendes. In 1992, while world leaders met for the UN Earth Summit in fashionable Rio de Janeiro, Human Rights Watch publically proclaimed that few of the homicides that took place in the Amazon were brought to trial at all and even fewer, if any, of those charged with the homicides were found guilty.[29] In May 2011, two environmentalists and extractivist workers José Cláudio Ribeiro da Silva and Maria do Espírito Santo, husband and wife, were killed in a sadly familiar ambush in the state of Pará, after repeatedly denouncing the illegal logging in the region.[30] High profile cases such as these and the killing of the American nun Dorothy Stang in 2005 are more likely to reach some sort of judicial resolution, but they are exceptions. Violence in the Amazon has many reasons—and the environmental conflicts just add to those. The region is large and well beyond the ability and capacity of the Brazilian's enforcing agencies. Furthermore, violence, fraud, land grabbing and slave labour are all intertwined in the history of the occupation of the region, which necessarily bring consequences in the way the Amazonian elites see the federal state and their right of access to the local power structures.[31] The predatory exploitation of natural resources was, from their point of view, merely an extension of their power over society and their predatory exploitation of human labour. It is not surprising that local resistance to human exploitation also implied resistance against the exploitation of natural resources.

Nevertheless, while dramatically common, Chico Mendes's killing was singular for the impact it had on the environmental movement in Brazil. In part, the time was ripe for a change. The climax of the confrontation between the rubber tappers and landowners which resulted in the Mendes' murder overlapped a critical moment in the Brazilian history, that is the transition from military dictatorial rule to a more democratic regime. Mendes was killed in 1988, the same year a new democratic constitution was signed. The Workers' Party with which he was affiliated was greatly involved in the creation of the document—and so was a myriad of environmental activists, many recently returned from exile. In fact, Brazilian civil society in the 1980s turned the limited liberalization controlled by the military into a 'full-scale democratic transition'.[32] United in this common goal, progressive organizations collaborated fully with each other and the result was an exchange of ideas and agendas as had rarely occurred. A rich and diverse set of environmental struggles arose from this collaboration, in which environmental ideas also migrated to more traditional social movements. In fact, as Eduardo Viola and Victor Leis point out, environmentalism itself in Brazil could not be contained within a narrow definition of an 'environmental movement', but rather constitutes a multi-sectorial mosaic of environmental ideas and struggles via a variety of private and public actors.[33]

In previous decades, often with the support of Theology of Liberation-committed priests and preachers, rubber tappers in the Amazon had already collaborated with several other traditional populations in the Amazon called forest peoples. Their ability to create and feed networks was vital for the survival of the movement in local, national and global spheres.

During the 1980s, this collaboration helped shape the way the constitution would frame the right to property and exploration of natural resources. The 1988 Constitution recognized the right of traditional peoples to land and to their livelihood in very broad terms. The elaboration of new constitution was part of an on-going process which combined environmental concerns—which were new in the Brazilian society—and social concerns which were not new at all. Social equity and participation were as important for Brazilian environmentalists as protecting the environment. As Hochstetler and Keck stated, these movements focused on 'socio-environmentalism', 'a homegrown set of ideas that emerged more or less simultaneously out of struggles in Brazil, India, Indonesia and a few other developing countries.... Opposed to purely expansionist capitalism on social *and* ecological grounds, it argues that empowering poor people and responding to their demands for social equity must be an integral part of any solution to environmental problems'.[34]

In global terms, the 1980s were also critical for the global environmental movement. As news of large-scale deforestation of the Amazon reached households in the Europe and North America, the forest was brought to the central focus of international NGOs such as Greenpeace, the Environment Defense Fund and the Friends of the Earth. At the same time, local actors protested that these NGOs often practiced 'ecological imperialism', that is they imposed their own ideas of wilderness and nature protection upon communities and countries based on their own trajectory and history of relationship with nature. Global environmental networks, connecting South and North NGOs, therefore, were an important strategy which developed fully in the 1980s and shaped much of the international environmental movement. On the one hand, they provided the Northern NGOs with the legitimacy and local knowledge they lacked in working in the tropical rainforest; on the other hand, they provided grassroots organizations such as the rubber tappers' union with resources and international clout for their own local agendas. This international backing from the networks was crucial in the late 1970s and early 1980s during the military dictatorship while domestic channels of communication between state and civil society were strained and the threat of violence came from state as well as non-state actors. In fact, it is a classic example of Keck's and Sikkink's 'boomerang' pattern of international influence in which grassroots are able to push forward their agendas by using their international allies to pressure local governments.[35]

International NGOs adopted part of the socio-environmentalism promoted by the grassroots organizations and these networks were powerful in advancing both agendas.[36] In the case of rubber tappers, these networks brought their struggles to a larger audience and helped Chico Mendes to win support in 1985 from the World Bank and the Interamerican Bank of Development for the concept of extractive reserves even before the Brazil's larger environmental movement had really focused on the proposal. Only two years later in 1987, the Ministry of Agrarian Reform and Development introduced the legal framework for the creation of the reserves. That same year, Mendes was awarded the United Nations Environmental Programme's Global 500 Award presented to grassroots activists and environmental organizations for their efforts on environmental protection.[37]

The extractive reserves proposal

The international recognition of the rubber tappers' movement in the 1990s, however, cannot be attributed simply to good timing and a charismatic leader. There were more than community grievances in the rubber tappers' struggle. There was also a proposal regarding the forest, the communities' engagement with nature and the entire concept of land use that was new, challenging and quite remarkable. In fact, what differentiated the rubber tapper movement from several other grassroots movements was their willingness to put forward the concept of the 'extractive reserves' and their success in presenting these reserves as an alternative to the model of predatory exploitation that had dominated development projects in the Amazon region.

The decade after Chico Mendes's assassination marked a different but equally critical period in the rubber tapper organizations. Mendes had seen the creation of the first extractive reserves in Brazil during his lifetime in February and March of 1988, but they were not regulated and the Brazilian government resisted the idea. Only after Mendes's death as a reaction to the international outcry for his murder, did the President of Brazil José Sarney sign the bill which defined the criteria for the establishment and regulation of future extractive reserves.

By 1992, Mary Allegretti, the young anthropologist who had worked closely with Mendes in the previous years, was the head of the Amazonian Studies Institute with direct access to the Ministry of the Environment, José Lutzenberger.[38] Her role in promoting the extractive reserves as a viable project both before and after Chico Mendes's murder cannot be overstated.

Lutzenberger himself, also an iconic name within the Brazilian environmental movement, supported Allegretti in establishing extractive reserve models for many products other than rubber and Brazil nuts, and for areas beyond Acre.[39] This move solidified the concept of extractivism well within the official strategies of environmental protection for the Amazon.

Other forest peoples have fought for land and resource access in the Amazon. Few have succeeded in obtaining at least some respite in the overwhelming advance towards the Amazon frontier. Rubber tappers realized that resistance required more than simply halting the expansion of deforestation into their lands; they needed alternative models for land use in which their experience and their presence mattered. When in 1985 Mendes and Allegretti convinced the Rubber Tapper National Council to frame their fight for land rights within a larger context of forest protection, they countered the mainstream discourse of inexorable progress with a discourse of superseding local and global rights. If it is true that the murder of Mendes was the turning point after which the defence of the rubber tappers' rights gained international consensus, this was only possible because they had an alternative model for forest use already in place: the extractive reserves.

The proposal for extractive reserves departed radically from the traditional concept of national parks which excluded human populations. More than merely static plots of land put aside from human use, extractive reserves demanded continuous activity. As Kathryn Hochstetler and Margaret Keck describe it, extractive reserves were:

> conservation units in which traditional extractive populations had the right to remain on the land and continue to engage in extractive activities such as rubber tapping and nut gathering, and where measures would be taken to safeguard these activities and make them economically viable. The extractive reserve embodies a classic enabling strategy in that both state and societal actors need to collaborate continually to achieve the reserves' ends... And everyday activities by resident populations are critical for providing the intended conservation and livelihood outcomes of the reserves. [40]

The proposal attracted and confounded many observers. On the one hand, it originated from the community itself, forged by their personal, bodily and communitarian experience in the forest. On the other hand, as Biorn Maybury-Lewis comments, it combined a 'premodern lifestyle—extractivism, hunting, fishing, subsistence farming—with a postmodern twist— entrepreneurialism, communitarianism, multiethnicity—all within an international framework'.[41] It was initially inspired by the model of Indian reservations more than by national parks. It daringly proposed rights for the collective use of land by rubber tappers and defined the forest as their means of production.[42]

The left, which was more nationalist and concerned about sovereignty in the Amazon, feared the extractive reserves would increase international control and halt what they deemed to be much-needed development; strict environmentalists instead feared they would bring the loss of wilderness in the area. The proposal did not fit their models of what should be done in the Amazon—but it was original, powerful and supported by a broad base of both local and global actors.

Domestically, the popularity of the extractive reserves proposal was partly a result, as mentioned earlier, of the elaboration of the 1988 Constitution. Furthermore, the model put forward in the 1970s by the military government supporting large cattle ranch operations in the Amazon had failed spectacularly in the 1980s. Deforestation in the Brazilian Amazon in 1988 was around 8.5 per cent, compared to 3.5 per cent in 1980 and less than 2 per cent in the 1960s.[43] These numbers diminished Brazil's standing within the international community, particularly in a decade when the social costs of the military period's development policies became evident and the economic growth was mediocre.

From a global perspective, the selection of Rio de Janeiro as the site for the United Nations Conference on Environment and Development in 1992 (also known as the 'Earth Summit') also established an equally important international landmark for Brazilian environmentalism. The Conference put environmental issues at the centre of diplomatic strategies for Brazil. Groups such as the National Rubber Tappers' Council had leverage to push forward their agendas, and the Conference increased this leverage. In fact, strengthened by the experience of the 1988 Constitution, grassroots organizations seized the Earth Summit as an opportunity to reinforce and renew domestic and international networks, building them into the backbone of the Brazilian civil society. Supported by the Association for the Progress of Communication, a progressive NGO from San Francisco, CA, IBASE (*Instituto Brasileiro de Análises Sócio-Econômicas* or Brazilian Institute for Socio-Economic Analyses) provided training and infrastructure for web-based communication among Brazilian non-profit organizations in a period when commercial internet had not yet made its appearance in Brazil. As a result, civil society organizations in Brazil take the Earth Summit as a reference point for the construction of alliances and collaborative networks even when their own priorities do not include directly environmental issues.

After 1992, the model of extractive reserves gained worldwide recognition. It proposed a kind of relationship between working communities and nature which attributed a high priority to the conservation of natural resources. Yet the extractive reserves are not an end in themselves. There are still many questions regarding their economic viability and the possibilities of replication in areas with larger human density or closer to urban centres.[44] Synthetic rubber has lower prices in the international market than Amazon rubber which places serious limitations to the potential of the extractive reserves when not subsidized to improve the material conditions of rubber tappers' lives. For the rubber tappers' communities, however, they represent a real alternative for survival in a healthy forest.

Legacy and challenges

The rubber tappers' movement offers a narrative that is simultaneously local, national and global. Their success placed the extractive reserves at the central focus of most projects for the definition and use of Amazon for the governments in the late twentieth century. When the Worker's Party leader Luiz Inácio Lula da Silva was elected president of Brazil in 2002, he drew heavily on his 'Acre connection' to form his environmental policy staff. During his centre-left administration, 'deforestation in the Amazon was reduced by more than 70 per cent (from 27,800 to 7,500 sq. km)'.[45] His Minister for the Environment, Marina Silva, created almost one hundred conservation units, including several extractive reserves. In many venues, however, the early twentieth-first century has brought as much disappointment as hope for the Amazon forest activists and for the rubber tappers. Lula's 'Acre connection' was much less influential than expected, particularly in his second term. The labelling of ecologically friendly products, a top priority for Marina Silva, was soundly defeated within the government. The advance of the soy agroindustry in the Southern frontier in the Amazon has been hailed as the cause of a boom in the Brazilian economy.[46] Local governments have enthusiastically promoted road building in the Amazon forest, and their development priorities have not changed since the military rule. Violence, as we have seen, is still much of a daily concern for rubber tappers and other forest people.

Nevertheless, there is little doubt that rubber tappers made their mark on the history of environmentalism in Brazil. Like most grassroots movements, its trajectory is very linked to its own time and place and cannot be easily replicated. Perhaps they would agree with the Mexican Zapatistas that each local movement may find support and inspiration in others, but must also find their own path. The rubber tappers' path was not without heavy human losses. For each leader such as Chico Mendes and Wilson, there were many unnamed rubber tappers who lost their lives in this endless conflict. But their struggle represents a success story of a community who fought for and achieved survival against tremendous odds.

Notes

1 Richard White, 'Are you an environmentalist or do you work for a living?' in William Cronon (ed.), *Uncommon Ground: Rethinking the Human Place in Nature* (New York: W. W. Norton, 1996), 174.

2 J. Timmons Roberts and Nikki Demetria Thanos, *Trouble in Paradise: Globalization and Environmental Crises in Latin America* (New York: Routledge, 2003), 132.
3 Greg Grandin, *Fordlandia: The Rise and Fall of Henry Ford's Forgotten Jungle City* (New York: Metropolitan Books, 2009).
4 Timmons and Thanos, *Trouble in Paradise*, 143.
5 Marcos Vinicius Neves, 'Uma breve história da luta acreana', in Carlos Carvalho and Sinara Sandri (eds), *Chico Mendes Vive—Caderno Povos da Floresta* (Rio Branco: Secretaria Executiva Comitê Chico Mendes, 2003), 13.
6 Neves, 'Uma breve história da luta acreana', 17. Caboclos are Brazilian of mixed ethnicity, usually European and Indian ancestry.
7 Xenia Wilkinson, *Tapping the Amazon for Victory: Brazil's 'Battle for Rubber' of World War II* (Doctoral diss., Unpublished. Washington, DC: Georgetown University, 2009), 136.
8 Gomercindo Rodrigues, *Walking the Forest with Chico Mendes: Struggle for Justice in the Amazon* (Austin: University of Texas Press, 2007).
9 Rodrigues, *Walking the Forest with Chico Mendes*, 35.
10 Rodrigues, *Walking the Forest with Chico Mendes*, 51.
11 Rodrigues, *Walking the Forest with Chico Mendes*,108.
12 Rodrigues, *Walking the Forest with Chico Mendes*, 111.
13 There is some debate on the date of this first *empate* in Brasiléia. Gomercindo Rodrigues claims it took place in 1973, while Sinara Sandri writes it happened in 1976, after the creation of the rubber tappers' union. Rodrigues, *Walking the Forest with Chico Mendes*, 111; Sinara Sandri, 'A assustadora década de 70', in Carvalho and Sandri (eds), *Chico Mendes Vive*, 25.
14 Elson Martins, 'Wilson Pinheiro e Chico Mendes: Semelhança que dói', in Carvalho and Sandri (eds), *Chico Mendes Vive*, 34.
15 Rodrigues, *Walking the Forest with Chico Mendes*, 115.
16 Rodrigues, *Walking the Forest with Chico Mendes*, 106.
17 Timmons and Thanos, *Trouble in Paradise*, 155.
18 Chico Mendes often claimed that the Catholic Church was the first voice to denounce crimes against rubber tappers. Sandri, 'A assustadora década de 70', 27.
19 Rodrigues, *Walking the Forest with Chico Mendes*, 127.
20 José Augusto Pádua, 'Chico Mendes Foi um Herói Ambiental?' *O Eco*, 11 July 2007. Available at: http://www.oeco.org.br/jose-augusto-padua-lista/17234-oeco23068 [accessed 12 May 2013].
21 Pádua, 'Chico Mendes Foi um Herói Ambiental?'
22 Rodrigues, *Walking the Forest with Chico Mendes*, 128.
23 Stefania Barca, 'On working-class environmentalism: A historical and transnational overview', *Interface: A Journal For and About Social Movements* 4:2 (November 2012), 61–80.
24 Barca, 'On working-class environmentalism: A historical and transnational overview', 73.
25 Rodrigues, *Walking the Forest with Chico Mendes*, 45.
26 Cristina Scheibe Wolff, *Mulheres da Floresta—Uma Historia Alto Jurua Acre (1890–1945)* (São Paulo: Hucitec, 1999), 19.
27 Rodrigues, *Walking the Forest with Chico Mendes*, 117.

28 Ramachandra Guha and Joan Martínez Alier, *Varieties of Environmentalism: Essays North and South* (London: Earthscan Publications, 1997).
29 Timmons and Thanos, *Trouble in Paradise*, 163.
30 Bernardo Loyola and Felipe Milanez (dir.), *Toxic Amazon*, Documentary (Vice Media, 2011). Available at: http://www.vice.com/toxic/toxic-amazon-full-length.
31 Kathryn Hochstetler and Margaret E. Keck, *Greening Brazil: Environmental Activism in State and Society* (Durham, NC: Duke University Press, 2007), 151.
32 Hochstetler and Keck, *Greening Brazil*, 12.
33 Eduardo J. Viola and Hector R. Leis, 'O ambientalismo multissetoral no Brasil para Além da Rio-92: O desafio de uma estratégia globalista viável', in Eduard J Viola. et al. (eds), *Meio Ambiente, Desenvolvimento e Cidadania: Desafios para as Ciências Sociais* (São Paulo: Cortez, 1995), apud Hochstetler and Keck, *Greening Brazil*, 65.
34 Hochstetler and Keck, *Greening Brazil*, 13.
35 Margaret E. Keck and Kathryn Sikkink, *Activist Beyond Borders: Advocacy Networks in International Politics* (Ithaca, NY: Cornell University Press, 1998).
36 Lise Fernanda Sedrez, *A Meeting of Minds: Coalitions, Representations and American Non-Governmental Organizations in the Brazilian Amazon* (Unpublished MSc thesis. Newark: New Jersey Institute of Technology, 1998); Hochstetler and Keck, *Greening Brazil*, 37.
37 Hochstetler and Keck, *Greening Brazil*, 165.
38 Hochstetler and Keck, *Greening Brazil*, 60.
39 Laure Emperaire and Jean-Paul Lescure list 24 species which are objects of extractive activities in the Brazilian Amazon, with variable degrees of sustainability, although not necessarily in extractive reserves. According to the authors, about one-third of the rural population in the Amazon practices extractive activities, which are necessary to the subsistence of their families. Laure Emperaire and Jean-Paul Lescure, 'Introduction', in Laure Emperaire (ed.), *A Floresta em Jogo—O Extrativismo na Amazônia Central* (São Paulo: UNESP, 2000), 16.
40 Hochstetler and Keck, *Greening Brazil*, 162.
41 Biorn Maybury-Lewis, 'Introduction to the English Edition', in Rodrigues (ed.), *Walking the Forest with Chico Mendes*, 16.
42 Catherine Aubertin, 'As reservas extrativistas: Inventário', in Emperaire (ed.), *A Floresta em Jogo*, 162.
43 Emperaire and Lescure, 'Introduction', 17.
44 Hochstetler and Keck, *Greening Brazil*, 168; Aubertin, 'As reservas extrativistas: Inventário', 162.
45 José Augusto Pádua, 'The politics of forest conservation in Brazil: A historical view', *Nova Acta Leopoldina* 114:390 (2013), 45.
46 Hochstetler and Keck, *Greening Brazil*, 180. Most of the area occupied by soy plantations is in the Cerrado ecosystem or transitional biomes, not in the Amazon forest. But the disintegration of local communities in the affected areas is depressingly similar to the process that took place in the 1970s in the Amazon, and it has expanded.

Further reading

Coomes, Oliver T. and Bradford, Barham. 1994. 'The Amazon rubber boom: Labour control, resistance and failed plantation development revisited', *Hispanic American Historical Review* 74:2, 231–257.

Dean, Warren. 1987. *Brazil and the Struggle for Rubber: A Study in Environmental History*. Cambridge: Cambridge University Press.

Gross, Tony (ed.). 1992. *Fight for the Forest: Chico Mendes in His Own Words*. 2nd ed. London: Latin America Bureau.

Hall, Anthony L. 1997. *Sustaining Amazonia: Grassroots Action for Productive Conservation*. Manchester: Manchester University Press.

Hecht, Susana and Cockburn, Alexander. 1990. *The Fate of the Forest: Developers, Destroyers and Defenders of the Amazon*. London: Penguin.

Hochstetler, Kathryn and Keck, Margaret E. 2007. *Greening Brazil: Environmental Activism in State and Society*. Durham, NC: Duke University Press.

Keck, Margaret E. 1995. 'Social equity and environmental politics in Brazil: Lessons from the rubber tappers of Acre', *Comparative Politics* 27:4, 409–424.

Revkin, Andrew. 2004. *The Burning Season: The Murder of Chico Mendes and the Fight for the Amazon Rain Forest*. 3rd ed. Washington, DC: Island/Shearwater.

Rodrigues, Gomercindo. 2007. *Walking the Forest with Chico Mendes: Struggle for Justice in the Amazon*. Austin: University of Texas Press.

Stanfield, Michael Edward. 1998. *Red Rubber, Bleeding Trees: Violence, Slavery, and Empire in Northwest Amazonia, 1850–1933*. Albuquerque: University of New Mexico Press.

8

Garbage Under the Volcano: The Waste Crisis in Campania and the Struggles for Environmental Justice

Marco Armiero

A global tale of damnation and redemption

On 26 March 2009, Prime Minister Silvio Berlusconi inaugurated the incinerator in the town of Acerra, the only incinerator operating in Campania and the fulcrum of the entire governmental plan to deal with the waste crisis in the region.[1] That ceremony, very theatrical as usual in Berlusconi's style, came after fifteen years of emergency regime in the management of waste in Campania—the fifteen years during which Naples and its region had become a global icon of environmental bankruptcy, gripped between illegal toxic waste and piles of urban garbage accumulated in the streets. After damnation—and Naples was damned indeed by the mass media from all over the world[2]—the city needed its redemption; and there is no doubt that Berlusconi viewed himself as the perfect redeemer. After all, he had won the 2008 national election in part by promising to solve the long-running garbage crisis in Campania, overcoming the indecisions and contradictions which had paralyzed the centre-left coalition in power at both the national and local levels.

The inauguration ceremony for the new incinerator was planned as a celebration of that redemption; modernity and technology, embodied in the incinerator, were the keys to exit the waste crisis. However, as in every sacred representation, to make the redemption glittering, it was necessary to pass through the damnation, to retell the story of the perdition in which the city was immersed. In other words, celebrating the incinerator as the ultimate solution to the crisis implied condemning those who were guilty of opposing it, thereby delaying its realization. Pushing the red button which, according to the choreography of the event, would have switched on the incinerator, Berlusconi solemnly declared that it was possible to inaugurate the plant because 'the State [was] back and [was] determined to defend legality also employing its force, even using the Army'. Just to clarify his thought, as if there were the need to do so, Berlusconi openly stated that demonstrations against waste facilities would not be tolerated any more.[3]

Later on during the redeeming celebration, Berlusconi and other speakers stressed that same point; building the incinerator in Acerra was a difficult deed because of politics, and not for technical reasons. According to that narrative, social opposition from local communities, long bureaucratic processes to obtain permissions and, finally, judicial investigations all conspired in slowing down the realization of the incinerator. Looking at the story of the waste crisis from that perspective, Berlusconi defined the managers of the corporation in charge of building and managing the incinerator in Acerra as 'heroes', brave and strong enough to persist and accomplish their mission.[4] Apparently, building the incinerator in spite of controls from public bodies and of social consensus was the main goal rather than actually solving the waste crisis in Campania.

Indeed, the inauguration of the incinerator in Acerra was conceived as a cathartic moment; the region exited from the darkness of garbage and entered into a new time of cleanness and modernity. As in a cartoon, the hero pushed the red button and the city was saved while the villains were definitively defeated; nevertheless, this time the gang of bad guys regrouped as a strange troop of local activists, radical politicians, public prosecutors and other public officials guilty of applying the normal rules even to those who were building the road to salvation, that is the incinerator. Here I do not need to stress the disruptive character of such public absolution of the managers of the corporation who were on trial. Actually, they were depicted not only as innocents but even as heroes fighting against all kinds of adversities, including judicial investigations.

The 26 March ceremony is an eloquent metaphor about the waste crisis in Campania and the struggles coming from it; of course, it mirrors the specificities of Italian society, especially in Berlusconi's age.[5] The attacks against the public prosecutors were not new arguments in Berlusconi's rhetoric. Nevertheless, the Campania story has a wider significance that goes beyond Italy, Berlusconi and his difficult relationships with the Italian judges. In fact, the inauguration of the Acerra incinerator also tells a global story about waste, power and grassroots resistance.

Garbage wars occur everywhere following the expansion of social metabolism and urbanization. As Joan Martínez Alier has repeatedly argued, in post-industrial societies, no dematerialization has actually occurred; those societies still consume large amounts of raw materials and energy and produce a remarkable quantity of waste.[6] Therefore, the problem of where to find raw materials and energy sources and where to put waste is absolutely crucial in the contemporary world. Conflicts over natural resources and waste facilities are the main by-product of this pattern of producing–consuming–disposing. While the former occur essentially at the external frontier of capitalism, the latter are also visible within it; the frontier of waste is located everywhere that a marginal, poor community exists which can be transformed into the ultimate dump for any kind of garbage.

In this chapter, I will not address the international dimension of waste trafficking, that is the illegal exportation of toxic materials, generally from rich to poor countries.[7] Instead, I will examine how the waste issue has contributed to creating a new awareness in subaltern communities about the connections between environmental and social injustices. In other words, I will explore the raising of the environmental justice movement from an eccentric perspective, that is from the unusual vision of the Neapolitan landscape filled with toxic contamination, piles of rubbish, pickets of activists and riot police. Of course this is not the standard Neapolitan scenery with its bay and Vesuvius, nor is it actually the classical background of the environmental justice tales. Black neighbourhoods in a US city, preferably in the South, or a Latino barrio in Los Angeles or any other minority island in the ocean of WASP America are the typical locations for those stories; after all, the environmental justice movement (EJM) was born precisely there in the 1980s when communities of colour began to resist to environmental injustice and racism.

The history of the EJM is deeply rooted in the history of the US civil rights movement; we might say that it is a unique variety of environmentalism strictly connected to the racial arrangement of the US society. Nevertheless, the EJM has also expanded beyond US society to become a global framework of another kind of environmentalism.

The vision of environmentalism as a pluralistic movement and the need to explore the role of subaltern social groups in shaping it are the main arguments of this chapter. Hence, take Naples, for instance.

Waste city

When in 2009 Berlusconi pushed the red button, Naples and the Campania region had already been under an emergency regime regarding the management of waste for fifteen years. Only such a gangrenous situation could have required an impressive staging such as that of 26 March in Acerra; a theatrical celebration was badly needed in order to erase years of failures in the management of waste, the negative images of the city submerged by garbage and the criticism of those who had opposed the incinerator and the government exit strategy from the crisis.

The waste emergency had officially started in 1994 when, facing the inefficiency of the local institutions, the national government took the management of waste upon itself, creating an ad hoc agency, the Committee for the Waste Emergency (*Commissariato di governo per l'emergenza rifiuti* in Campania, hereafter CWE).[8] The declaration of the state of emergency with the creation of the CWE implied that special measures were needed in order to solve the waste crisis in Campania; evidently regular procedures were not enough. As a matter of fact, the government granted special powers to the CWE which, in the name of the emergency, could violate European, national and regional rules and procedures, including environmental impact assessment.[9] Due to the combination of extraordinary power and an almost unlimited availability of funds, the CWE affected not only the management of waste but also the politics and economies of the entire region for about twenty years. Generally, the logic of emergency regimes does not mesh with democracy. Emergency regimes call for rapid solutions, strong decision-makers and minimum discussions; many times emergency regimes have entailed even martial law or, at least, some form of military repression with a suspension of citizens' rights. Mediations and scientific debates do not fit in the emergency framework. Those authoritarian aspects of the emergency regime are all present in the Campania case, which, as D'Alisa et al. have rightly said, is a crisis of democracy even more than an environmental crisis.[10]

Nevertheless, the assumption that complicated situations such as the waste crisis in Campania can only be solved with special measures which reduce the space of democracy has proved to be wrong. Despite its special powers and gigantic budget, the CWE has never delivered any solution for the crisis. The case of the 1998 public tender for the construction of waste facilities and the management of the entire cycle is emblematic; as Paolo Rabitti, consultant for the public attorney, has demonstrated, instead of seeking the most efficient technology and plan, the CWE awarded the tender to the bidder promising the lowest cost and quickest implementation of the project.[11] Furthermore, the 'delivery or pay' provision, which requires each municipality to send a certain amount of garbage to the incinerator or pay a penalty, has actually contributed to the low rate of recycling in Naples and Campania. The legacy of about twenty years of the CWE regime is the squandering of an incredible amount of Euros—in 2004 it was evaluated at 1.5 billion—and the million tons of *ecoballe*[12] piled up in the outskirts of Naples and Caserta.[13] Moreover, urged on by the cyclical waves of emergency which flooded Naples with thousands of tons of garbage, the CWE concentrated on finding short-term solutions—that is where to place

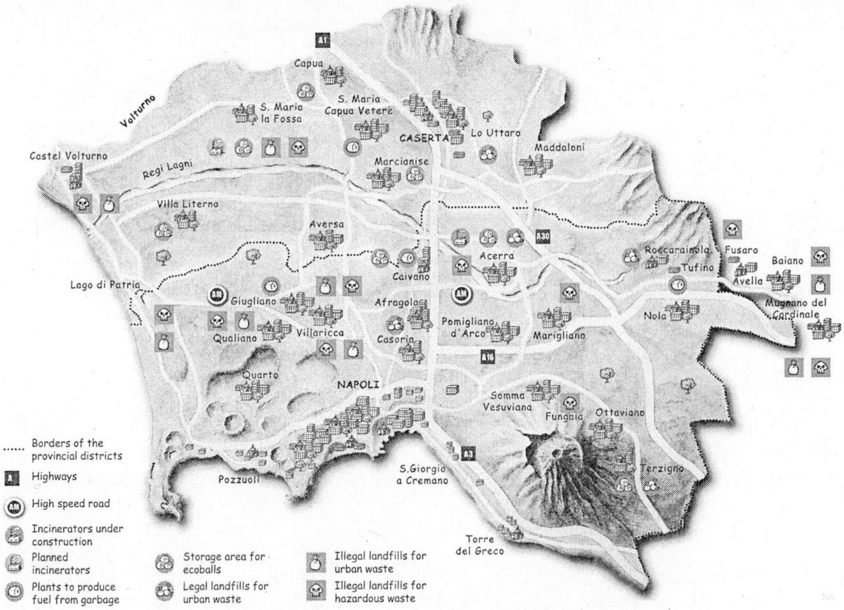

MAP 8.1 *The geography of waste in Campania.*
Author: Massimo Di Dato for Napoli Monitor. *Napoli Monitor* is a bimonthly magazine and a website, published by the association Cavalcavia. It publishes surveys, news, reports and cartoons about Naples and the world. Courtesy of Napoli Monitor (http://napolimonitor.it/).

the waste—without taking into due consideration safety measures in the building and management of garbage storage sites (Map 8.1).

The very idea that the waste crisis was an emergency is misleading. In fact, the roots of the waste crisis must be found in the 1980s when the Camorra, the Neapolitan Mafia, became interested in garbage. At that time the Camorra discovered that the disposal of toxic waste could become a far more lucrative business than urban waste collection, in which it has always had some interest. They were right: as a matter of fact, in 2011 the revenues from eco-criminal activities reached 16.6 billion Euros.[14] Specialized among other things in the extraction of rocks and sand for the building sector, the Camorra controls several quarries that can be transformed into gigantic dumps for all kinds of waste. In the dualistic structure of the Italian society,[15] the South found its position within the capitalistic trade-mill of production, becoming the cheap trash can of the factories from the North. Several criminal investigations have uncovered the illegal traffic of toxic waste from the industrial North to the semi-rural South, managed by the Camorra with the complicity of corrupt politicians.[16] According to the Italian NGO Legambiente, which coined the term 'ecomafia', about thirteen million tonnes of waste have been illegally disposed of in Campania between 2006 and 2008.[17] It is due to those criminal activities that Campania today has the largest contaminated areas in the entire nation, consisting in all of about 2,500 highly polluted sites. According to the journal *Sapere*, almost the entire province of Naples needs to be decontaminated.[18] While the diffuse presence of illegal dumps in Campania is a fact,[19] it remains challenging and rather controversial to establish any kind of causal correlation between them and health issues among the inhabitants of Campania. In 2004, *Lancet Oncology* published an article entitled 'The Triangle of Death' which supported the thesis of a correlation between illegal dumping and specific illness,[20] but it was criticized by several scholars for its methodological weaknesses.[21]

Nevertheless, after that article other studies have been published on the health effects of illegal dumping in Campania. In 2004, a team of researchers published an article in the academic journal *Epidemia e prevenzione* arguing that in the area of Villaricca and Qualiano municipalities the death rate for lung, larynx, bladder, liver and brain cancer, as well as for cardiovascular diseases and diabetes, was significantly higher than the national average.[22] According to another research project in the province of Caserta, the areas most affected by illegal dumping were also more exposed to foetal distress, low birth weight and childhood cancers.[23] Scientifically proving a definite causal association between toxic waste and health issues is difficult. Nevertheless, the abnormal number of cases of specific diseases or birth defects in the areas most affected by illegal dumping should be an alarm bell calling for deeper research. Instead, too often that alarm has been covered and only thanks to the mobilization of activists have new studies and tools been implemented. For instance, in 2008, the region sponsored the first biomedical research on contamination in human blood and milk which was the institutional response to the popular anxiety on that matter[24]; in 2012, under the pressure of activists and public opinion, the regional government of Campania approved the creation of a centralized register of cancer cases,[25] a decision which still awaits approval from the national government.[26]

However, for a long time this contamination haunting soil, air, water and bodies in Campania has remained hidden, completely absent from the mainstream narrative about the waste emergency. Indeed, the emergency was only about the visible: that is, the piles of trash bags in the streets of Naples. Therefore, incinerators and landfills were the solution, the magic boxes with which to make the garbage disappear; decontamination and biomedical research on the effects of toxic waste were not on the emergency agenda. Again, it was thanks to the activists' mobilization that those issues entered into the public discourse about the waste crisis in Campania, although without affecting the State's intervention in terms of reclamation and public health policies. The incinerator was indeed inaugurated, but as for the decontamination, the Campania inhabitants still have to wait.

Environmental injustice, or it never rains but it pours

The waste crisis of Campania entails two complementary environmental injustices; on one hand, Campania, one of the poorest regions in Italy,[27] has been chosen to be the sacrifice zone for the rest of the country, supporting the economic growth of the North by hosting its toxic waste. On the other hand, the most marginal, already contaminated and poor communities in the region have become the target of a government and corporate plan to solve the so-called waste emergency. Hence, while the entire region was filled with toxic waste from the North, some specific communities became the ideal location for any kind of waste facilities, such as incinerators, landfills and storage sites for million tonnes of ecoballe, that is fuel from garbage. It is no surprise that those communities were also the most affected by illegal dumping; as everywhere, also in Campania the path of least resistance has always led towards the same communities.

Acerra, for instance, the location for the impressive celebration of 26 March 2009, and, above all, the town chosen to host the incinerator, was already polluted before the arrival of the new waste facility. In 2001, the regional agency for environmental protection detected that 21 per cent of 117 wells in Acerra were polluted,[28] while in 2003 the ENEA[29] found a significant concentration of dioxin in the soil exactly in the area destined to host the incinerator[30]; finally, public prosecutors have sequestrated 25 illegal dumps situated in the municipalities of Nola, Marigliano and Acerra.[31] The case of Acerra is not an exception; in another case the CWE decided to open a landfill in exactly the same area as an illegal dump.[32] After all, an already contaminated territory seemed the perfect location for further contamination.[33] The same pattern occurred in Pianura, a working-class neighbourhood at the western periphery of Naples, where a gigantic landfill had operated for about fifty years, from the 1950s to the 1990s, swallowing all kinds of urban and toxic waste. While the promised reclamation of the area was never implemented, in 2007 the CWE tried to reopen that landfill but failed due to strong popular opposition and a judicial investigation into the epidemic and environmental disaster related to the Pianura dump.[34] Again, reopening a site that had been so deeply contaminated appeared the best option to address the emergency. The same can be said about the storage of ecoballe; Giugliano, the town that came to host the largest area of ecoballe, is part of the so-called Land of Fires where illegal dumps of toxic waste are continuously burned by eco-criminals. In his report for the public prosecutor Alessandro Milita, who is investigating the waste crisis, the geologist Giovanni Balestri has confirmed the pollution of water and soil in Giugliano; Balestri bluntly defines that situation as an 'environmental disaster'.[35]

Acerra, Pianura and Giugliano had been chosen to become the terminal of waste in the Campania region because they were already contaminated, but the choice actually also involved a range of other environmental and social reasons. In fact, besides being polluted, those communities seemed also socially weak, able to be easily bribed with the offer of jobs or even primary services as compensation, such as sewage system and public illumination.[36]

Instead those communities have showed an incredibly high resistance to the government-corporate plan aiming at transforming their territories in dumps. In Acerra, Pianura and Giugliano, as well as elsewhere in Campania, activists have confronted repression and blandishments while proposing different solutions to the waste crisis.[37] Therefore, the story of the waste crisis in Campania is also the story of a new form of environmentalism that has been defined as the environmental justice movement, or subaltern environmentalism.

As Laura Pulido has observed, 'subaltern environmentalism is embedded in material and power struggles, as well as questions of identity and quality of life'.[38] This is an environmentalism that brings together social and environmental issues, assuming that only through social changes will it be possible to attain a better environment for everyone. As an organized and self-conscious movement, the EJM was born in the United States around the beginning of the 1980s; most of the stories of the movement start with the protests in Afton, North Carolina, when the local African-American community began to resist a planned mega-dump for highly toxic polychlorinated biphenyls (PCBs). Although the protesters failed to stop the project, the Afton movement nevertheless became very influential in revealing the unequal distribution of environmental burdens across the entire nation.[39] Following the Warren County mobilization, several studies were produced on the social and racial patterns of environmental inequalities in the United States, proving the existence of what Benjamin Chavis called 'environmental racism'.[40] According to those studies, racial minorities were more likely to live in contaminated environments and pay with their health for economic growth. Race has always been at the core of the EJM as the connection to the civil rights movement clearly demonstrates. While there is a never-ending debate among scholars about the predominance of race or class in the causes of environmental injustice,[41] I agree with Laura Pulido that economic relations, race and ethnicity and cultural identity are key analytical categories in understanding those subaltern environmental struggles.[42]

For this reason, I believe that the expression 'subaltern environmentalism' is extremely powerful, encompassing all the varieties in non-mainstream environmentalism.[43] Love Canal, for instance, was one of the earliest and most dramatic environmental justice struggles in the United States, involving a highly toxic dump buried mostly under the local elementary school, but that conflict was not framed in terms of race, at least not by the key actors involved in the struggle.[44]

This is also the case in Campania, where the racial issue is essentially absent; the residents of Acerra, Giugliano and Pianura, and more in general the inhabitants of Campania are mostly white, and they do not belong to any ethnic minority.[45] Instead, as I have already argued, Campania as a whole and specifically the communities more affected by both legal and illegal dumping are poorer in terms of income and marginal in relation to the metropolitan powers, that is Naples at the regional level and the industrialized North at the national level.

Apart from the racial issue, the Campania case is a potent example of subaltern environmentalism. First of all, it opens up the canon of 'environmentalism', going far beyond its standard definition. The majority of the activists I have interviewed prefer not to be defined as environmentalists; according to them, being an environmentalist would limit their activism, while they feel that their struggles go beyond the classical ecological battles. Even in terms of political biographies, the majority of the Campania activists do not have any 'green' background; rather, a large number of them come from some kind of leftist culture while others simply do not have any previous political experience. As in the emblematic environmental justice movement, also in Campania the 'environment' has been redefined by those activists in a broader sense. In the United States, environmental justice activists used to say that the environment is where one lives, studies, plays and prays, intending therefore to overcome the dichotomy between the space of daily life and that of nature.[46] In other words, they are not interested in an environmentalism that protects wilderness somewhere far away and neglects the problems of their daily environments.

The environmental justice activists, in Campania as everywhere, are able to see the connections linking places, bodies, power and science; defending their neighbourhoods, they defend their health, they challenge the 'normal science',[47] and they criticize the power relationships among groups and territories. Although their environmentalism—if they would accept calling it environmentalism—is extremely anthropocentric, nevertheless it incorporates the basic notion of ecological thinking, that is the awareness that everything is connected with everything else.[48] In the environmental justice framework, the city is connected to the countryside, the production of goods to the disposal of waste, social structures to pollution and health.

Basically, the environmental justice movement uncovers the deep connections linking ecological problems and social issues; as the domination of nature always entails the domination of other human beings, the solutions for environmental problems come not only from technological-scientific expertise but must also be political, entailing social changes.

With this I do not want to dismiss the significance of science in environmental justice controversies; it is evident that in these cases both activists and their adversaries always make extensive use of science. Experts of all kinds are mobilized to support opposing visions; however, while corporate and government bodies have access to an extraordinary arsenal of officially recognized expertise to sustain their claims, generally things are more challenging for activists. They do not have experts, laboratories and research teams working for them; by and large academic research has not gone in the directions they want to explore; and even when they are able to bring a case in court, public prosecutors do not always have the resources to scientifically address such complex issues.[49] The activists' critique of scientific knowledge does not question science per sé but rather the politics of science and the construction of authority in the scientific discourse; above all, activists claim their rights to be part of production and validation of knowledge. American scholar Jason Corburn defines activists' knowledge as 'street science', which, in his words, is a 'practice of science, political inquiry and action'.[50] Even if Corburn does not explicitly theorize it, I believe that street science is deeply connected to the conflict for environmental justice; after all, without any struggle, there would be no need for exploring other ways of knowing and legitimizing knowledge. First of all, before creating an alternative knowledge, environmental justice activists have experienced what Boaventura de Sousa Santos calls the 'internal plurality of science',[51] that is the fact that scientists disagree on controversial matters, even if too often some theories—generally those supporting corporate or government interests—have become stronger in both the academic and the public spheres. In Campania, activists have sought support from official experts; they have badly needed geologists, physicians, biologists, engineers and others who could scientifically demonstrate the validity of their concerns. Lay people know through stories, smells, smoke and experiences; they have drawn maps of contaminations and illness; they have collected medical records which testify to years of exposure to toxins; nevertheless, they aim at translating—better off, validating—that knowledge within a scientific discourse. Hence, activists' knowledge, or as Corburn defines it, 'street science' does not deny the necessity of official science, rather it seeks to influence the agenda of scientific research; what is denied is the neutral character of science and technology and the theoretically apolitical nature of the researcher. On the ground, the relationships between activists and scientists have been rather complicated; the local university in Naples has strongly avoided any 'contamination' with the activists' movement, even refusing to host the international conference on Zero Waste in 2009. In interviews several activists have lamented the minimal level of collaboration from the Neapolitan academics. 'They are all barons', stated Crescenzo referring to the faculties of the Neapolitan universities,[52] while Roberto argues that they have been just indifferent to the crisis.[53] The few experts who have stood by the activists' side confirm the indifference or even the hostility of the academic establishment. Antonello Petrillo, professor of sociology and author of an excellent Foucauldian account of the waste crisis,[54] says in the interview that:

> Probably our research is the only one on the subject coming from the social sciences and humanities. The behaviour of the Neapolitan intellectuals has been really bad. In the local newspapers the big names were all against the movements. It is the two cities, again, the well-educated city, in contact with the world, and the plebeian city which acts as ballast for the other.[55]

Angelo Genovesi, professor at the Veterinary School, speaks of the indifference of his colleagues and the difficulties in advancing his academic career (even if more connected with his independent thinking rather than just with his involvement in the waste movements),[56] while Alberto Lucarelli, professor of public law, recognizes the risks connected with standing at the activists' side if one wishes to pursue an academic career.[57] Although he cannot see any special pressure from the academy on him for his work with the activists, geologist Franco Ortolani refers that some Italian geologists have criticized his support for the protesters during a very popular television talk show.[58] According to Antonio Marfella, medical researcher at the National Institute for the Study of Tumors Fondazione G. Pascale, his public exposition in the struggles over incinerators and landfills has affected—negatively, of course—his career.[59] According to Alfredo Mazza, the publication of his famous article 'The Triangle of the Death'[60] ended his career in the Italian Civil Protection.[61]

However, those stories can also be read in a different way; while on one hand they prove the difficult relationships with the official science, on the other, they also testify to the existence of a network of scholars supporting activists' claims. In the case of Campania, activists and scholars have created a sort of popular university, the Assise di Palazzo Marigliano, which has organized weekly meetings, a periodical publication and several pamphlets on every aspect of the waste crisis.[62] Almost all the activists and experts interviewed in our oral history project have referred to the Assise as a point of reference in their personal and collective experience. The Assise has been a sort of collective brain aimed at supporting the struggles with strong scientific arguments; today, many people recognize that one of the fruits of the crisis in Campania has been the amazing competence developed by ordinary citizens regarding waste. I would say that while several times experts have become activists—or have gone back to their history of activism—almost always activists have turned out to be experts, able to address complicated issues in a competent way. The websites of the grassroots organizations are full of 'scientific' materials produced by both experts and the activists themselves.

Conclusion

According to David Harvey, garbage is an excellent metaphor for the postmodern condition representing the changing forms of capitalism and, particularly, its instantaneity.[63] Goods and values are produced to be trashed and any attachment to things, people and spaces is overcome by a consumerist practice.

The production of waste implies also the production of space; dumps must be created, changing the ecology and identity of places. Indeed garbage is a powerful maker of places; nothing remains the same when it arrives. Garbage draws the hierarchies among spaces and groups, clearly defining on the ground winners and losers, rich and poor, subalterns and elite. As David Pellow has remarked, 'in most parts of the world, those social groups that consume the most natural resources and create most of the waste and pollution are the least likely to have to live or work near the facilities that manage those environmental "bads"'.[64] The environmental justice movement or, in a broadened sense, any form of subaltern environmentalism has arisen from that unequal condition. Those movements have questioned the separation between social and environmental issues; according to that vision, the exploitation of nature always occurs through the exploitation of subalterns. Actually, social inequalities have become spatial and environmental inequalities inscribing patterns of injustice even into bodies through exposure and illness. Hence, the poor and the subaltern share a huge part of the environmental costs of economic growth and urbanization, but this is not news, we already knew this. Instead the news is that they fight back; the assumption that they were too poor, ignorant or powerless to care about environmental issues was proven wrong. Of course, a subaltern vision of environmental issues has changed the very content of what we mean by 'environmental issues'. Well known is the reaction of mainstream environmentalist organizations to the quest for help coming from a coalition of Latino women fighting against an incinerator in Los Angeles: according to them, those women raised a public health issue and not an environmental one.[65] If today this answer would seem awkward even for the majority of mainstream environmentalists—probably with the exception of the most conservative ones—it is because subaltern environmentalism has been able to affect the general understanding of nature and of its relationships with social structures, and, above all, it has changed the environmentalist movement. Choosing to focus on the struggles in Campania, I argue that this shift in environmentalism has not affected only the United States where the environmental justice movement was born and is particularly strong; Joan Martínez Alier has demonstrated that the environmentalism of the poor actually involved a large majority of people defending their livelihood and health in the South. The story of the waste crisis in Campania shows that subaltern environmentalism is neither only a matter of the US racialized society nor of the global South; it is now worldwide and it is adapting to the different social and natural environments.

By definition, the movements for environmental justice are generally rather local; they are strongly connected to specific places or problems. Nevertheless, they have often been able to build larger coalitions. In the case of Campania, activists have created coalitions among various grassroots committees, generally avoiding an egoistic NIMBY approach; as they say in their slogans, the incinerator should be built 'neither here nor elsewhere'. Furthermore, in many cases starting from the issue of garbage, those grassroots organizations have enlarged their field of action to other and wider issues; they are part of a larger movement against a certain type of modernization based on huge infrastructures, thereby exchanging support with the communities fighting against the High Speed Train in the Susa Valley. Many of those grassroots organizations have started to frame their struggles around the issue of commons and broaden its definition to include health, education, water and the right to a job. I have learnt this lesson from Mena, one activist I interviewed; I asked Mena how it happened that she got interested in waste and she replied to me: 'I am not an activist on garbage, but on commons.'[66]

With the rise of the movement for climate justice, environmental justice has moved beyond its local/small-scale approach. Once again as in the past, subaltern environmentalism is challenging the mainstream environmental narrative on climate change; facing a rampant depoliticization of that discourse, subaltern environmentalism has put power and social inequalities back in the picture. Hopefully climate justice will be able to change the environmentalist discourse on climate change just as the environmental justice movement has been able to affect mainstream environmentalism.

Acknowledgements

The research project 'Lares—Landscape of Resistance. Science, Power, and Environmental Justice in the Struggle over Garbage and Incinerators in Contemporary Naples, Italy' has been funded by the Marie Curie Intra European Fellowship under the Seventh Framework Programme for Research (FP7). Research for this paper benefited also from the People Program ENTITLE (European Union's Seventh Framework Programme, REA agreement No. 289374). Many thanks to Veronika Fukson and Peder Roberts for their editorial work on the language. Finally, my respectful thanks to the activists in Naples who have helped me in understanding the garbage crisis.

Notes

1 'Rifiuti, Berlusconi inaugura il termovalorizzatore di Acerra: Lo Stato c'è', *Il Sole24ore* 26 March 2009. Available at: http://www.ilsole24ore.com/art/SoleOnLine4/Italia/2009/03/acerra-berlusconi-termovalorizzatore.shtml?uuid=931a50c8–19fe-11de-b1e2–5d56434cd0c1DocRulesView=Libero.

2 On this, see Marco Armiero and Giacomo D'Alisa, 'La ciudad de los residuos. Justicia ambiental e incertidumbre en la crisis de los residuos en Campania (Italia)', *Ecologia Politica* 41 (2011), 95–96.

3 I am referring here to a press conference with Prime Minister Silvio Berlusconi in October 2010. Available at: http://wwww.ansa.it/web/notizie/rubriche/politica/2010/10/28/visualizza_new.html_1727172260.html.
4 Parts of Berlusconi's discourse are available at: http://tg24.sky.it/tg24/cronaca/2009/03/26/Termovalorizzatore_Acerra_Berlusconi_Lo_Stato_ce.html.
5 On the Italian society in Berlusconi's age, see Paul Ginsborg, *Berlusconi: ambizioni patrimoniali in una democrazia mediatica* (Turin: Einaudi, 2003); Michael E. Shin and John A. Agnew, *Berlusconi's Italy: Mapping Contemporary Italian Politics* (Philadelphia, PA: Temple University Press, 2008).
6 Joan Martínez Alier, *The Environmentalism of the Poor. A Study of Ecological Conflicts and Valuation* (Northampton, MA: Edward Elgar, 2002) 54, 100.
7 Don Liddick, 'The traffic in garbage and hazardous wastes: An overview', *Trends in Organized Crimes* 13:2–3 (2010), 134–146.
8 Cabinet order, 11 February 1994.
9 As a matter of fact, in a hearing of the Parliamentary Committee on the Waste Cycle an officer from the Ministry of the Environment stated that '[for the incinerator in Acerra] we are not doing a classic environmental impact assessment. Rather we are intervening in a process in which there is a general necessity which has led to some decisions, which for us is a starting point'. In Parliamentary Committee for Waste Cycle XXXIII/17, 14.
10 Giacomo D'Alisa, David Burgalassi, Hali Healy and Mariana Walter, 'Conflict in Campania: Waste emergency or crisis of democracy', *Ecological Economics* 70:2 (2010), 239–249.
11 Paolo Rabitti, *Ecoballe* (Rome: Aliberti, 2008).
12 The term 'ecoballe' indicates balls of packed garbage which should be prepared and sorted properly in order to be burnt in incinerators. The suffix 'eco' would imply that they would not harm the environment or human health. Actually, the parliamentary and judicial investigations have demonstrated that those ecoballe were not well prepared and harmless. In the Parliamentary Committee on Waste, one can read: 'They [the ecoballe] contained too high a percentage of both arsenic and humidity, and entire objects have been found in them, for instance, a wheel with rim and tire, which proves the absence of any kind of screening'; in Parliamentary Committee for Waste Cycle, XXIII/12, 32. See also Court of Naples, Office of the Judge for Preliminary Investigations Rosanna Saraceno, SECTION XXXIII, RG.R.N. No. 15940/03; RG.GIP No. 21810/04.
13 The Corte dei Conti (the Italian institution for safeguarding public finance) has stigmatized the waste of public money made by the CWE with sentence no. 4174/07, Corte dei Conti—Sezione Giurisdizionale per la Regione Campania. See also Marco Armiero, 'Seeing like a protester: Nature, power, and environmental struggles', *Left History* 13:1 (2008), 64–66.
14 Data from Legambiente website: http://www.legambiente.it/contenuti/comunicati/ecomafia-2012-le-storie-e-i-numeri-della-criminalita-ambientale.
15 As it is well known, historically, Italy has been represented as a dichotomic country composed by two macro regions, the richer and more industrialized North and the poorer and backward South. In the 1980s, not only a group of scholars, especially historians, but also economists and sociologists

criticized that trenchant narrative about the Italian South; they started a new interdisciplinary journal *Meridiana* which for a long time became the expression of their revisionistic approach to the Italian South. In English, see Robert Lumley and Jonathan Morris (eds), *The New History of the Italian South* (Exeter: Exter University Press, 1997).

16 The most important among these investigations are Adelphi, Cassiopea, Re Mida, Green, Terra mia, Ultimo atto, Madre terra and Eldorado.

17 Legambiente-Osservatorio Ambiente e Legalità, *Ecomafia 2009. Le storie e i numeri della criminalità ambientale* (Città di Castello: Genesi, 2009), 79.

18 Consiglio Nazionale delle Ricerche, Relazione sullo stato delle conoscenze in tema di ambiente e salute nelle aree ad alto rischio in Italia, 2007, p. 6. Available at: http://www.cnr.it/documenti/83_Relazione_aree_a_rischio.pdf.

19 In the early 2000, several scientific investigations proved the presence of dioxin contamination in the milk of cows, goats and sheep. On this, see Leopoldo Iannuzzi et al., 'Chromosome fragility in two sheep flocks exposed to dioxins during pasturage', *Mutagenesis* 19:5 (2004), 355–359; Angela Perucatti et al., 'Increased frequencies of both chromosome abnormalities and SCEs in two sheep flocks exposed to high dioxin levels during pasturage', *Mutagenesis* 21:1 (2006), 67–75. Less 'scientific' but very effective was the television documentary 'Allarme cibo avvelenato', first broadcast 15 December 2007 by La7 Network. Available at: http://www.la7.it/blog/post_dettaglio.asp?idblog=ILARIA_DAMICO_-_Exit_15&id=1509.

20 Kathryn Senior and Alfredo Mazza, 'Italian "Triangle of death" linked to waste crisis', *The Lancet Oncology* 5:9 (2004), 525–527.

21 Fabrizio Bianchi et al., 'Italian "Triangle of death"', *The Lancet Oncology* 5:12 (2004), 710; Benedetto Terracini, 'Discariche, triangoli e aree calde', *Epidemia e prevenzione* 28:6 (2004), 300.

22 Pierluigi Altavista et al., 'Mortalità per causa in un'area della Campania con numerose discariche di rifiuti', *Epidemia e Prevenzione* 28:6 (2004), 311.

23 The data regarding this report are quoted here from Altavista et al., 'Mortalità per causa in un'area della Campania con numerose discariche di rifiuti', 314.

24 Elena De Felip and A. Di Domenico (eds), *Studio epidemiologico sullo stato di salute e sui livelli d'accumulo di contaminanti organici persistenti nel sangue e nel latte materno in gruppi di popolazione a differente rischio d'esposizione nella Regione Campania* (Roma: Dipartimento Ambiente e connessa Prevenzione Primaria, Istituto Superiore di Sanità, 2010).

25 *Bollettino Ufficiale della Regione Campania*, No. 44, 16 July 2012—regional law No. 19.

26 M. La Penna and G. Ausiello, 'Registro tumori Campania, il governo chiede lo stop: costa troppo', *Il Mattino* 16 September 2010.

27 The average per capita GDP in Campania is the lowest of the country—about 67 per cent of the national average. The employment rate for people of working age fell for the first time below 40 per cent and in 2010 the proportion of households in which no one of the members was employed has raised of more than 27 per cent. Finally in 2009, the 25.1 per cent of the families lived in condition of relative poverty, that is one out of four families. Data from Istituto Nazionale di Statistica www.istat.it and from

Caritas (2010), Dossier regionale sulla povertà, available at: http://www.caritascampania.it/index.php?option=com_k2&view=item&id=1:dossier-regionale-della-caritas-2010-sulle-povert%C3%A0-in-campania&Itemid=101.

28 Alessandro Iacuelli, *Le vie infinite dei rifiuti* (Altrenotizie.org, 2007), 121–122.

29 ENEA stands for Italian National Agency for New Technologies, Energy and Sustainable Economic Development.

30 Iacuelli, *Le vie infinite dei rifiuti*, 124.

31 Parliamentary Committee on the Waste Cycle, XIV, 53.

32 This is the case of Castelluccio in the Salerno province; see the hearing of the sub commissioner Attilio Buonomo in front of the Parliamentary Committee, XIII, transcripts of the mission in Campania, 17 September 1997.

33 Robert Bullard, *Dumping in Dixie. Race, Class, and Environmental Quality* (Boulder, CO: Westview Press, 1990), 143.

34 On Pianura, see Marco De Biase, 'Lo stato attacca, Pianura risponde. Scenari, strategie, tattiche e azioni anti-discarica nella periferia occidentale napoletana', in Antonello Petrillo (ed.), *Biopolitica di un rifiuto. Le rivolte anti-discarica a Napoli e in Campania* (Verona: Ombre Corte, 2010).

35 I was unable to access the original of that report; the quotation is from Daniela De Crescenzo, 'Veleni nella cava. Il Dossier choc', *Il Mattino* 27 June 2010, 34.

36 In a focus group I have organized in Pianura with a group of activists, more or less all of them stated that the state offered such basic services as compensation for the reopening of the landfill.

37 Some examples of possible alternative solutions to the waste crisis are available at: http://www.rifiuticampania.org/rifiuticampania/indices/index_76.html and http://www.allarmerifiutitossici.org/.

38 Laura Pulido, *Environmentalism and Economic Justice. Two Chicano Struggles in the South West* (Tucson: The University of Arizona Press, 1996).

39 Bullard, *Dumping in Dixie*, 30.

40 Benjamin F. Jr Chavis, 'Preface', in Robert Bullard (ed.), *Unequal Protection: Environmental Justice and Communities of Color* (San Francisco, CA: Sierra Club Books, 1994), xi–xii.

41 Sheila Foster, 'Justice from the ground up: Distributive inequities, grassroots resistance, and the transformative politics of the environmental justice movement', *California Law Review* 86:4 (1998), 793–798.

42 Pulido, *Environmentalism and Economic Justice*, p. XX.

43 'Varieties of environmentalism' was the title chosen by Joan Martínez Alier and Ramachandra Guha for their book on the various streams of the environmental movement (London: Earthscan Publications, 1997).

44 On Love Canal in general, see Thomas Fletcher, *From Love Canal to Environmental Justice* (Peterborough: Broadview Press, 1985); Murray Levine and Lois Gibbs, *Love Canal. My Story* (New York: Grove Press, 1982). For a revision of the story with a race, class and gender perspective, see Elizabeth D. Blum, *Love Canal Revisited. Race, Class, and Gender in Environmental Activism* (Lawrence: University of Kansas, 2008).

45 Actually, Antonello Petrillo, referring to a longstanding tradition of political discourse which has 'racialized' the differences between Northern and

Southern Italy, has argued that a racial narrative is hidden in the Campania case; in Antonello Petrillo, 'Le urla e il silenzio. Depoliticizzazione dei conflitti e parresia nella Campania tardo liberale', in Antonello Petrillo (ed.), *Biopolitica di un rifiuto. Le rivolte anti-discarica a Napoli e in Campania* (Verona: Ombre Corte, 2009), 20–23. According to that characterization, the South was a provincial but still radical otherness, repository of primitiveness, savagery and archaism, the archetypal land of any kind of pre-modern rebellion; on this, see Marco Armiero, *A Rugged Nation. Mountains and the Making of Modern Italy* (Cambridge: White Horse Press, 2011), 62–75. The same concepts, imaginaries and keywords have been employed to stigmatize the current waste crisis.

46 Patrick Novotny, *Where We Live, Work and Play: The Environmental Justice Movement and the Struggle for a New Environmentalism* (Westport: Praeger Publisher, 2000).

47 The concept of 'normal science' comes from Thomas Kuhn and implies the centrality of scientific paradigms which actually fix the limits of the scientific inquiry.

48 This is the first of the four laws of ecology as formulated in Barry Commoner, *The Closing Circle* (London: Cope 1972).

49 This is the case of the criminal investigation on the Pianura landfill in Naples which was interrupted due to the lack of financial resources for the experts.

50 Jason Corburn, *Street Science. Community Knowledge and Environmental Health Justice* (Cambridge, MA: The MIT Press, 2005), 44.

51 Boaventura de Sousa Santos, 'Beyond abyssal thinking. From global lines to ecologies of knowledges', *Review* xxx:1 (2007), 70.

52 ACE, Interview with Crescenzo, in the author's possession.

53 ACE, Interview with Roberto, in the author's possession.

54 Petrillo, 'Le urla e il silenzio'.

55 ACE, Interview with Antonello Petrillo, in the author's possession.

56 ACE, Interview with Angelo Genovesi, in the author's possession.

57 ACE, Interview with Alberto Lucarelli, in the author's possession.

58 ACE, Interview with Franco Ortolani, in the author's possession. The talk show was *Porta a Porta* broadcasted by RAI1 on 10 January 2008.

59 ACE, Interview with Antonio Marfella, in the author's possession.

60 Senior and Mazza, 'Italian "Triangle of death" linked to waste crisis', 2004.

61 ACE, Interview with Alfredo Mazza, in the author's possession.

62 Available at: http://www.napoliassise.it/.

63 David Harvey, *The Condition of Postmodernity: An Enquiry into the Origins of Cultural Change* (Oxford: Blackwell, 1989), 286. I own this reference to Julie Sze, *Noxious New York. The Racial Politics of Urban Health and Environmental Justice* (Cambridge, MA: The MIT Press, 2007), 117.

64 David N. Pellow, *Garbage Wars: The Struggle for Environmental Justice in Chicago* (Cambridge, MA: The MIT Press, 2002), 1.

65 Giovanna Di Chiro, 'Nature as community. The convergence of environmental and social justice', in William Cronon (ed.), *Uncommon Ground. Rethinking the Human Place in Nature* (New York: W. W. Norton, 1995), 299.

66 ACE, Interview with Mena, in the author's possession.

Further reading

Bullard, Robert. 1990. *Dumping in Dixie: Race, Class, and Environmental Quality*. Boulder, CO: Westview Press.

Cole, Luke W. and Foster, Sheila R. 2001. *From the Ground Up. Environmental Racism and the Rise of the Environmental Justice Movement*. New York: New York University.

Gottlieb, Robert. 1993. *Forcing the Spring. The Transformation of the American Environmental Movement*. Washington, DC: Island Press.

Gottlieb, Robert. 2001. *Environmentalism Unbound: Exploring New Pathways for Change*. Cambridge, MA: The MIT Press.

Hofrichter, Richard. 1993. *Toxic Struggles. The Theory and Practice of Environmental Justice*. Philadelphia: New Society Publishers.

Hurley, Andrew. 1995. *Environmental Inequalities. Class, Race, and Industrial Pollution in Gary, Indiana, 1945–1980*. Chapel Hill: University of North Carolina Press.

Martínez Alier, Joan. 2005. *The Environmentalism of the Poor: A Study of Ecological Conflicts and Valuation*. New Delhi: Oxford University Press.

Melosi, Martin. 1981. *Garbage in the Cities: Refuse, Reform, and the Environment: 1880–1980*. College Station: Texas A&M University Press.

Melosi, Martin. 2000. 'Equity, eco-racism and environmental justice movement', in J. Donald Hughes (ed.), *The Face of the Earth. Environment and World History*. New York: Armonk-M. E. Sharpe.

Sandler, Ronald and Pezzullo, Phaedra C. (eds). 2007. *Environmental Justice and Environmentalism. The Social Justice Challenge to the Environmental Movement*. Cambridge, MA: The MIT Press.

Shaw, Randy. 2008. *Beyond the Fields: Cesar Chavez, the UFW, and the Struggle for Justice in the 21st Century*. Berkeley: University of California Press.

Szasz, Andrew. 1994. *EcoPopulism: Toxic Waste and the Movement for Environmental Justice*. Minneapolis: University of Minnesota Press.

Sze, Julie. 2007. *Noxious New York: The Racial Politics of Urban Health and Environmental Justice*. Cambridge, MA: The MIT Press.

9

The Great Fear: European Environmentalism in the Atomic Age

Hein-Anton van der Heijden

Introduction

In the 1970s, millions of committed citizens in more than thirty countries worldwide took to the streets and construction sites in order to prevent the introduction of nuclear power in their countries, or to fight for its abandonment.[1] The anti-nuclear movement that gave shape to this resistance could be considered as one of the most influential social movements of the past decades.[2] Its action campaigns resulted not only in a fundamental rethinking of nuclear technology as one of the three strategic technologies of postwar modernity,[3] but also in a basic reconsideration of the very institutional features of modernity itself: capitalism, industrialism, surveillance and military power.[4] Apart from this, the anti-nuclear movement has largely contributed to the emergence of a completely new type of political parties in major European countries: green parties.

During the forty years following the emergence of the anti-nuclear movement, apart from innumerable smaller incidents, one major nuclear accident (Three Miles Island 1979) and two full-blown global nuclear disasters have occurred: Chernobyl (1986) and Fukushima (2011). All three events resulted in increasing doubts about nuclear energy as a reliable future energy source, but not into its complete opting out. Whereas some politicians keep considering nuclear energy as a necessary—whether or not transitory—alternative to fossil fuels in order to stop climate change, other politicians, as well as the environmental and anti-nuclear movement, do not stop to argue that the nuclear alternative discourages a plain choice in favour of renewable energy choices like solar and wind.

In this chapter, the history of the European environmental movement against nuclear energy will be analysed. The story starts with the large-scale grassroots resistance in the 1970s and early 1980s in a number of West European countries, by which the anti-nuclear movement as a new social movement established its fame. However, despite the magnitude of the resistance, the successes of the anti-nuclear movement largely differed from one country to another. In order to explain these differences, the concept of Political Opportunity Structure (POS) will be introduced, and the different kinds of impacts of the anti-nuclear movement will be analysed accordingly. In the section thereafter, the history of the European anti-nuclear movement from Chernobyl (1986) to Fukushima (2011) will be told. Whereas in the years up to Chernobyl anti-nuclear movements in Central and Eastern Europe hardly existed, in the second half of the 1980s they played a pivotal role in undermining the legitimacy of the communist state-bureaucratic regimes in the former Soviet Union and in some Central and East European countries. In Western Europe, apart from Germany, large-scale grassroots resistance against nuclear energy was restricted to a short period of time after the Chernobyl disaster. In the years to follow, apart from Germany again, the European anti-nuclear movement lost much of its strength, and environmental movement organizations like Greenpeace and Friends of the Earth largely took over the baton. One important new feature of the movement, however, was its gradual turn from a '*movement against*' (nuclear energy) into a '*movement in favour of*' (sustainable energy). The final section of this chapter shortly assesses the history of the European anti-nuclear movement after the Fukushima disaster: Which activities did the movement display, what role does nuclear energy play in Europe after Fukushima, and how can its future be conceived of?

The anti-nuclear movement as a new social movement

From the end of the Second World War to the first oil crisis (1973), Western Europe experienced a period of uninterrupted economic growth, going along with a rapidly increasing need of energy, and in major European countries nuclear energy was seen as the very option to cover future energy demands.

In some countries, especially Belgium and France, in the early 1970s nuclear energy already provided for a major part of national energy needs, and in many other countries detailed programmes existed for the construction of numerous new nuclear plants. These programmes reflected the high level of 'technological progress optimism' that was so characteristic of that period.

In France, for instance, Pierre Messmer, the then prime minister, announced that by the year 2000 France would operate 170 nuclear reactors supplying 85 per cent of all national electricity production.[5] In the Netherlands, a 1972 government memorandum assumed the necessary construction of 35 new nuclear plants, each with a capacity of 1,000 megawatt, by the year 2000.[6] The 1973 oil crisis painfully revealed that West European governments for continuing their economic growth were heavily dependent on oil from the Middle East. This made them highly vulnerable. Consequently, new nuclear energy programmes, or increased implementation of the existing ones, were deemed necessary, but at the same time these programmes increased the cleavage between the existing social order and the environmental/anti-nuclear movement.

The anti-nuclear movement could be considered as the archetype of a 'new social movement'. Challenging the scientifically hegemonic, US-based Resource Mobilization Approach (RMA), from the late 1970s onwards West European social movement scholars started to define the recently emerged women's, environmental, peace and other social movements as a 'qualitatively new type of social movement' (New Social Movement Approach). New social movements distinguished themselves from 'old' (labour, farmers, religious, regional)[7] movements by six specific features.[8]

1. An emphasis on 'post-materialist' rather than materialist values.
2. A constituency disproportionately belonging to the 'new middle class'.
3. A structure of organization characterized by decentralized networks of grassroots groups, granting direct participation to all the ones involved.
4. A fundamental distrust in the established political and economic system.[9]
5. A new, unconventional action repertoire, a core feature of which is that activists deliberately deploy their own bodies.
6. Activists not only engage in new social movements in order to change society; their engagement also produces new ideas and more sophisticated forms of political consciousness, resulting in the development of new, individual and collective, identities.

How do these features recur in the anti-nuclear movement?

1. Post-materialist rather than materialist values. In the way the resistance against nuclear energy in Western Europe has been framed, seven different ways of framing nuclear energy could be distinguished, all of which reflect post-materialist rather than materialist values.[10] In many cases, these definitions occurred complementary to one another.

a. *A local definition*. In this conception, a nuclear plant in or nearby a small village or township is considered to be an ultimate threat of the particular character of a local community. A nuclear plant has a big impact on community life, and supervising such plants goes far beyond the competencies of the local authorities. The final result would be a huge reduction of local autonomy.

b. *An anti-technological definition*. Because of the lack of knowledge about the consequences of a nuclear disaster, as up to now no satisfying solution to fundamental problems like the storage of nuclear waste has been found. According to the anti-technological definition, nuclear energy should be considered as an unreliable energy source and, consequently, should be declined.

c. *An anti-industrial definition*. According to this frame, nuclear energy neatly fits within the dominant philosophy of the modern, industrial era. Natural resources and people's rights to health and safety are sacrificed in order to enable limitless industrial expansion and economic growth. The anti-industrial definition challenges this hegemonic worldview.

d. *An anti-authoritarian definition*. In order to minimize the risks of accidents and sabotage, nuclear energy requires ever more control and, consequently, ever more centralization of power. The result is an increasing militarization of society ('the atom state'), and this is definitely not the kind of society in which people can optimally develop themselves.

e. *An anti-capitalist definition*. From this perspective, nuclear energy is considered to be an important instrument to combat the economic crisis by the late capitalist system as a whole, and by multinational corporations in particular. Consequently, contesting nuclear energy and contesting the capitalist system should go hand in hand.

f. *A pacifist definition*. According to this definition, the development of, on the one hand, 'peaceful' nuclear energy, and, on the other hand, developing nuclear weapons are intimately connected. Supporting nuclear energy implies supporting the further development of weapons of mass destruction and, therefore, should be rejected.

g. *A rational perspective*. According to this—explicitly non-ideological—perspective, nuclear energy is an outdated technology which is neither safe nor profitable. Consequently, it should be declined.[11]

Most of the definitions reflect 'post-materialist' rather than materialist values, and also challenge the hegemonic capitalist 'growth imperative'.

2. New middle-class constituency.

During the 1970s, most trade unions, communist parties, as well as large parts of social-democratic parties still firmly believed in straightforward economic growth and, thus, in the advantages, or even indispensability, of nuclear energy. Rural populations, such as farmers and fishermen, belonging to the old middle class, appear as frequent carriers of early protests, especially in countries like France, Germany, Italy and Norway (local definition). The lion's share of the resistance against nuclear energy, however, was carried out by conservation and political ecology groups, far-left political splinter parties, students groups, religious organizations, academic study groups and other predominantly new middle-class groups. In Austria, for instance, a large number of these groups joined forces, and the Austrian configuration of groups can be seen as emblematic for most West European countries.

The Citizens' Initiative against Atomic Hazards (BIAG), an offspring of conservative middle-class organizations like the World Alliance for the Protection of Life and the Nature Conservation Alliance, cooperated with the left-dominated Study Group Atomic Energy Linz. Whereas it was not possible to reconcile right and left in every respect, clashes especially marked the relationship between the BIAG, on the one hand, and the Maoist Communist Alliance Linz and its offshoot Action Committee against the Construction of the Nuclear Plant in St. Pantaleon, on the other hand. On site, the activists received support from groups that had formed in other regions, such as the Study Group Ecology in Salzburg and the Study Group Atomic Energy in Vienna.[12]

The names of the groups neatly reflect the activities and ideological orientations characteristic of the new middle class of those days all over Western Europe: study group, citizens' initiative, political ecology, Maoism, communism. Consequently, it is not difficult to reconstruct the different ways in which nuclear energy was defined, not only in Austria but also elsewhere in Western Europe. One only has to replace the names of countries, cities and nuclear sites in order to get a complete picture of the very exponents of the anti-nuclear resistance and its, heterogeneous, rationale all over Western Europe.

3. Decentralized networks of grassroots groups.

A (new) social movement has been defined as a network linking a number of quasi-autonomous groups and individuals through belief, values or common practices that engage in communication and exchange to negotiate a collective identity and opponent.[13] Although in Western Europe in the early 1970s, numerous new environmental movement organizations (EMOs) had been founded, the nuclear energy conflict was mainly fought out by men and women not belonging to any existing EMO. In the Netherlands, for instance, in the height of the conflict the radical part of the anti-nuclear movement consisted of 300 so-called basic groups, each of them having about fifteen members.[14] The only EMO clearly taking part in the conflict in several countries was Friends of the Earth (FoE), and in one case (Britain) FoE even took the initiative.

In some countries (Germany, France) the conflict emerged at the local level and was started by local and regional groups (Breisach and Whyl in Germany, the Alsace in France). Whereas in those countries no national umbrella organizations were founded, in most other countries during the 1970s national level anti-nuclear organizations developed themselves from the local level. Examples include the United Action Committees to halt Nuclear Energy (VAKS) in Belgium; the Anti-Nuclear Campaign (ANC) in Britain; the National Energy Group Stop Kalkar (LLSK) in the Netherlands; and the Initiative of Austrian Adversaries of Nuclear Energy (IOAG). In contrast to other national-level EMOs, however, these national anti-nuclear umbrella groups were rather weak, and until deep in the 1980s the anti-nuclear movement would remain a textbook example of a decentralized network of grassroots groups.

4. Distrust in the established political and economic system.

The emergence of anti-nuclear movements followed the end of the late 1960s to early 1970s protest cycle. In most cases, therefore, anti-nuclear protest developed in a political context which was deeply affected by a new emphasis on participatory democracy and the spread of critical political orientations to large sectors of society.[15] The boundaries between the women's, environmental, peace, squatters, anti-nuclear and other social movements were fluid; activists easily switched from one movement to another, dependent on which actual issue was at stake at a given place and time. One could even argue that all these activities reflected *one* broad social movement that challenged the very features of the established political and economic system. This is reflected in, for instance, the anti-technological, anti-industrial, anti-authoritarian and anti-capitalist framings of nuclear energy, all of which reflected a counter-hegemonic definition of reality.

5. Unconventional action repertoire.

As for the action repertoire, one may conclude that during the course of the conflict literally all available strategies from the social movement action repertoire have been applied.[16] Some forms of action, however, were more appropriate in some countries than in others, dependent on a country's specific political system. Local opposition, site occupations and mass demonstrations were key features in France and West Germany, whereas participation in hearings and public inquiries was the main course of action pursued in the United Kingdom. Litigation played an important role in West Germany. Other options were only available in certain countries: national referenda determined much of the conflict in Switzerland, Austria, Sweden and, indirectly, also in Denmark.[17] In most countries, strategies in the early years of the conflict (1971–1976) were relatively moderate, especially in countries with an open political system like Sweden where the movement mainly tried to influence decision making by lobbying. In countries like Spain, the Netherlands, France and Germany, however, in the second half of the 1970s and in the early 1980s the movement organized mass demonstrations that attracted tens of thousands of participants. Examples include the demonstrations in 1977 in Bilbao (Spain) (200,000 participants); in 1978 in Almelo (the Netherlands) (40,000 participants); in 1978 in Malville (France) (50,000 participants) and in 1981 in Brokdorf (Germany) (100,000 participants).

Especially in Germany and France, demonstrations sometimes ended in violent confrontations with the police. In Brokdorf, for instance, 100,000 demonstrators came face to face with 10,000 police officers.[18] In June 1976, during a demonstration in Plogoff in Brittany (France), property of the energy company EDF was demolished, access roads were blocked and the site was temporarily occupied. During the 1978 demonstration in Malville, police forces and the National Guard blocked demonstrators and started frontal attacks. Gas grenades were fired. One demonstrator was killed; three people lost a hand or a foot, and about 100 other demonstrators were injured.[19]

6. New individual and collective identities.

For many thousands of youngsters all over Western Europe, participation in the anti-nuclear movement has been a decisive element in their personal and political development. As the anti-nuclear movement is a textbook example of a grassroots movement, this development first of all took place in action committees at the local level, where all participants personally knew one another. New individual and collective identities typically were formed by means of 'learning by doing', although in daily practice this 'doing' used to be preceded by endless discussions. Topics to deal with by movement activists included, for instance, the way in which the further development of nuclear energy should be framed; the way decisions were made (majority or unanimity); the question whether to work with or without leaders, representatives or spokesmen; the level of autonomy of the group vis-à-vis other local, regional or national groups; the division of labour within the group, among which that between women and men; the nature of the action repertoire, among which the principle of nonviolence; the relationship with political organizations (socialist, communist, Maoist, etc.); the organization and the content of publicity and movement media; the contacts with 'official' media and public opinion; the question whether or not to install distinct women's groups; the contacts with other grassroots groups: peace, squatters, environmental and so on; the contacts with local politics and politicians. All these discussions and activities were part of the further development of the identity of the individual activists (micro level), the grassroots groups (meso level) and of the anti-nuclear movement as a whole (macro level).

Explaining the outcomes of the anti-nuclear movement: Political opportunities from the early 1970s to Chernobyl

In most West European countries, resistance against nuclear energy emerged in the early 1970s, whereas the most important confrontations with the government took place at the end of that decade. The way the conflict developed in individual countries in Western Europe and the specific outcomes of the conflict were decisively influenced by the political structures of those countries. During the past couple of decades, the political opportunity structure (POS) approach has developed into a powerful instrument for analysing the organizational structure, the action repertoire, the frames and, most importantly, the impacts of anti-nuclear and other social movements.[20]

In social movement studies, four different kinds of impacts have been distinguished: procedural, substantive, structural and sensitizing impacts. *Procedural impacts* point to access to the system by social movements or SMOs, for instance, by formal recognition or by their participation in consultation or negotiation procedures.[21] The participation of anti-nuclear groups in public inquiries in the United Kingdom, as touched on in the former section, could be seen as an example of such a procedural impact. *Substantive impacts* refer to the material successes of a social movement or SMO, for instance, the anti-nuclear movement preventing the construction of a new nuclear plant or enforcing the closing down of an existing one. *Structural impacts* refer to the changing of specific institutional structures due to movement or SMO activities, for instance, the introduction of referenda about nuclear energy that occurred in several European countries.[22] Another example of a structural impact could be the foundation of a new (green) political party due to social movement activity. Obtaining *sensitizing impacts*, finally, means that a social movement or SMO is able to put an issue on the public or political agenda or that, due to the movements of SMO's efforts, the attitudes of the public regarding a specific issue (for instance, the desirability of nuclear energy) change. In social movement studies, a number of hypotheses has been developed about the relationship between political opportunity structures and these different kinds of impacts.[23]

Political opportunity structures have been conceived in many different ways.[24] The basic distinction Eisinger made was between open and closed POS, pointing to the responsiveness that movements could expect from government institutions.[25] According to Kitschelt, conceptualizations like

Eisinger's are one-sided as they only consider the input processes, not the—largely varying—capacity of political systems to convert demands into public policy.[26] As the output phase of the policy cycle also shapes social movements and offers them points of access and inclusion in policy making, POS should be considered as the sum total of political input *and* output structures. This results into a typology with two variables (Table 9.1).

Table 9.1 Political opportunity structure: The Kitschelt typology[27]

	Political input structures	
Political output structures	**Open**	**Closed**
Strong	Example: Sweden	Example: France
Weak	Example: United States	Example: West Germany

As for anti-nuclear movements, the empirical object of Kitschelt's analysis, Kitschelt concludes that in countries where political input structures were open and responsive to the mobilization of protest, like Sweden and the United States, a search for new policies was triggered. Where they were closed, as in France and West Germany, governments insisted more intransigently on a predetermined policy course.[28] Where, as in West Germany, state capacities to implement policies were weak, the anti-nuclear movement had at least a chance to disrupt the nuclear policy. Where political capacities were stronger, as in Sweden and France, nuclear policy was shielded from most of the attack on its implementation.[29]

According to Kriesi et al.,[30] a country's POS is determined not only by its formal institutional structure (open or closed), but also by its informal *elite strategies* (integrative or exclusive). By means of integrative strategies (facilitation, assimilation, cooperation), political elites try to integrate their challengers into the political system; by using exclusive strategies (repression, polarization, confrontation), they try to exclude them. Based on these two variables, again a fourfold typology can be constructed, and contemporary nation-state examples can be tentatively identified (Table 9.2).

According to this theory, in countries with integrative elite behaviour the strategies of the anti-nuclear movement will also be assimilative rather than confrontational, and its procedural impacts will be significant. In countries where exclusive elite strategies prevail (France, Germany) there will be less procedural impacts, and the movement strategies will be confrontational rather than procedural.

Also in Tarrow's theory political elites play an important role in a country's POS. However, rather than distinguishing between integrative or exclusive elite strategies, Tarrow takes the coherence or dividedness of a country's

Table 9.2 Political opportunity structure: The Kriesi Typology[31]

	Informal elite strategies	
Formal institutional structure	**Integrative**	**Exclusive**
Open	Example: Switzerland	Example: Germany
Closed	Example: Netherlands	Example: France

political elite as a key variable in a country's POS (his other variable, similar to Kriesi's, is 'formal institutional structure').[32] Tarrow, however, prefers to conceive the different dimensions of political opportunity structure as continua (ordinal variables) rather than reflecting merely as polar opposites (typology).

Similar to Tarrow, Kolb argues in favour of an analysis of POS in ordinal terms rather than as a typology. Whereas according to Kolb institutional structures definitely matter, he suspects that studies working with typologies might have overestimated their impact because of a bias with case selection.[33]

Kolb's two variables include a country's 'Political Institutional Structure' (PIS), and, similar to Tarrow, the degree of elite conflict within a country. As for the 'Political Institutional Structure' Kolb distinguishes between six different indicators, each of which can have values between zero and two (relationship between the executive and legislative branches of government; degree of federalism; existence of bicameralism; possibility of popular referendum; strength of judicial review; effective number of political parties). The higher the index score for a country, the more open its Political Institutional Structure and, thus, the more vulnerable it will be to the influence of social movements.[34] As the first column of Table 9.3 shows, Switzerland and Germany do have the most open PIS, whereas the United Kingdom, France and Ireland have the most closed ones.[35]

The degree of elite conflict over nuclear power, Kolb's second variable, is defined as the existence of controversy about nuclear energy among and within political parties (0: no conflict at all; 3: strong conflict). Kolb's hypothesis is that the more elite conflict exists within a country, the greater the impact of the anti-nuclear movement will be. As the second column of Table 9.3 reveals, Ireland, Luxembourg, the Netherlands and Sweden do have the highest level of elite conflict with respect to nuclear power, whereas in France such conflict does not occur at all.

The third, fourth and fifth columns of the table refer to the strength of the anti-nuclear movement in the fifteen countries. This strength is measured by two indicators: the level of mass mobilization against nuclear power and the strength of local and regional resistance to the construction of nuclear facilities. Each national movement could attain a score between zero and four on each indicator. As the fifth column shows, between 1975 and 1986

Table 9.3 Political context, performance and substantive impacts of the West European anti-nuclear movement, 1975–1986[36]

Country	PIS	Elite conflict	Mass mobilization	Local resistance	Sum	Programme deviation (%)
Austria	3	2	3	1	4	100
Belgium	4	1	0	1	1	0
Denmark	4	2	3	2	5	100
Finland	4	1	0	2	2	20
France	1	0	4	4	8	0
Germany	8	2	4	4	8	34
Ireland	1	3	3	2	5	100
Italy	7	2	2	2	3	25
Luxembourg	2	3	1	3	4	100
Netherlands	5	3	2	1	3	60
Norway	2	2	1	4	5	100
Spain	5	2	2	3	5	38.8
Sweden	2	3	3	1	4	7.6
Switzerland	10	2	3	4	7	44.4
United Kingdom	0	1	1	1	2	0

France, Germany and Switzerland did have the strongest anti-nuclear movements, whereas Belgium, Finland and the United Kingdom had the weakest ones. The last column, (nuclear) programme deviation, expresses the substantive impact of the anti-nuclear movement: the deviation in the realized nuclear programme size compared to attempted programme size during the period 1975–1986.[37]

Apart from procedural and substantive impacts, which we discussed above, and apart from structural impacts, which will be dealt with later, a fourth kind of impact has to be addressed: sensitizing impacts. This kind of impact is an important variable in Kolb's analysis, as will be shown shortly. What are the attitudes of the public with respect to nuclear energy, and to what extent has the anti-nuclear movement succeeded in changing these attitudes? Obviously, anti-nuclear movements are not the only factor influencing public opinion on nuclear energy; nuclear accidents like the ones in Chernobyl and Fukushima are probably much more important. However, in some cases anti-nuclear movement campaigns produce a much better climate for changes in public opinion than in other cases, or they better use the new objective conditions to promote their case. In Table 9.4, the quantitative differences between adherents of and opponents to nuclear energy over a time period of more than three decades is shown.[38]

Which conclusions can be drawn from Kolb's data, and how do they relate to other POS-based anti-nuclear movement studies? The overall hypothesis resulting from Kolb's theoretical and analytical framework is that a combination of an open institutional structure, a high degree of elite conflict and a strong anti-nuclear movement would result in the highest level of programme deviation. On the other hand, a combination

Table 9.4 Net majority of nuclear opponents/proponents 1978–2010[39]

	Before Chernobyl (1978, 1982, 1984)	After Chernobyl (1986, 1987, 1989)	Just before Fukushima (2010)
Austria	1	76	62
Belgium	9	13	23
Denmark	16	48	22
Finland	21	32	−1
France	−14	2	25
Germany	−4	21	45
Ireland	24	60	17
Italy	−4	50	7
Luxembourg	10	60	33
Netherlands	17	27	5
Norway	72	−0	−0
Spain	10	27	50
Sweden	−4	40	11
Switzerland	−1	−0	−0
United Kingdom	−13	9	−2

of a closed institutional structure, no elite conflict and a weak anti-nuclear movement would predict no programme deviation at all. This last hypothesis is most explicitly confirmed by the Belgian and British cases. According to Kolb, however, significant programme deviation was obtained through a combination of sustained anti-nuclear mobilization, elite support as well as, as an additional variable, through an anti-nuclear majority (see Table 9.4, first column) in Austria, Denmark, Ireland, Luxembourg, the Netherlands, Norway and Spain. In Italy, Germany and Switzerland, significant nuclear change was obtained by a combination of sustained mobilization and open institutional structure.[40] In France, a closed PIS, a united political elite and a pro-nuclear majority prevented any programme deviation despite a high level of anti-nuclear mobilization.

If we compare Kolb's operationalizations, data and findings with other research findings mentioned before, two conclusions can be drawn.

1. The level of nuclear programme deviation in France as expected by Kitschelt and Kriesi et al. is identical to Kolb's, and is confirmed by his empirical findings. The level of programme deviation in West Germany, the Netherlands and Switzerland as predicted by Kolb is not dissimilar to that of Kitschelt and Kriesi et al.
2. Explanations based on POS theory seem to work better, and to give more evidence, in the form of POS typologies like Kitschelt's and Kriesi's, than in the form of Kolb's ordinal variables. Kolb introduces quite a number of explanatory variables, and with respect to a number of countries his findings are rather inconclusive. Kolb's wealth of data, however, is unequalled.

The last kind of impact we have to address are *structural impacts*. The most important structural impact of the anti-nuclear movement has been the foundation of Green parties. Around 1980, going along with the settlement of the anti-nuclear energy conflict in a number of countries, activists increasingly became aware that activism was a necessary, but not a sufficient condition to influence political decision making. In most West European countries, Green parties were founded, and from the mid-1980s onward they would become serious competitors of existing political parties. Both the Austrian and the Swedish Green party had their origin in the referendum campaigns against nuclear energy, and also in Finland, Luxembourg, Germany and France the anti-nuclear movement had a decisive influence on the origin and development of Green parties. In many cases, however, the foundation of these parties went along with lots of conflict. Could a political party really be a means to realize the kind of society envisioned by the anti-nuclear movement? How could a movement, whose main characteristic features were grassroots democracy, anti-parliamentarism and an eagerness to radically change society, deal with concepts like party organization, coalition building and strategic negotiations? In many countries, the solution was found in the pragmatic, hybrid concept of *movement party*, a political party that would be involved in the political game but, at the same time, would maintain its features of a social movement.[41]

The political influence of Green parties was decisively shaped by national political opportunity structures, in particular the nature of the electoral system. In countries with a majority system (e.g. the United Kingdom), it is very difficult to obtain seats in Parliament, and the Ecology Party never succeeded in doing so. In countries with a system of proportional representation, however, Green parties turned out to be very successful, most of all in Germany where between 1998 and 2005 a Red-Green government coalition was in charge. Apart from this, at the turn of the century three out of four of the largest West European countries (Germany, France and Italy) had a Green minister for the environment.

From Chernobyl to Fukushima

On 26 April 1986, the world's worst nuclear power accident so far occurred at Chernobyl in the former USSR (now Ukraine). An explosion and a following fire released large quantities of radioactive contamination in the atmosphere, which spread over large parts of Europe. Apart from the deadly victims directly attributed to the accident, scientists estimated that among the hundreds of millions of people living in broader geographical areas, there would be 50,000 excess cancer cases resulting in 25,000 extra cancer deaths. For this broader group, an authoritative 2006 report predicted 30,000 to 60,000 extra cancer deaths, and a Greenpeace report even put the figure at 200,000 or more.[42]

The Chernobyl disaster had a far-reaching impact on nuclear energy politics, on public opinion with respect to nuclear power, on the anti-nuclear movement and even on the stability of the Soviet and Eastern European political systems. In this section, these impacts and, in particular, the role of the anti-nuclear movements after Chernobyl will be discussed.

Eastern Europe

At the time of the Chernobyl disaster, four Soviet republics had nuclear plants: Armenia, Lithuania, the Ukraine and Russia. During the time of Perestroika, converging with the period immediately following the Chernobyl disaster, anti-nuclear movements not only played an important role in the struggle to halt nuclear energy, but in Armenia and Lithuania the struggle was part of a larger attempt to obtain national independency.

In Armenia, the anti-nuclear movement demanded the closing down of the republic's one and only nuclear station, the Medzamor plant, and in 1988 the USSR Council of Ministers decided to close down the plant.[43]

In Lithuania, the anti-nuclear association Zhemina focused on the nuclear power station in Ignalina, a station with two 1.5 MW reactors and a third one being planned. Like in Armenia, opposition to nuclear energy soon developed into resistance against Soviet politics in general and, after Chernobyl, against 'the threat of "genocide" of the Lithuanian people by Moscow'. In September 1988, the newly founded Lithuanian perestroika movement Sajudis organized a mass protest rally at the Ignalina station. Lithuanians formed a human chain around the station which they called a 'ring of life', and celebrated their Lithuanian national identity and heritage. Consequently, the construction of the third reactor was postponed.

In contrast to Armenia and Lithuania, the Ukraine lacked a strong nationalist movement striving for independence. Besides, the Ukraine had not just one but numerous nuclear power stations scattered around the republic, among which is the Chernobyl station. Consequently, because of the necessity to struggle at different places at once, the Ukrainian anti-nuclear movement originally was fragmented into a number of separate but linked local movements, but in 1989 the umbrella organization Zelini Svit (Green World) was founded. During the height days of the anti-nuclear resistance (1989–1990), local groups circulated petitions, blockaded stations and held mass rallies to protest the continued construction of new nuclear facilities. Eventually the Ukrainian Supreme Court declared a five-year moratorium on these facilities.[44] In contrast to the Ukraine and Lithuania, however, and due to the unusual strength of anti-nuclear sentiment in Ukraine compounded with the weakness of the nationalist movement, the anti-nuclear movement was prevented from being used as a surrogate for nationalism.[45] In Russia, finally, the premier republic of the Soviet Union, the anti-nuclear movement from its very start onward became closely linked with demands for more local autonomy. In 1990, the Russian Supreme Soviet responded to popular pressure by imposing a five-year moratorium on the construction of new nuclear reactors in the republic.[46]

Whereas the movements in the four Soviet republics mentioned above initially thus achieved substantial successes in forcing the Soviet government to curtail its nuclear programme, after the collapse of the USSR the anti-nuclear movements largely withered away and their substantive impacts were reversed. In Armenia, the government decided to reopen the country's sole nuclear power station in Medzamor (closed in 1988), whereas in Lithuania steps were taken to ensure the continued operation of its powerful Ignalina facility.[47] The decision of the Ukrainian Parliament to close the Chernobyl nuclear power station was tabled in October 1993, and in Ukraine and Russia dozens of nuclear power stations already functioning in the USSR period continued to operate.[48]

In Central and Eastern Europe around the turn of the century, the share of nuclear energy in the total energy mix was 51 per cent in Hungary, 35 per cent in Bulgaria and 28 per cent in Czechoslovakia, whereas also in Romania and Poland the nuclear share was considerable. In Poland, which had particularly been affected by the fall-out of the explosion at Chernobyl, organized protest better succeeded in escaping harassment than any other country of the Soviet bloc. In September 1990, the government decided to abandon the nuclear power plant under construction at Zarnowiec, where protest demonstrations had become a regular feature after Chernobyl.[49] In other Central and Eastern European countries, however, the nuclear issue became less subject to public controversy. On the one hand, the anti-nuclear movement acknowledged the immanent danger of nuclear energy; on the other hand, in the present situation nuclear energy was seen as the only realistic alternative to the primitive and highly polluting gaining of energy from fossil fuels.

Western Europe

In Western Europe, the Chernobyl catastrophe led to more protest and movement mobilization than in Eastern Europe and the Soviet Union, but the level of protest largely differed from one country to another. The same applies to changes in the nuclear programmes that individual Western Europe enforced.

Why was the impact of Chernobyl so different across countries, and thus, why did the accident open a window for nuclear reform only in some countries? An obvious explanation would point to the statistically significant correlation between the amount of radioactive fall-out and the increase in opposition to nuclear energy. This explanation, however, does not explain the low level of crisis intensity in Belgium, the Netherlands and Sweden in contrast to, first of all, Germany.[50] That no changes in nuclear programmes occurred in France and the United Kingdom while nuclear energy was completely abandoned in Austria and Italy can, according to Kolb, better be explained by variations in public support for nuclear energy,[51] and also by different levels of movement mobilization. In Italy, for instance, in May 1986 in Rome 150,000 to 200,000 people marched to protest against the Italian nuclear programme, and in 1987 resounding victories in three anti-nuclear referenda virtually ruled out nuclear energy as a policy option for the foreseeable future.[52]

In explaining the different reactions of the anti-nuclear movement to the Chernobyl disaster, Koopmans and Duyvendak suggest an interesting and theoretically innovative connection between the explanatory models of, on the one hand, the political opportunity structure approach and, on the other hand, the social-constructivist approach to social movements.[53]

Although the degree to which West European countries suffered objectively from increased levels of radiation considerably differed, such differences hardly applied to the neighbouring countries Switzerland, France, Germany and the Netherlands. Nevertheless, the authorities reacted very differently. 'On one side of the Rhine bridge, at Kehl in West Germany, children were forbidden to play on the grass and lettuces remained uneaten in the ground. On the French side of the bridge, however, around Strasbourg, very similar lettuces were declared harmless'.[54] Similarly, in the same four countries only Germany witnessed a spectacular rise in the number of anti-nuclear protest events; in France and Switzerland only a small increase took place, whereas in the Netherlands no change at all could be observed.[55]

Thus, whereas people demonstrated in German Saarbrucken against the nuclear power station in French Cattenom, the same station remained unchallenged in France itself; and while the power station in North German Brokdorf—in an area only lightly affected by radiation—became the object of mass demonstrations, all was quiet around the two Dutch nuclear power stations.[56]

Whereas, according to the social-constructivist approach to social movements, the way an issue is framed can explain the level of movement mobilization, Koopmans and Duyvendak suggest that framing functions primarily as a mechanism translates existing structural conditions, constraints or opportunities into articulated discontent and dispositions towards collective action.[57]

In some countries, such as the Netherlands or Denmark, the anti-nuclear movement's point of view that nuclear energy is both dangerous and unnecessary has become the dominant one among the general public, the news media and most political parties. In other countries, such as West Germany, no clear winner has emerged from the debate between pro-nuclear and anti-nuclear interpretations, and the struggle for hegemony continues. In still other countries, with France as the best-known example, anti-nuclear forces have lost the discursive struggle, and have been marginalized by a discourse that emphasizes the safety of the national nuclear industry and the need for nuclear power as a guarantee of economic independence and as a source of national *grandeur*.[58] Consequently, Koopmans and Duyvendak conclude that political opportunities determined the degree of success of challenges to the ambitious nuclear programmes formulated in the 1960s and the 1970s, and in turn, success proved to be a powerful determinant of both anti-nuclear grievances and mobilization.[59]

Kolb's analysis covers much more countries. According to him, in the four years following the Chernobyl accident no changes occurred in France and the United Kingdom; weak changes in Finland, Spain and Sweden; medium changes in Germany, the Netherlands, Switzerland and Belgium; and strong changes in Austria and Italy, where the whole nuclear programme was disbanded.[60] Extremely closed institutional structures in the United Kingdom and France, Kolb argues, might help to understand why nuclear expansion continued.[61] Public opinion, however, remains the explanatory variable with the strongest impact on change in nuclear programmes in the years immediately following the Chernobyl disaster.[62]

Returning to the anti-nuclear movement, with respect to the period from Chernobyl to Fukushima two developments should be mentioned: the shift in action targets from nuclear plants to nuclear waste, and the cautious renaissance of nuclear energy due to climate change, to which the movement had to define its position. I'll assess these developments one after another.

Chris Rootes and his collaborators have surveyed the incidence of all kind of environmental protest in seven European countries in the period 1988–1997.[63] This survey, first of all, reveals a remarkable difference between Germany, on the one hand, and countries like France, Britain, Italy, Spain and Sweden, on the other hand. Whereas in Germany nuclear issues were raised in a majority of all environmental protests, in France they were raised in about 20 per cent of all environmental protests, and in Britain even in fewer than 5 per cent. Another difference, Rootes observes, is that in Germany a number of national environmental movement organizations as well as more local campaign networks raised nuclear issues, whereas in Britain, anti-nuclear protests were mostly the preserve of one single organization—Greenpeace—whose actions were oriented towards putting pressure on governments and corporations by attacking the attention of mass media rather than towards stimulating mass protest.[64]

An important difference with the previous period refers to the specific issues raised in anti-nuclear energy protests. Whereas anti-nuclear mobilizations in, for instance, France during the 1970s were mainly directed against specific plants,[65] in the 1980s and 1990s the focus shifted to the problem of nuclear waste storage, which came to account for about half of all protests concerning nuclear energy.[66]

A similar observation can be made with respect to Germany. During the 1970s and 1980s, activism in Germany was mainly geared to preventing the construction of nuclear power stations, but the overriding issue in the years thereafter was the transport and temporary storage of nuclear waste.[67] In October 2008, 15,000 people disrupted the transport of radioactive nuclear waste from France to a dump in Germany. One year later, on 5 September 2009, a convoy of 350 farm tractors and 50,000 protesters took part in an anti-nuclear rally in Berlin. The marchers demanded that Germany not only close all nuclear plants by 2020, but also close the Gorleben radioactive dump. For many years, Gorleben had been the focus of the German anti-nuclear movement, which has, for instance, tried to derail train transports of waste and to destroy or block the approach roads to the site. Two above-ground storage units in Gorleben house 3,500 containers of radioactive sludge and thousands of tons of spent fuel rods.[68]

In a few other cases, however, nuclear plants themselves rather than nuclear waste remained a mobilizing issue. In January 2004, 15,000 anti-nuclear activists marched in Paris against a new generation of nuclear reactors, the European Pressured Water Reactor (EPWR). On 17 March 2007, simultaneous protests organized by the group *Sortir du nucleaire* were staged in five French cities to protest construction of EPWR plants: Lille, Lyon, Rennes, Toulouse and Strasbourg.[69] In Germany on 24 April 2010, 120,000 people built a human chain between the nuclear plants at

Krummel and Brunsbuttel in order to question the plans of the CDU/FDP government to extend the life of nuclear power reactors.[70]

In Britain, finally, in October 2010 the government revealed the names of eight sites it considered suitable for future nuclear power stations. This resulted in a number of protests at some of the sites. The Scottish government, backed by the Scottish Parliament, stated that no nuclear power stations will be constructed in Scotland.[71]

Another recent development that should be mentioned is closely related to climate change. Since the turn of the century, the nuclear industry has undertaken a large-scale media and lobbying campaign to promote nuclear power as the very solution to the greenhouse effect and climate change, as nuclear plants emit no or only negligible amounts of carbon dioxide. Anti-nuclear groups, however, argue that only reactor operation itself is free of carbon dioxide emissions. All other stages of the nuclear fuel chain—mining, milling, transport, fuel fabrication, enrichment, reactor construction, decommissioning and waste management—use fossil fuels and hence emit carbon dioxide.[72] As Greenpeace International puts it,

> building enough nuclear power stations to make a meaningful reduction in greenhouse gas emissions would cost trillions of dollars, create tens of thousands of tons of lethal high-level radioactive waste, contribute to further proliferation of nuclear weapons materials, and result in a Chernobyl-scale accident once every decade. Perhaps most significantly, it will squander the resources necessary to implement meaningful climate change solutions.[73]

Consequently, from the early 1990s onward, a significant change in strategy within parts of the anti-nuclear movement can be observed. Rather than being just *against* something (nuclear energy), anti-nuclear and environmental organizations have closely cooperated to be also *in favour* of something else (renewable energy), an alternative that, however, would require a basic restructuring of the energy sector. As Vasi observes with respect to the German environmental movement, this movement has already influenced the restructuring of the energy sector and the growth of the wind energy industry through three major campaigns: the campaigns against nuclear energy that started in the early 1970s; the campaigns against acid rain that started in the early 1980s; and the campaigns against global climate change that started in the 1990s.[74]

How could, finally, the sensitizing impacts of the anti-nuclear movement during this period be assessed? According to a 2009 Eurobarometer survey, less than one respondent in five all over the EU still believed that the share of nuclear energy in the energy mix should be increased. Thirty-nine per cent of the European population preferred to maintain it at the current level, while 34 per cent wished it to be reduced.[75] The largest percentages of adversaries occurred in Austria (66 per cent), Greece (65 per cent), Germany (52 per cent) and Spain (49 per cent). However, in eight countries the percentage of opponents in 2009 was lower than it was just after the Chernobyl disaster; only in four countries (Belgium, France, Germany, Spain) it was higher.[76] Would the Fukushima disaster change these attitudes?

Fukushima, the anti-nuclear movement and the future of nuclear energy

On 11 March 2011, after an earthquake and a tsunami, a series of equipment failures and nuclear meltdowns in the Fukushima nuclear power station led to the release of huge quantities of radioactive material, not only in the atmosphere but also into ground and ocean water. The disaster, that lasted several days, was the largest nuclear disaster since Chernobyl.

Just one day after its beginning, on 12 March 2011, 60,000 Germans formed a 45 km human chain from Stuttgart to the Neckarwestheim power plant. On 14 March, 110,000 people protested in 450 other German towns. One day later, Angela Merkel announced the temporary closing down of seven nuclear power plants which went on line before 1980.[77] The Fukushima accident also gave cause to the largest anti-nuclear demonstration Germany ever had seen. In March 2011, on the eve of state elections, more than 200,000 people took part in anti-nuclear protests in four large German cities.[78]

In Britain on 10 March 2012, the first anniversary of the Fukushima disaster, hundreds of anti-nuclear activists formed a symbolic chain around Hinkley Point to express their opposition to new nuclear power plants, and to call on the Conservative/Libdem coalition government to abandon its plan for seven other new nuclear plants across the United Kingdom. Similar protests took place against new nuclear plants at Wylfa in North Wales and Heysham in Lancashire.[79]

In other European countries, the Fukushima accident led to considerably less anti-nuclear activism. Transnational environmental movement organizations like Greenpeace and Friends of the Earth Europe (FoEE), however, adequately articulated the great fear as well as the anger of large parts of the European population and challenged the position of nuclear energy. In its report 'Lessons from Fukushima', Greenpeace argued that although the great East Japan earthquake and the following tsunami triggered it, the key causes of the Fukushima accident lie in the institutional failures of political influence and industry-led regulation. According to Greenpeace, the Fukushima accident not only marks the end of the 'nuclear safety' paradigm, it also exposes the deep and systemic failure of the very institutions that are supposed to control nuclear power and protect people.[80]

Specifically with respect to nuclear plants in Europe, in 2012 Greenpeace hired a number of independent consultants to analyse the results of the EUcommissioned 'stress tests' carried out in nine countries. The most important threats were the alarming shortfalls in back-up power for nuclear plants, including multiple reactors relying on single emergency diesel generators in case of disaster. Some plants were found to be incapable of handling challenging earthquake or flood conditions. Radiation shielding was woefully inadequate in dangerous spent fuel storage across the continent. Secondly, the consultants found that testers have ignored multiple disaster scenarios, like that of Fukushima. Most also ignored plane crashes and all ignored emergency evacuation plans, despite the fact that plants are as close as 10 km to European cities.[81]

Friends of the Earth Europe called upon the European Commission to demand a genuine, open process to bring about the end of the nuclear age in Europe, and for the introduction of phase-out laws at national level. Measures to be taken immediately, according to FoEE include: (a) closure of reactors without full pressure containment like Dukovany in the Czech Republic and Paks in Hungary; (b) closure of old reactors, or those with outdated designs, like numerous reactors in Germany; (c) closure of reactors in seismica areas like Krsko in Slovenia; (d) no life-time extension for old reactors.[82]

How could the present situation with respect to nuclear energy in Europe be assessed, and what conclusions could be drawn about the role of the European anti-nuclear movement?

As of 30 March 2012, in 31 countries worldwide 436 nuclear power plant units with an installed electric net capacity of about 370 GW were in operation, and 63 plants with an installed capacity of 60 GW in 15 countries were under construction. The total number of plants in Europe, including the Russian Federation, amounted to 186, with an installed capacity of 162 GW (Table 9.5).

How do these numbers relate to the strength of the anti-nuclear movement? As Kolb has observed, a small nuclear programme, or no nuclear programme at all, does not necessarily mean that the anti-nuclear movement in that country has been more successful than in a country with a larger programme.[83] For instance, despite the remaining nine nuclear plants, of all European anti-nuclear movements the German movement is by far the strongest one. In fact, it is the only one which has succeeded in maintaining an almost uninterrupted process of anti-nuclear mobilization for more than forty years. The only other constant factor in the resistance against nuclear energy has been Greenpeace and Friends of the Earth, which have continued to articulate an anti-nuclear discourse even in times when national-level anti-nuclear movements remained deeply silent. Remarkably, in the four decades that have passed since the early 1970s, the terms of the anti-nuclear discourse have hardly changed although, due to Chernobyl and Fukushima, the anti-technological and rational definitions of nuclear energy at present definitely have become the dominant ones.

Table 9.5 Nuclear power plant units in Europe in operation and under construction, March 2012[84]

Country	Number in operation	Output, MW	Number under construction	Output, MW
Belgium	7	5,927	–	–
Bulgaria	2	1,906	2	1,906
Czech Republic	6	3,766	–	–
Finland	4	2,736	1	1,600
France	58	63,130	1	1,600
Germany	9	12,068	–	–
Hungary	4	1,889	–	–
Netherlands	1	482	–	–
Romania	2	1,300	–	–
Russian Federation	33	23,643	10	8,203
Slovakian Republic	4	1,816	2	782
Slovenia	1	688	–	–
Spain	8	7,567	–	–
Sweden	10	9,326	–	–
Switzerland	5	3,263	–	–
Ukraine	15	13,107	2	1,900
United Kingdom	17	9,736	–	–

Source: ENS 2012

Finally, the sensitizing impacts of anti-nuclear activism have to be mentioned one more time. Partly due to the action campaigns of the anti-nuclear movement and partly due to the Chernobyl accident, in most West European countries between 1978 and 2010 the net majority of nuclear opponents has increased by tens of per cent, for instance, in Austria (by 61 per cent; France (39 per cent); Germany (49 per cent); and Spain (40 per cent) (see Table 9.4). In most Central and Eastern European countries, however, in 2009 the number of nuclear *proponents* still surpassed that of the opponents, for instance, in the Czech Republic (by 14 per cent), Bulgaria (16 per cent), and Hungary (7 per cent).[85] It is no coincidence that in these countries the anti-nuclear movement is still in its infancy.

As for the future of the European anti-nuclear movement, we have to conclude that apart from Germany, after Fukushima large-scale mobilization hardly has occurred. Resistance to nuclear energy, however, is sustained by EMOs like Friends of the Earth and Greenpeace, which do not stop to look for ways to offer alternatives for nuclear energy. I would conclude with an example of such a mobilizing effort, a website coordinated by Friends of the Earth Scotland with news and information about the UK nuclear industry. Some years ago the website launched a campaign '50 ways to help stop nuclear power', including, for instance, saving energy around the house, installing solar photovoltaics and joining a number of action campaigns of FoE, Greenpeace and WWF.[86] It is not difficult to find in these examples strong resemblances to the core features of the new social movements as assessed in the first section of this chapter: local-level action campaigns; distrust in the established political and economic system and a preference for 'do it yourself' solutions. Maybe it is by these kind of campaigns that the anti-nuclear struggle will and can be fought in the years to come.

Notes

1 Felix Kolb, *Protest and Opportunities. The Political Outcomes of Social Movements* (Frankfurt: Campus, 2007), 193.

2 There is disagreement among social movement scholars whether the anti-nuclear movement should be seen as an independent social movement or as a part of the environmental movement broadly defined. Still other scholars emphasize the connection between the peace movement, opposing nuclear weapons, and the anti-nuclear energy movement. In my opinion, answers to this kind of disputes are largely time- and place-dependent. At present, as transnational social movement organizations like Greenpeace play a leading role in the resistance to nuclear energy, I would define the anti-nuclear movement as part of the environmental movement. Because of space restrictions, in this chapter no attention could be paid to the, equally important, anti-nuclear weapons movement.

3 The other two are information technology and biotechnology.

4 Anthony Giddens, *The Consequences of Modernity* (Cambridge: Polity Press, 1990).

5 Dieter Rucht, 'The anti-nuclear movement and the state in France', in Helena Flam (ed.), *States and Anti-Nuclear Movements* (Edinburgh: Edinburgh University Press, 1994), 139.

6 Hein-Anton Van der Heijden, 'The Dutch nuclear energy conflict 1973–1989', in Helena Flam (ed.), *States and Anti-nuclear Movements*, 109.

7 Old social movements emerged from the nineteenth-century industrial and national revolutions. The industrial revolution, producing the cleavages between labour and capital and between the city and the countryside, subsequently gave birth to the labour and farmers' movements. The national revolution, producing the cleavages between church and state and between centre and periphery, gave birth to religious and regional movements.

8 Hein-Anton van der Heijden, *Social Movements, Public Spheres and the European Politics of the Environment* (Houndmills: Palgrave, 2010), 19–20.
9 Alberto Melucci, *Nomads of the Present. Social Movements and Individual Needs in Contemporary Society* (Philadelphia, PA: Temple University Press, 1989).
10 Van der Heijden, *Social Movements, Public Spheres and the European Politics of the Environment*, 99.
11 Van der Heijden, *Social Movements, Public Spheres and the European Politics of the Environment*, 99.
12 Max Preglau, 'The state and the anti-nuclear movement in Austria', in Helena Flam (ed.), *States and Anti-nuclear Movements*, 47.
13 Ian Welsh, 'Anti-nuclear movements: Failed projects or heralds of a direct action milieu?' *Sociological Research Online*. Available at: http://www.socresonline.org.uk/6/3/welsh2.html [accessed 24 October 2012].
14 Hein-Anton van der Heijden, 'The Dutch nuclear energy conflict 1973–1989', 113.
15 Mario Diani, and Hein-Anton van der Heijden, 'Anti-nuclear movements across states: Explaining patterns of development', in Helena Flam (ed.), *States and Anti-nuclear Movements*, 357–358.
16 Diani and Van der Heijden, 'Anti-nuclear movements across states', 357 ff.
17 Wolfgang Rudig, *Anti-nuclear Movements. A World Survey of Opposition to Nuclear Energy* (Hanlow: Longman, 1990), 7.
18 Wikipedia, 'Anti-nuclear movement'. Available at: http://en.wikipedia.org/wiki/Anti-nuclear-movement [accessed 27 July 2012].
19 Rucht, 'The anti-nuclear movement and the state in France', 144.
20 Herbert Kitschelt, 'Political opportunity structures and political protest: Anti-nuclear movements in four democracies', *British Journal of Political Science* 16 (1986), 57–85; Hanspeter Kriesi et al., *New Social Movements in Western Europe. A Comparative Analysis* (Minneapolis: University of Minnesota Press, 1995); Hein-Anton van der Heijden, 'Political opportunity structure and the institutionalisation on the environmental movement', *Environmental Politics* 6:4 (1997), 25–50.
21 Kriesi et al., *New Social Movements in Western Europe*, 210.
22 Flam (ed.), *States and Anti-nuclear Movements*.
23 Kitschelt, 'Political opportunity structures and political protest', 62; Kriesi et al., *New Social movements in Western Europe*, 210.
24 Peter Eisinger, 'The conditions of protest behavior in American cities', *American Political Science Review* 67:1 (1973), 11–28; Sidney Tarrow, *Power in Movement. Collective Action and Politics* (Cambridge: Cambridge University Press, 1994); Kolb, *Protest and Opportunities*; Kitschelt 'Political opportunity structures and political protest', 62; Kriesi et al., *New Social movements in Western Europe*, 210.
25 Eisinger, 'The conditions of protest behavior in American cities'.
26 Kitschelt, 'Political opportunity structures and political protest', 62.
27 Kitschelt, 'Political opportunity structures and political protest', 63.
28 Kitschelt, 'Political opportunity structures and political protest', 84.
29 Kitschelt, 'Political opportunity structures and political protest', 84.
30 Hanspeter Kriesi et al., 'New social movements and political opportunities in Western Europe', *European Journal of Political Research* 22:2 (1992), 219–244.

31 Kriesi et al., 'New social movements and political opportunities in Western Europe', 219–244.
32 Tarrow, *Power in Movement*.
33 Kolb, *Protest and Opportunities*, 206.
34 Kolb, *Protest and Opportunities*, 206.
35 Remarkably, whereas Kitschelt labels the Swedish Political Input Structure as open, according to Kolb it is closed.
36 Kolb, *Protest and Opportunities*, 198.
37 Kolb, *Protest and Opportunities*, 198.
38 In order to measure public opinion, Kolb used the net majority of nuclear opponents/proponents, calculated as the percentage difference between supporters and opponents of nuclear energy. Most data in the first two columns, and all data in the third column, are from Eurobarometer surveys (Kolb, *Protest and Opportunities*, 210–211; Eurobarometer, *Europeans and Nuclear Safety. Report* (Brussels: TNS Opinion and Social, 2010).
39 Kolb, *Protest and Opportunities*, 211; Eurobarometer, *Europeans and Nuclear Safety*.
40 Kolb, *Protest and Opportunities*, 228.
41 Closely related to the strategic discussions about these matters was the discussion about the party's willingness to reach compromises with other political parties. In Germany, this discussion has become known as the discussion between *Fundamentalists* ('Fundis') and *Realos* ('Realists').
42 Wikipedia, 'Chernobyl disaster'. Available at: http://en.wikipedia.org/wiki/Chernobyl_disaster [accessed 20 September 2012].
43 Jane Dawson, 'Anti-nuclear activism in the USSR and its successor states: A surrogate for nationalism?' *Environmental Politics* 4:3 (1995), 451.
44 Dawson, 'Anti-nuclear activism in the USSR and its successor states: A surrogate for nationalism?' 456.
45 Dawson, 'Anti-nuclear activism in the USSR and its successor states: A surrogate for nationalism?' 457.
46 Dawson, 'Anti-nuclear activism in the USSR and its successor states: A surrogate for nationalism?' 458–459.
47 Dawson, 'Anti-nuclear activism in the USSR and its successor states: A surrogate for nationalism?' 443.
48 Dawson, 'Anti-nuclear activism in the USSR and its successor states: A surrogate for nationalism?' 459.
49 Michael Waller and France Millard, 'Environmental politics in Eastern Europe', *Environmental Politics* 1:2 (1992), 177.
50 Kolb, *Protest and Opportunities*, 214.
51 Kolb, *Protest and Opportunities*, 230.
52 Mario Diani, and Francesca Forno, 'Italy', in Christopher Rootes (ed.), *Environmental Protest in Western Europe* (Oxford: Oxford University Press, 2003), 135.
53 Ruud Koopmans and Jan Willem Duyvendak, 'The political construction of the nuclear energy issue and its impact on the mobilization of anti-nuclear movements in Western Europe', *Social Problems* 42:2 (1995), 235–251.
54 Nigel Hawkes et al., *The Worst Accident in the World. Chernobyl: The End of the Nuclear Dream* (London: Pan Books/William Heinemann, 1986), quoted in Koopmans and Duyvendak, 'The political construction of the

nuclear energy issue and its impact on the mobilization of anti-nuclear movements in Western Europe', 238.

55 Koopmans and Duyvendak, 'The political construction of the nuclear energy issue and its impact on the mobilization of anti-nuclear movements in Western Europe', 238.
56 Koopmans and Duyvendak, 'The political construction of the nuclear energy issue and its impact on the mobilization of anti-nuclear movements in Western Europe', 238.
57 Koopmans and Duyvendak, 'The political construction of the nuclear energy issue and its impact on the mobilization of anti-nuclear movements in Western Europe', 242.
58 Koopmans and Duyvendak, 'The political construction of the nuclear energy issue and its impact on the mobilization of anti-nuclear movements in Western Europe', 243.
59 Koopmans and Duyvendak, 'The political construction of the nuclear energy issue and its impact on the mobilization of anti-nuclear movements in Western Europe', 249.
60 Kolb, *Protest and Opportunities*, 200.
61 Kolb, *Protest and Opportunities*, 231.
62 Kolb, *Protest and Opportunities*, 236.
63 Rootes (ed.), *Environmental Protest in Western Europe*.
64 Rootes (ed.), *Environmental Protest in Western Europe*, 240.
65 Fessenheim and Bugey in 1971; Creys-Malville in 1977; Golfech and Chooz in 1979; Plogoff in 1980.
66 Olivier Fillieule, 'France', in Rootes (ed.), *Environmental Protest in Western Europe*, 62.
67 Dieter Rucht and Jochen Roose, 'Germany', in Rootes (ed.), *Environmental Protest in Western Europe*, 104.
68 Wikipedia, 'Anti-nuclear movement', 12–13.
69 Wikipedia, 'Anti-nuclear movement', 12.
70 Wikipedia, 'Anti-nuclear movement', 13.
71 Wikipedia, 'Anti-nuclear movement in the United Kingdom'. Available at: http://en.wikipedia.org/wiki/Anti-nuclear_movement_in_the_United_Kingdom [accessed 27 July 2012].
72 Wikipedia, 'Anti-nuclear movement', 5.
73 Greenpeace International, *Nuclear*. Available at: http://www.greenpeace.org/international/en/campaigns/nuclear [accessed 27 September 2012].
74 Ion B. Vasi, *Winds of Change. The Environmental Movement and the Global Development of the Wind Energy Industry* (Oxford: Oxford University Press, 2011), 55–60.
75 Eurobarometer, *Europeans and Nuclear Safety*, 24; see also Table 9.4, column 3.
76 In 2010, one year before Fukushima, in several countries nuclear energy had become a relatively depoliticized political issue. The figures reflect the differences between those who think that the current level of nuclear energy as a proportion of all energy sources should be reduced, on the one hand, and be increased, on the other hand. Many respondents, however, think that it should remain the same. In Belgium, Finland, France, Italy, Luxembourg, the

Netherlands and the United Kingdom, their percentage exceeds the percentage of explicit opponents and/or adherents of nuclear energy.

77 Wikipedia, 'Anti-nuclear movement', 14.

78 Wikipedia, 'Anti-nuclear movement', 14.

79 Wikipedia, 'Anti-nuclear movement in the United Kingdom'.

80 Greenpeace, *Lessons from Fukushima*, Greenpeace.org., 2012, 5.

81 Greenpeace, 'Nuclear stress tests – flaws, blind spots and complacency'. Available at: http://www.greenpeace.org/eu-unit/en/Publications/2012/stress-tests-briefing/ [accessed 27 September 2012].

82 FoEE, 'Europe must phase-out nuclear'. Available at: http://www.foeeurope.org/press/2011/Mar15_Europe_must_phase-out_nuclear.html [accessed 27 September 2012].

83 Kolb, *Protest and Opportunities*, 195.

84 European Nuclear Society, 'Nuclear power plants, world-wide'. Available at: http://www.euronuclear.org/info/encyclopedia/n/nuclear-power-plant [accessed 27 September 2012].

85 Eurobarometer, *Europeans and Nuclear Safety*, 26.

86 No2NuclearPower, '50 Ways to Help Stop Nukes'. Available at: http://www.no2nuclearpower.org.uk/help/help_stop_nukes.php [accessed 27 September 2012].

Further reading

Downey, Gary. 1986. 'Ideology and the clamshell identity: Organizational dilemmas in the anti-nuclear power movement', *Social Problems* 33:5, 357–373.

Flam, Helena (ed.). 1994. *States and Anti-Nuclear Movements*. Edinburgh: Edinburgh University Press.

Kitschelt, Herbert. 1986. 'Political opportunity structures and political protest: Anti-nuclear movements in four democracies', *British Journal of Political Science* 16, 57–85.

Koopmans, Ruud and Duyvendak, Jan Willem. 1995. 'The political construction of the nuclear energy issue and its impact on the mobilization of anti-nuclear movements in Western Europe', *Social Problems* 42:3; 235–251.

Opp, Karl Dieter. 1986. *Soft Incentives and Collective Action: Participation in the Anti-nuclear Movement*. Cambridge: Cambridge University Press.

Rootes, Christopher. (ed.). 2003. *Environmental Protest in Western Europe*. Oxford: Oxford University Press.

Rucht, Dieter. 1990. 'Campaigns, skirmishes and battles; anti-nuclear movements in the USA, France and West Germany', *Organization & Environment* 4:3, 193–222.

Rudig, Wolfgang. 1990. *Anti-Nuclear Movements. A World Survey of Opposition to Nuclear Energy*. Hanlow: Longman.

Touraine, Alain. 1980. *La Prophétie Anti-nucléaire*. Paris: Seuil.

Van der Heijden, Hein-Anton. 2010. *Social Movements, Public Spheres and the European Politics of the Environment*. Houndmills: Palgrave.

INDEX

Note: The letters 'n' following locators refer to notes respectively